Catholics, Slaveholders, and the Dilemma of American Evangelicalism,

1835–1860

Catholics, Slaveholders,

and the Dilemma

of American Evangelicalism,

1835–1860

W. JASON WALLACE

University of Notre Dame Press
Notre Dame, Indiana

Library of Congress Cataloging-in-Publication Data

Wallace, William Jason.
Catholics, slaveholders, and the dilemma of American evangelicalism,
1835–1860 / W. Jason Wallace.
p.   cm.
Includes bibliographical references (p.   ) and index.
ISBN-13: 978-0-268-04421-3 (pbk. : alk. paper)
ISBN-10: 0-268-04421-X (pbk. : alk. paper)
1. United States—Church history—19th century.   2. Evangelicalism—
United States—History—19th century.   3. Catholic Church—
United States—History—19th century.   4. Slavery—United States—
History—19th century.   5. Christianity and politics—United States—
History—19th century.   I. Title.
BR525.W34   2010
282'.7509034—dc22

2010024340

For Meg

Contents

Acknowledgments

This book germinated over a period of years through the encouragement of a number of important people in my life. I am grateful for the guidance I received at the University of Virginia from my former professors Gerald Fogarty, Augustine Thompson, Heather Ann Warren, and Bill Wilson. Their criticisms and counsel improved my thinking, my writing, and my desire for excellence in scholarship. I also owe a special debt of gratitude to Darryl Hart, formerly of Westminster Theological Seminary, Philadelphia. Darryl is a gifted scholar whose insights into history and theology profoundly influenced my understanding of church history. I can only hope my own work will stand the test of time as I know his work will. Special thanks also to my colleagues in the history department at Samford University for their friendships and encouragements while I slowly put the manuscript together. Likewise, thanks to the wonderful staff at the University of Notre Dame Press for their invaluable advice. Finally, I thank my wife, Meg. She, more than anyone I know, understands the dilemma of American evangelicalism; and she, more than anyone else, has my utmost gratitude for her support through the years.

When a religion seeks to found its empire only on the desire for immortality

that torments the hearts of all men equally, it can aim at universality;

but when it comes to be united with a government,

it must adopt maxims that are applicable only to certain peoples.

So, therefore, in allying itself with a political power,

religion increases its power over some

and loses the hope of reigning over all.

—ALEXIS DE TOCQUEVILLE, *Democracy in America*

Introduction

Between 1835 and 1860, evangelical pulpits and religious journals in the North aggressively attacked slaveholders and Catholics as threats to American values. Criticisms of these two groups could often be found in the same northern evangelical journal, if not on the same page. Words such as "despotism" and "tyranny" described both the theological condition of the Catholic Church and the political condition of the South. Slavery and Catholicism were labeled incompatible with republican institutions and bereft of the virtues necessary to sustain a democratic people. They were remnants of an old order, the depraved relics of monarchy, clerisy, and feudalism. Beginning in the 1830s, the northern evangelical campaign against Catholicism and slavery initiated a twenty-five-year political and religious struggle that culminated with the collapse of the Second Party System and the conflagration of the American Civil War.[1]

Although tremendously influential, the northern evangelical moral crusaders did not go unchallenged. There were many Christians who did not agree with the social ideals preached in the pulpits of the North. There were also those who disagreed with northern evangelical theological assumptions. The two groups who received the brunt of evangelical ire, Catholics and proslavery southern conservatives, put forth substantial and at times similar arguments challenging what they believed to be an erroneous and ill-conceived Protestant political theology.

In the decades leading up to the American Civil War, large numbers of Catholics in both the North and the South found themselves politically aligned with southern proslavery apologists. Alignment, however, should not be confused with alliance. Between Catholics and southerners, most of whom were Protestants, there were no explicit treaties to bridge the theological chasm that had separated the two groups and their ancestors for some three hundred years. Indeed, vitriolic bantering between leading southern Catholic and southern Protestant theologians sometimes equaled and exceeded that of their northern counterparts.[2] What little common ground they had came in the form of lucid arguments outlining the value of a stratified social order grounded in orthodoxy. The reason for this strange concord is that both Catholics and southern Protestants believed, for many of the same as well as their own distinct reasons, that northern evangelicals threatened sound Christian teaching and secure political arrangements.[3]

Ironically, northern evangelicals never doubted that they were doing anything less than reinforcing sound Christian teaching and secure political arrangements. As champions of the idea that Christianity should influence public values, they believed that social ills could be corrected through the moral influence of the church. Not all Christians, however, saw northern evangelical causes as beneficial. In particular, the American Catholic hierarchy resisted their Protestantized ideal of a Christian society. The hierarchy believed that northern evangelicals overestimated Protestantism's ability to serve as the moral conscience of the state. Northern evangelicals were dangerous, said Catholics, because they vilified the contributions of the pre-Reformation Church while simultaneously championing the notion that American political values represented the zenith of Protestant historical development.

In the antebellum period, northern evangelicals developed a distinctly Americanized Protestant political identity. Rhetorically, they upheld the legal separation between church and state. Their case for public virtue, however, rested on the idea that evangelical Protestantism alone guaranteed the proper balance between freedom and personal responsibility. In formulating their unique Protestant political identity, northern evangelicals went to great lengths to demonize the medieval heritage of the Catholic Church as well as the Church's loyalty to Rome. At the same time, they strived to prove that certain American principles, such as liberty and equality, were products of the Protestant Reformation.

Here, however, northern evangelicals ran into a significant problem. Southern evangelicals might agree about the blessings of the Protestant Reformation, but they had to reconcile those blessings to a society that depended on enslaved labor, a society, it should be noted, that until the 1830s faced only moderate criticism from complicit and at times sympathetic northern industrialists. Put simply, southern evangelicals did not share the same vision of liberty and equality as their northern counterparts. Evangelical social reformers in the Northeast tried to justify their activism by appealing to the Bible. Southern evangelicals, who at times commiserated with issues of personal morality such as temperance, but never favored the immediate abandonment of slavery, also appealed to Scripture to justify their position.[4]

Ongoing disagreements over the correct interpretation of the Bible with regard to social and political issues created a serious quandary for those who wanted their faith to provide the moral underpinnings for republican political values. Evangelical arguments over slavery and the role of the church in a free society undermined the idea that the Bible alone was useful for forming social and political ethics. As a result, American Protestants found themselves vulnerable to the perennial criticism that troubled every Protestant country since the Reformation: the problem of unity and authority when there was more than one claimant to ecclesiastical authority.

This book explores a series of dilemmas that emerged within antebellum American evangelicalism. Despite efforts to define the young country as a Christian nation united in its commitment to Protestant ideals, northern evangelicals could not reconcile the place of Catholics or slaveholders in their narrative. Catholicism and slavery exposed serious disagreements in the nation's fastest growing denominations. These divisions became increasingly apparent as evangelicals in the North and the South used the Bible to justify their respective political and social positions. One result of this discord was that Catholics and southern evangelicals found themselves in strange relationship. Theologically, they were worlds apart, yet they shared a common nemesis in the northern evangelical social reformer.

The first three chapters of this book profile the way in which northern evangelicals constructed a national narrative after their own image.

Chapter 1 looks at the rapid changes America faced as immigration and industrial advances shaped political loyalties. As the country struggled to find a truly national identity, personalities and arguments emerged that defined the northern evangelical agenda. In the Northeast, evangelical Protestantism became increasingly identified with revivalism, social activism, and modification of traditional Calvinist teaching on original sin and human depravity. New England, in particular, produced a spate of preachers who were optimistic that both their political and religious commitments would shape the future of the country.

New England's quest for a comprehensive Protestant nationalism was tempered, however, by the presence of an articulate and intellectually gifted Catholic hierarchy. Behind the hierarchy, New England evangelicals argued, stood Europe, and behind Europe's political problems, stood Rome. Current events in Europe as well as Europe's pre-Reformation history loomed large in the northern evangelical imagination, and northern evangelicals devoted a great deal of intellectual energy on interpreting that history in ways that best fit their agenda. Included in their agenda was the notion that the United States was to be a Christian republic that served as a corrective to the social arrangements of the Old World. These themes are traced in chapter 2.

In the decades leading up to the Civil War, southern slaveholders, like Catholics, found themselves relentlessly attacked in the northern evangelical press. Chapter 3 looks at the way in which denominational journals portrayed the slave system of the South as equally subversive of American institutions as Catholicism. Journals such as the *Downfall of Babylon, Zion's Herald,* the *New York Evangelist,* the *New York Observer,* the *Christian Watchman and Examiner,* and the *Oberlin Quarterly Review,* though published by different denominations, voiced in equal measure a deep hostility toward Catholicism and slavery. Directly and indirectly, northern evangelicals compared the immoral authoritarianism of the Catholic priest to the immoral authoritarianism of the slaveholder. Both were portrayed by the press as brutal, lecherous, and most importantly, un-American.

Chapters 4 and 5 examine the responses of both southerners and Catholics to northern evangelical aggression. Southerners, along with Catholics in the North and the South, shared a mutual distaste for northern evangelical abolitionism, and specifically, they disliked the social agenda promoted from northern pulpits. Both were quick to compare northern evangelical political sympathies with radical movements in Europe, and both took care to outline what they believed to be the distinct responsibilities of the church and the state. The hierarchy of the Catholic Church and proslavery southern evangelicals challenged northern evangelical reformers in two important ways. First, southern evangelicals by and large rejected northern evangelicals' faith in both theological and political "progress." In doing so, they exposed a fundamental tension in evangelicalism that belied attempts to present American Protestantism as the univocal moral conscience of the nation. Second, Catholic intellectuals took on northern evangelicals' caricature of Europe and the papacy by articulating the enormous contributions made by the pre-Reformation Church to the western political tradition. Between 1835 and 1860, northern evangelicals had to confront sophisticated arguments about the meaning of European religious and political history that resisted their challenges to abrogate spiritual hierarchy and to rescind caste-based social control.

Chapter 4 looks at Catholicism in the South and the dilemmas faced by southern evangelicals in the decades prior to the Civil War. Southern evangelicals were conservative in temperament, yet they shared with northern evangelicals the belief that the United States was a nation founded upon and perpetuated through Protestant values. Disagreements with northerners, however, exposed that American evangelicals were not united in their understanding of Protestant values. In the main, southern evangelicals overwhelmingly rejected northern evangelicals' revisions to received Christian doctrine and, likewise, rejected all attempts by northern evangelicals to associate Christianity with social egalitarianism. Still, southern evangelicals did not entirely reject the idea that Protestantism played an important role in shaping the character of the nation. With the crises of secession and war, evangelicals in the South were as resolute as evangelicals in the North were that their understanding of Christianity provided a moral template for political republicanism.

While the American Catholic hierarchy disparaged Protestant triumphalism in both the North and the South, it was especially critical of northern evangelical hubris. Questions surrounding slavery, freedom, and the relationship between religion and politics had long preoccupied Catholic thinkers. Chapter 5 shows the way in which leading Catholic intellectuals interpreted contributions made by the Catholic Church to American prerogatives such as religious liberty and the separation of church and state. Chapter 5 also explores how these same intellectuals vigorously defended the Catholic Church against accusations of divided loyalty between the pope and the Constitution.

The published writings and private correspondence of members of these three antebellum groups—northern evangelicals, southern evangelicals, and Catholics—suggest that divisions among them stemmed, at least in part, from disagreements over the role religious convictions played in a free society. When northern evangelical leaders challenged the place of Catholics and proslavery southerners in the republic, and the latter responded in kind to northern evangelicals, they were often debating the public meaning of Christianity. Central to these debates are the proper relationship between church and state in a country where there was no established church—and where Christianity itself had, in effect, become democratized—and the memory of European religious and political heritage in the midst of a growing national consciousness hostile to aristocratic and hierarchical concerns.

CHAPTER ONE

New England Sets a Pattern

A Tale of Two Cities

On the evening of July 29, 1835, Charleston, South Carolina's post-master, Alfred Huger, dutifully opened mail sacks delivered direct from New York City on the steamship *Columbia*. Once every two weeks the *Columbia* made the run between New York and Charleston, and for Huger, the monotony of sorting through stacks of letters on a balmy evening promised no more excitement than previous summer deliveries from New York. The night, however, took a turn when Huger made a re-markable discovery. The mailbags were full of pamphlets, thousands of pamphlets, with titles such as *Human Rights,* the *Anti-Slavery Record,* the *Slaves' Friend,* and *Thoughts on African Colonization.* Huger quickly de-termined that the literature had been sent to South Carolina courtesy of the American Anti-Slavery Society, and he decided that this mail could not be delivered to the citizens of Charleston. The vigilant postmaster believed the pamphlets to be incendiary documents sent by abolitionists in an effort to prompt slaves to revolt against their masters. Delivering such mail would be tantamount to calling for black revolution. Huger quarantined the documents and petitioned Postmaster General Amos Kendall of the Jackson administration to advise him on his next move.[1]

Within twenty-four hours, Charleston's citizens learned of the se-questered propaganda. Unlike Huger, they were not willing to wait for in-structions from the president. A mob of about three thousand people, led by an ex-governor of South Carolina, broke into the post office, seized the controversial mail, and congregating outside the nearby citadel, piled the pamphlets below a mock gallows from which hung the effigies of three northern abolitionists: William Lloyd Garrison, Samuel H. Cox, and Arthur Tappan. A balloon signaled to the crowd that mob leaders were about to ignite the papers, and with that, the mail served as tinder for a large public bonfire on the parade grounds of Charleston.[2]

As the antislavery pamphlets poured into other cities throughout the South, southerners were quick to imitate the reaction of their neighbors in South Carolina. Throughout the month of August 1835 (a month that happened to mark the fourth anniversary of the Nat Turner slave insurrection in Virginia), anti-abolitionists held rallies in almost every large city.[3] Citizens of New Orleans, Richmond, Norfolk, and Mobile believed Yankee fanaticism had crossed a tacit but understood line of political respectability, and leading southern statesmen decried the abolitionists' postal campaign as an evil that had to be resisted, even to the point of disunion if necessary.[4]

In Richmond, several prominent citizens asked the postmaster to refuse to deliver the pamphlets, and the *Richmond Whig* demanded that civil authorities deport the financier of the literature, Arthur Tappan, from New York to Virginia for trial. The postmaster of Raleigh, North Carolina, did not have to be asked not to deliver the mail; he simply refused on his own. Farther south in Alabama, planters and farmers from the city of Greensborough gathered in angry mobs in the fall of 1835 to protest the distribution of the antislavery newspaper the *Emancipator*. When copies of the *Emancipator* arrived in Tuscaloosa County, Alabama, a grand jury demanded that its editor, Robert G. Williams, be served with an indictment in New York for "circulating pamphlets and papers of a seditious and incendiary character."[5] In New Orleans, a group called the Louisiana Constitutional and Anti-Fanatical Society formed for the sole purpose of printing and distributing literature that countered the abolitionists' arguments. Also in Louisiana, one parish posted a $50,000 reward for Arthur Tappan to be delivered dead or alive.[6]

Recognizing the severity of the situation, Postmaster General Kendall and President Jackson formulated a plan within weeks of the first

Charleston deliveries that would allow postmasters to confiscate suspect letters until citizens demanded delivery. The hope was that those persons who insisted on receiving dubious material would be made known to their communities "as subscribers to [a] wicked plan of exciting the negroes to insurrection."[7] A public record would be kept of those citizens who demanded the controversial letters, and they in turn would find themselves so socially ostracized that only the most resolute of them could withstand the disapproval of their fellow southerners. President Jackson and Postmaster General Kendall understood that they were calling for censorship of the mail service, but the gravity of the situation, they believed, demanded a swift and earnest response from the federal government. The South, in the summer and fall of 1835, faced the first in a series of crises prompted by abolitionist agitation. If government agents did not act to censor, then angry mobs would.

In the mid-1830s, the South was not the only region of the country to confront the problem of mob violence. Almost one year to the day before the mail controversy created an uproar in Charleston, South Carolina, a northern city—Charlestown, Massachusetts—faced its own conflict involving overheated public sentiment. A small community six miles north of Boston, Charlestown was known primarily for its brickyards and close proximity to the famous battle site Bunker Hill. Another feature of Charlestown was a large convent school built on top of Mt. St. Benedict overlooking the city. The convent school had been founded by Ursulines after they settled in Charlestown in 1818. Although a Catholic school, the convent attracted many of its students from the wealthier Protestant families of Boston who found the Congregationalist-controlled public school system too uncompromising. In fact, many girls attending the school came from Unitarian families who disdained the evangelical sympathies that dominated much of the political culture of the region.[8]

The disgust New England Unitarians felt toward evangelical rigidity was equally matched by evangelical contempt for Unitarian latitudinarianism. In Charlestown, this mutual antipathy boiled because many of its citizens were working-class and middle-class Calvinists, albeit modified Calvinists, who believed that two of their worst theological enemies had united in a cloistered educational enterprise. And Charlestown was not alone in its distrust of the Ursulines. Nearby Boston also took no-tice of the success of the convent school. As the number of liberal Prot-estant Boston families enrolling their daughters in the convent school grew, more and more conservative clergy from Boston and the surround-ing area began to express concerns over the extent of Catholic influence in New England. The 1834 meeting of the General Association of the Con-gregational Church of Massachusetts adopted a resolution that urged ministers to actively confront "the degrading influence of Popery." Like-wise, periodicals produced by the Boston religious press warned that if the influence of Catholic schools was not controlled, then Massachusetts would face the calamity of seeing many of its prominent citizens come under the influence of Rome.[9]

To add to these concerns, a young girl named Rebecca Reed began to circulate malicious stories around Charlestown and Boston about life in the convent.[10] Rebecca Reed claimed to have escaped from the convent, and she depicted life within its walls as one of priestly licentiousness and psychological torture. It mattered not that the Ursulines dismissed Ms. Reed from their employ after she served only a short time there as a custo-dian. Her stories appealed to the popular imagination, and when, in July 1834, a nun named Elizabeth Harrison briefly left the convent due to fa-tigue and other health concerns and then returned at her own request, Re-becca Reed's grim tale appeared even more inauspicious. A rumor circu-lated that Ms. Harrison had been returned to the convent by force and that she was now a prisoner held in the cellar against her will.[11]

In the midst of the melodrama generated by tales of "escaped" nuns, it did not help matters that the Reverend Lyman Beecher returned to Boston from Ohio in early August to plead his cause for funding Protes-tant schools and seminaries in the Western Reserve to counter Catholic expansion. On Sunday, August 10, Beecher preached three anti-Catholic sermons in three different churches. All the churches were filled beyond capacity, and each audience was treated to a barrage of denunciations of the pope, Rome, and Catholicism. Other evangelical clergy in and around Boston followed Beecher's lead that day, and some directly denounced the Ursuline convent. The Sabbath ended without incident, but the fol-lowing night the suburbs of staid Boston found themselves in the middle of a loud and disturbing commotion.[12]

On the evening of August 11, an angry mob gathered outside the convent shouting anti-Catholic slogans while several of its leaders went directly to the Mother Superior and demanded to see the sisters they believed to be imprisoned there. The mob leaders were told to come back when the sisters were not sleeping, and the crowd gradually dissipated. Later that night, however, around eleven o'clock, a pile of tar barrels was ignited in a field adjacent to the convent. Recognizing the fire as a signal, a crowd again swarmed the Ursuline's property. By midnight the school was on fire. The nuns quickly evacuated the children from the building and fled for refuge. Apparently not satisfied with the destruction wrought the first night, another mob returned the night of August 12 and burned fences and trees surrounding the convent. Three nights after the initial aggression, a rumor spread that Irish laborers were about to launch a counterattack in Boston. This hearsay prompted over one thousand Bostonians to take to the streets as self-appointed guardians of public safety. Though the Irish attack never took place, angry Protestant rioters released their pent-up anxiety by burning a hovel in Charlestown occupied by poor Irish families.[13]

After the assault on the convent, Lyman Beecher expressed regret for the violence, but he denied that his sermons were responsible for inciting the mob. He argued that he preached "two or three miles distant from the scene, and not an individual of the mob, probably, heard the sermon or knew of its delivery." Moreover, the excitement that produced the riot "had no relation whatever to religious opinions, and no connection with any denomination of Christians."[14] Beecher contented himself with the belief that the riot would have occurred regardless of his sermons about the dangers of popery. He was not, however, as easily satisfied with the opinion that Catholics did not retaliate with violence because the bishop of Boston restrained them:

> Has it come to this, that the capital of New England has been thrown into consternation by the threats of a Catholic mob, and that her temples and mansions stand only through the forbearance of a Catholic bishop? There can be no liberty in the presence of such masses of dark mind, and of such despotic power over it in a single man. Safety on such terms is not the protection of law, but of single-handed despotism.[15]

Apart from the incendiary violence, the episodes in Charlestown, Massachusetts, in the summer of 1834 and in Charleston, South Carolina, in the summer of 1835 appear to have little in common. The cities were separated geographically and culturally. The circumstances leading up to the actions of the mobs were very different, as were the objects of their respective scorn. Nevertheless, despite the differences, there are striking similarities between the two events that cannot be dismissed and deserve further examination.

The people of Charleston and the South, as well as the people of Charlestown and Massachusetts, believed that something fundamental about their way of life was being threatened by outside forces. For southerners, a small group of northern agitators—with little or no reflection about the enormous complexities involved in its demands—was using a public trust, the mail service, to try to overturn the slave system. For Bostonians, the success of a Catholic convent school horrified the heirs of the Puritans who held that a Protestant education was essential for continuing their social project. Both southerners and New Englanders believed that they were facing a potential crisis that contained a number of unknown variables. How many more "outsiders" might threaten their respective ways of life? Who would agree with them? What kind of influence would they have? Furthermore, both southerners and New Englanders found themselves challenged by persons who did not share the common heritage, values, and political sympathies that gave an identity and a purpose to their respective regions. Abolitionists knew as much about cotton production as Catholics did about Calvinist predestination. Who were they to make their presence felt so far from their proper spheres of influence?[16]

Beyond being responses to perceived threats, both protests involved evangelicals who believed that responsible Christians were to concern themselves with the pressing social issues of the day and that this concern could and should be organized into a program of political persuasion.[17] In the 1830s, the strength of this type of Christianity was concentrated in the Northeast, and practitioners could be found across the four largest Protestant denominations: Methodist, Baptist, Presbyterian, and Congregational.[18]

Two principal players in the stories of the mail riots and the convent burning, Arthur Tappan and Lyman Beecher, are representative of these evangelical convictions. They were well-known leaders of moral reform movements in the Mid-Atlantic states and New England. They actively campaigned for causes such as temperance, maintenance of Sabbath laws, distribution of religious tracts and Bibles, and Protestant control of public education.[19] Both men desired to transcend denominational differences in order to secure a vast network of local organizations dedicated to transforming society. They were allies in a struggle defined by a unique Christian commitment: not only the individual but also society could and should be regenerated.[20]

To accomplish the goal of social regeneration, Tappan and Beecher, and many others who shared their convictions, believed that civil authorities needed the guidance of churches, specifically evangelical Protestant churches, in matters of moral legislation. Furthermore, they held that evangelical churches could exercise a social influence, in Beecher's words, "distinct from that of the government, independent of popular suffrage, superior in potency to individual efforts, and competent to enlist and preserve the public opinion on the side of law and order."[21] In short, northern evangelicals believed that they had more to offer than salvation: they had a transforming worldview, and given the right means of moral suasion, their worldview could keep society from degenerating into anarchic lawlessness. In the summers of 1834 and 1835, however, citizens of South Carolina and Massachusetts had faced in the mail riots and the convent burning two frightening episodes of lawlessness, and northern evangelicals helped to incite both incidents.

The antebellum northern evangelical crusades against slavery and Catholicism were born over the same five-year period, in the same region, with many of the same leaders. Northern evangelicals embraced the causes of antislavery and anti-Catholicism with the same zeal that they brought to the causes of temperance and the enforcement of Sabbath laws. Both antislavery and anti-Catholic movements involved the application of theology to politics, and both had rather ugly beginnings. In Charleston, a northern evangelical mail campaign had incited the southern mob who opposed abolitionist activity in their community. In

Charlestown, northern evangelical preaching had provoked the northern mob who opposed a strong Catholic presence in their community.[22]

Joining Arthur Tappan and Lyman Beecher were a transdenominational group of ministers and laypersons who were dedicated to a social philosophy grounded in Christian activism. They were, in Ray Allen Billington's memorable phrase, "Protestant crusaders," rhetorical warriors who fought vigorously to sustain the idea that America had been providentially set apart to advance the twin causes of political and religious freedom.[23] Northern evangelicals viewed Catholics and slaveholders as much more than an anomaly on the American landscape; they were competitors in the race to define and control public space in a rapidly changing young country.

Immigration, Religion, and Politics

How fast was the country changing? In 1800, a traveler who wished to cross the territory between Lake Erie and New Orleans would need to set aside a month for the journey. By 1830, the same distance could be covered in two weeks. Likewise, a trip from Boston to Baltimore required three days at the turn of the nineteenth century, while thirty years later the same distance could be traveled in a day. Improvements in transportation and road conditions were making mobility, both physical and economic, a reality for many Americans. Better highways and the introduction of steam powered boats, locomotives, and canals inspired new possibilities of western expansion. Between 1810 and 1830, over two million people exited the eastern states for the Northwest Territory, and by 1840, one-third of the American population lived west of the Appalachian Mountains.[24]

The push west did not simply result in urban drain. Cities also grew between 1820 and 1850. Pittsburgh went from being a modest town of 7,000 to a large city of 46,000, and Cincinnati mushroomed from 9,000 to 115,000. On the eastern seaboard Boston's population increased from 42,000 to 137,000, New York's from 123,000 to 515,000, and the manufacturing suburbs of Philadelphia jumped from 45,000 people to just over 200,000.[25] The Northeast and the Midwest were growing. Charleston, South Carolina, and the rest of the South, at least the lower South, appeared sleepy and listless by comparison.[26] Between 1830 and 1850, the combined population of the three largest cities in the lower South—New Orleans, Charleston, and Mobile—remained under 200,000. At midcentury, a train trip from New Orleans to Charleston took an entire week, while a trip from western New York to Charleston could be made in five days.[27]

In New England, urban growth coincided with changes in industry. Improved technologies brought increased productivity to many northern manufacturers, and in turn, manufacturers needed a reliable supply of labor. The need for factory workers was met in part by local populations. By far, however, the greatest supply of industrial labor came from the 500,000 plus immigrants who arrived in the United States between 1828 and 1844. Most of the newcomers were from Europe with the largest percentage emigrating from Ireland and Germany. Statistics help to highlight the pattern. In 1820, annual emigration from Ireland totaled 3,614, whereas by 1852, that number increased to 159,548. Germans comprised a relatively small percentage of the immigrant population in 1820, totaling only 968 persons. By 1852, over 145,918 Germans were emigrating annually to the United States.[28] Irish immigrants settled in the large seaport cities of the Northeast, while German immigrants settled further west in both urban and rural areas. Both groups were exceedingly poor, congregating around the cheapest land or the cheapest housing available, and more often than not, they competed with each other for employment.[29]

New arrivals from Europe brought distinct customs, cultural habits, and peculiarities of language with them. They also brought their religious beliefs. Some were Lutheran, some Pietist; a handful of Protestants from Ulster were among the immigrant population, as were a few Jews, but by far the overwhelming majority of immigrants were Catholic. European Catholics stood out in Protestant America. They brought with them a continental disposition toward the use of alcohol. Apart from attending Mass, they treated the Christian Sabbath like any other day of the week. They also enjoyed music and dancing. These factors alone prevented most immigrants from quietly blending into the emerging industrial towns of New England. But beyond cultural peculiarities, Catholics, especially Irish-born Catholics, often faced deplorable living and working conditions. They were poor, and their poverty frequently subjected them to abysmal material circumstances. Wages were low, neighborhoods were unsanitary, and personal hygiene was inadequate due to the difficulties of their environment. Consequently, locals viewed them as uncouth and determined that they were the source of recurrent social unrest. Fighting, drunkenness, prostitution, and juvenile delinquency were all believed to have their worst manifestations in the foreign born.[30]

Even in the best conditions, the rapid collision of cultural differences strains the bonds that hold communities together. Suspicion, mistrust, and resentment are common reactions to large numbers of strangers moving into settled cities and towns. Antebellum Protestants in New England and the newly settled Midwest, however, faced a unique confluence of circumstances. Within the span of a generation, they had to confront accelerated changes that altered long-established patterns of agrarian economic and social life. At the same time, they had to deal with large numbers of newly arrived European Catholics who did not share their Protestant heritage. Perhaps most importantly they had to wrestle with how these changes fit with the exigencies of the American political system. Immigrants were potential voters, and how they participated in political life determined for many how they would be received.

In the 1830s and 1840s, political participation narrowed to two choices: either one was a Whig, or one was a Democrat. Democrats thought themselves more tolerant, populist, and religiously neutral than the Whig party. Whigs, by contrast, believed themselves to be direct descendants of the Federalists, and, like the Federalists, they carried the cause of conservative social values. They thought that the church should influence moral legislation; they supported an industrial aristocracy grounded in Protestant values; and they detested the legacy of Thomas Jefferson.[31] Furthermore, what the Whigs disliked about Jefferson the Democrat they absolutely abhorred in Andrew Jackson the populist.[32]

By and large, Irish immigrants were drawn to the Democratic Party with its reputation for Jeffersonian broadmindedness. They viewed the Whigs as the heirs of the Puritans, and as Catholics, this made choosing their political affiliation rather easy.[33] Northern evangelicals, by contrast, were sympathetic with Whig politics. They liked the notion that government action could be used to secure religious and moral improvement.

Religion provided a restraining social influence that tempered the liberating effects of political and economic freedom. Whigs were the party of economic progress and social conservatism, champions of freedom and personal responsibility. Rarely did their leadership discern the potential incompatibility between their love of progress and their desire for political constancy.[34]

French historian Alexis de Tocqueville recorded the unique religious impulse of American politics in his account of his travels through the United States in the 1830s. Tocqueville noted that in France he had witnessed the "the spirit of freedom and the spirit of religion pursuing courses diametrically opposed to each other . . . but in America they were intimately united." Although there was no established religion in the United States, religion was nevertheless "the foremost of the political institutions" because religion in America "facilitates the use of free institutions."[35]

Tocqueville offered the keen observation that nineteenth-century Americans, unlike nineteenth-century Europeans, did not see religious institutions and political institutions as contestants locked in a struggle for power. This was especially true for evangelical Whigs. In fact, socially conservative evangelicals believed religion was indispensable to the progress of the young country. "Unless our course of national glory be checked," wrote the Rector of Oldenwold, a minister from Boston writing under a pseudonym, "the present condition of our land is only a beginning of what it will be in years to come." The reason for his optimism, he continued, was that Americans were committed to the "circulation of the word of God among her people, to the exercise of the right of private judgment, and the spirit of peace."[36]

The Christian, like the country, was destined to move forward, and Presbyterians such as William Adams believed that anyone who earnestly studied the scriptures could not "imagine that the time will come when there will be a limit to his advancement."[37] Likewise, Henry Ward Beecher celebrated the "upward and progressive tendency of the great elements of good," and boldly declared that "constant Progress rests chiefly upon one Association, THE CHURCH."[38]

In Europe, religion might very well have conflicted with the interests of the state, but Europe was the Old World. In America, religion and the state were believed to be compatible because the authority of both rested on the same agency: the free assent of the individual. Presbyterian Albert Barnes succinctly summarized the situation in 1844: "This is an age of freedom, and men will be free. The religion of forms is the stereotyped wisdom or folly of the past, and does not adapt itself to the free movements, the enlarged views, the varying plans of this age."[39]

In the 1840s and 1850s, many evangelicals believed that Americans faced an exceptional historical opportunity. In the Old World, church and state had been, more often than not, contestants locked in a power struggle because people lived under the dictates of arbitrary religious coercion. In the United States, however, individuals were free to choose for themselves what they would believe. If free people could be convinced that their spiritual and political interests were one and the same, then there was real potential for harmony between Christian moral teaching and public order.

Northern evangelical leaders were conscious of the importance of the historical moment, but they were also aware that new opportunities presented new dangers. If Christianity was to be moral leaven in a nation consumed with the possibilities of freedom and progress, then Christian leaders had to avoid the ominous prospect that freedom and progress might eventually undermine self-restraint. Alexis de Tocqueville well understood the problem. While Americans were no doubt a religious people, they still have "no traditions, or common habits, to forge links between their minds." Moreover, as New England cities swelled with Catholic immigrants from Europe, and as scores of peoples migrated westward, Tocqueville speculated, "there is nothing of tradition, family feeling, or example to restrain them. . . . The woof of time is broken and the track of past generations lost."[40]

The Evangelical Dilemma and the National Identity Crisis

Antebellum evangelical conservatives faced a substantial dilemma. How was one to maintain a shared understanding of the common good in a culture that elevated the prerogatives of individualism and egalitarianism over the authority of tradition? More pointedly, how could one both champion the virtues of progress and at the same time insist that progress not disrupt social stability? New England evangelicals found these questions particularly urgent given the large numbers of European Catholics pouring into the Northeast after 1830. Immigration together with rapid economic changes challenged their support of both commercialism and social conservatism. In addition, the aggressive populism that characterized the age of Jackson exposed a fundamental problem for northern evangelical Whigs. On the one hand, as evangelicals, they were champions of individual conscience and the right of private opinion over and against the dictates of inherited authority. On the other hand, as socially conservative Whigs, they were suspicious of populism, and they doubted that the rabble of the cities and the frontier could survive without strong moral leadership.

Many New England ministers struggled with the tension created by their commitments to both progressive theology and conservative social paternalism. Eminent preacher and theologian Horace Bushnell of Hartford, Connecticut, worried that the social changes brought by immigration and populism would undermine public order. He warned that "emigration, or a new settlement of the social state, involves a tendency to social decline. There must, in every such case, be a relapse towards barbarism, more or less protracted, more or less complete."[41] He insisted that under the political conditions of democracy some stability had to be guaranteed.[42] In a lament that anticipated the work of Reinhold Niebuhr in the twentieth century, Bushnell said that partisanship in democracies had the subtle effect of convincing normally well-behaved individuals to "yield to impulse, to party spirit and policy, without any consideration of moral constraints and principles."[43] While he demonstrated a tendency toward social conservatism, he nevertheless rejected conventional theological systems such as Calvinism. He was convinced that modern Christianity had outgrown old confessional boundaries and that doctrinal disputes were futile because our "apprehensions of truth are here only proximate and relative." Bushnell limited his taste for experimentation to religion. When it came to politics, he sought firmer ground, believing it was his "duty" to "assert God's law."[44]

Like Horace Bushnell, Albert Barnes had difficulty reconciling his theology with his apprehensions about the social problems facing the young country. Pastor of the First Presbyterian Church in Philadelphia, Barnes was instrumental in the 1837 schism that split the Presbyterians into a New School (theologically progressive) side and Old School (theologically confessional) side. Over the course of a forty-seven-year career, he championed interdenominational cooperation and innovations in received Presbyterian doctrine. He also published caustic but effective social treatises on subjects such as prohibition, abolition, and the threat of Catholic immigration. His influence on nineteenth-century Protestant thought cannot be underestimated. Between 1832 and 1853, he published an eleven-volume theological tome entitled *Notes, Explanatory and Practical,* which sold over one million copies.[45]

Early in his career, Barnes challenged the doctrinal positions of the Westminster Confession of Faith by claiming that people are sinful by choice rather than by an inherited depraved nature.[46] In a blatant repudiation of Calvinist principles, Barnes argued that people have the potential to be good, or morally acceptable, before God.[47] Barnes' sanguine view of human nature translated into an equally confident view of America's role in world history. He declared that the American Constitution "is the last hope of the world" and that in due course "the spread of intelligence and virtue cannot fail ultimately to extend the same principles of government through the earth." Hardly understating his predilection for the idea of manifest destiny, he urged that "in the era of better things, which is about to rise in the world, our land shall be first; our counsels the guide of other nations; our countrymen everywhere the devoted advocates of the rights of men."[48]

Still, for all his optimism about human potential and national destiny, Barnes, too, apprehended Tocqueville's reservations about the problem of freedom and self-restraint. "America," he wrote, was "fast becoming a nation of drunkards," and if people did not sober up, the entire future of American civilization was in jeopardy. Likewise, he saw avarice as the besetting sin of the American character. As people migrate west, he lamented, "they go for gold . . . and they trample down the law of the Sabbath, and soon, too, forget the laws of honesty and fairdealing, in the insatiable love of gain."[49]

Rhode Island Baptist Francis Wayland shared Barnes' concerns. A native of New York, Wayland graduated from Andover Seminary in 1818 and worked for a time as a private tutor before accepting an invitation to serve as the pastor of the First Baptist Church of Boston. He returned to academic life in 1826, and soon after was elected president of Brown University, a post he held for almost thirty years. Wayland was a prolific writer whose 1835 textbook on moral philosophy, *Elements of Moral Science,* went through several editions in the United States and in England. He was quick to address political concerns, and he chastised Christians who failed to vote, or who argued that politics should be of no concern to ministers.[50]

In 1842 after Thomas Dorr led a populist movement to extend suffrage to Rhode Island's nonpropertied persons, Wayland assumed leadership of the party opposing Dorr's activity. He used his political platform to champion a number of social causes, including prison reform, care of the mentally ill, gradual emancipation, and public education. He also directed attention to the threat slaveholders presented to the interests of New Englanders. When the Kansas-Nebraska Act of 1854 broke the tenuous peace of the 1820 Missouri Compromise, Wayland added his voice to the many who believed that a minority of southerners had for too long dominated national politics. "The question," he wrote, "ceases to be whether black men are forever to be slaves, but whether the sons of the Puritans are to become slaves themselves."[51]

As a New Englander, Wayland found a natural political enemy in the slaveholding South. Yet, at the same time, he understood that slaveholders were not the only Americans subject to the impulse of greed. Eastern manufacturers could fall prey to the "love of gain" as well. Still, Wayland was a committed capitalist. Rather than condemn the unsavory consequences of laissez-faire economics as some radicals did, he tried to cast the principles of Adam Smith, David Ricardo, and John Stuart Mill in a favorable light. As one historian put it, Wayland "sought to harmonize classical economic thought with traditional religious principles" and his efforts resulted in two celebrated works, *Elements of Political Economy* and *The Moral Law of Accumulation.*[52]

These studies in political economy reflected the growing ambiguity surrounding the problem of freedom and moral authority in the antebellum period. As a disciple of liberalism, Wayland could unflinchingly declare that "every man be allowed to gain all that he can" and that "each has a right to use what is his own, exactly as he pleases." Yet, at the same time, he could not discard his evangelical moral sensibilities. He insisted after the financial panic of 1837 that people had violated God's laws for amassing wealth by "excessive avidity for the rapid accumulation of property."[53] He reasoned that Americans had the right to enjoy liberty, and to pursue the blessings of liberty, but personal freedom should never be elevated above the right of society to provide a check on unrestrained individualism. Some form of governmental paternalism was necessary in order for a democracy to function properly. Freedom provides "precious blessings. . . . But it is to be remembered, that no liberty can exist without restraint. . . . It therefore becomes all civil and judicial officers, to act as the guardians of society."[54]

Francis Wayland, Albert Barnes, Horace Bushnell, and other northern evangelicals were not simply conflicted social conservatives caught in the all too human trait of self-contradiction. Their optimism about the progressive potential of the young country and their pessimism about its moral stability reflected the concerns of many evangelical Whigs. Their contradictions reveal the complexity of pursuing normative ethical principles in a culture that has no explicitly agreed upon repository of moral wisdom. Antebellum evangelical leaders, as Tocqueville observed of nineteenth-century Americans in general, were trying to hold disparate values together. They esteemed social stability, public order, and biblical ideals. They also, however, revered industrial growth, territorial expansion, and progressive theology. The dilemma they faced was how to maintain the proper balance between their love for freedom and their conviction that only coercive moral authority could keep freedom from becoming socially destructive.

The problem was not unique to the North. Conservative evangelical Whigs could be found struggling with the issue in the South as well. The South, however, did not face to the same degree as the North the social disruptions created by immigration, industrial expansion, and market competition. Irish and German Catholics never populated the southern states with the numbers they did in the northern states. At midcentury, there were an estimated 181,500 Catholics in the four largest dioceses of the upper South combined, a figure roughly equal to the number of Catholics entering the Northeast annually. Similarly, in the lower South, the combined immigrant Catholic population of New Orleans, Mobile, Savannah, and Charleston was smaller than the number of Catholics in many individual cities in the North.[55] Furthermore, social conditions in the South, premised as they were on the relationship between master and slave rather than between labor and capital, were not as threatened by bourgeois individualism as was the North. Southerners valued caste and hierarchy, and thus they were less subject to the leveling effects of the marketplace that made it increasingly difficult to maintain a conservative social vision in the North.[56]

The problem of how to balance freedom with moral authority was not simply an abstract philosophical or theological question. It was a question relevant to the broader problem of American national identity and the development of nationalist ideology in the nineteenth century. The Jacksonian era was a period of uncertainty for many Americans. Evangelical Whigs recognized this uncertainty and spent a lot of political energy trying to capitalize on it. Complicating the Whig project was the fact that the United States was predominately a country of regions and regional interests, with the two most powerful regions being New England states and southern states.[57]

Between 1835 and 1860, the United States struggled to find a truly national character. Heroic tales from the American Revolution and the War of 1812 provided something of a touchstone of common origins. But there were also memories, some fresher than others, of the divisions brought about by the Federalists and Anti-Federalists debates; of the Hartford Convention's flirtation with the right of secession and their challenge to the president's power over state militias; of the Congressional debates on the Missouri Compromise of 1820; and of the explosive tariff and nullification controversy of 1832.[58]

In addition to political differences, there was the painfully obvious economic division of free labor versus slave labor. It is perhaps superfluous to note that before the Civil War there was no national consensus as to what type of economic system would govern the nation. Southern intellectuals spilled as much ink denouncing the horrors of capitalism and the free-labor system as Yankee abolitionists did condemning the brutality of slavery. Although many southerners agreed that slavery could indeed be vicious, and many New Englanders questioned the social consequences of market-driven relationships between capital and labor, in the main, geography determined one's commitment to a political economy of slavery or free labor.[59]

Similarly, the political economy set limits on how people interpreted Constitutional arrangements. In the case of the 1832–33 debates between Daniel Webster and John C. Calhoun, it framed how one understood the obligations of individual states to the Union. Even within the subregions of the North and the South there were disagreements over economics. New York City had a great deal of interest in the cotton market of the Deep South states, and New Englanders wanted to ensure a healthy commercial relationship between themselves and the newly settled Ohio Valley region. Likewise, the Mid-Atlantic states and the states of the upper South often shared material resources as well as the means for transporting them. The point is that no substantial accord existed between the different economic interests that comprised the Union, no nationwide preference for one kind of political economy over another.[60]

In addition to lacking a comprehensive economic identity, the various regions lacked a unifying cultural identity. While the implications of the term "culture" are legion, a helpful definition that narrows the scope of the term has been given by anthropologist Clifford Geertz. Geertz defined culture as "an historically transmitted pattern of meanings embodied in symbols, a system of inherited conceptions expressed in symbolic forms by means of which men communicate, perpetuate, and develop their knowledge about and attitudes towards life."[61] In effect, "culture" can be considered a way of conceiving oneself and one's society through the mediation of symbols that have been handed down from one generation to the next.

The problem for antebellum Americans was that, unlike Europeans, they lacked a significant repository of inherited symbols. Apart from the Fourth of July and the doughtiness of George Washington, there was little available for Americans of all regions to rally around. A prominent New York attorney lamented this fact by noting that the United States does not have "like England and France, centuries of achievements and calamities to look back on."[62] Ralph Waldo Emerson, in a celebrated speech before Harvard's Phi Beta Kappa society declared, "we have listened too long to the courtly muses of Europe. . . . The mind of this country, taught to aim at low objects, eats upon itself."[63] American culture, at least in the first half of the nineteenth century, had no shared accomplishments in literature, music, or art—no Petrarch, no Milton, no Mozart. America's cultural identity rested on two wars and abstract sentiments for liberty and union. As the decades passed, these sentiments were strained under differing sectional interpretations. As one historian described the situation, the North increasingly came to view "liberty and union" as a national mandate that justified political permanency as well as material and geographic expansion. The South, by contrast, while not opposed to wealth and geographic expansion, nevertheless understood "liberty and union" less as an idea of mission and destiny and more as an insurance policy against centralized abuse of governmental power.[64]

As well as lacking enduring cultural symbols, antebellum Americans lacked a significant common ancestry.[65] The *New York Times* noted that "the Cavaliers who emigrated to Virginia and the Puritans who planted themselves in New-England, may be regarded as presenting the most marked dissimilarities of character of the whole bulk of those who first populated America."[66] Unitarian minister and amateur historian John Gorham Palfrey concurred. He denounced the South's pretense at having established an alleged aristocracy and declared that it was in fact the founders of Massachusetts who were "of the noble and gentle blood of England," while the wretched settlers of Virginia were "much fitter to spoil and ruin a Commonwealth than to help raise or maintain one."[67] What little common genealogy antebellum Americans shared was eventually lost to regional biases. The very labels of "Cavalier" and "Yankee" give some indication of how each stereotype contributed to regional myth-making and the idea of separate origins.[68]

As the first half of the nineteenth century progressed, regional rather than national interests dominated the concerns of most Americans. Conflicting political and economic agendas as well as a feeble inheritance of symbolic cultural forms contributed to the fragmentation. Northerners and southerners sought opportunities to secure their respective regional identities as the nation's collective identity. In the northern states, evangelical Protestants with their Whig sympathies were at the heart of the quest to define the "meaning" of America. Their cause was all the more urgent because of the increased Catholic presence in their region. Their cause was also all the more conflicted because they struggled with the problem of how to maximize freedom and yet still maintain moral authority without a universally accepted religious inheritance.[69]

Northern Evangelicals and Christian Nationalism

In the 1830s, 40s, and 50s, northern evangelicals, most of whom were Whigs, tried to solve their dilemma by connecting their religious values to a larger meaning of America. The United States, they argued, was a Christian nation. Specifically, it was a Protestant Christian nation. It was not, however, a Protestant nation in the tradition of the Huguenots of South Carolina, or the German Reformed of Pennsylvania, or the Anglicans of New York and Virginia. Rather, the United States was a Protestant nation conceived in, and sustained through, the values of New England Protestantism.[70]

New England, said the Reverend D. F. Robertson in a discourse entitled "National Destiny and Our Country," is where "the external institution of Revealed Religion has existed in its *simple integrity, there* all the ends of civil organization have been attained to the highest degree; and there they have been perpetuated" (emphasis original).[71] Likewise, Horace Bushnell claimed that though many parts of the "Old World" may look upon New England society as "still in the rough," through the revitalizing power of New England religion "we are rising steadily into noon, as a people socially complete."[72]

The Reverend James P. Stuart shared Bushnell's optimism. He maintained that the Divine Laws of the Bible constituted the first assemblies of New England and that the legislatures of the region remained substantially devoted to the same. Because of New England's steadfast commitment to Protestant principles, "the United States are destined for new forms of society, a new form of the Church, a new form of the State, a new and higher type of Christianity."[73]

Noah Porter, a professor of moral philosophy at Yale, argued that the legacy of the New England Puritan was "freedom and independence of the individual man . . . not, however, a lawless freedom, but a liberty implied in that separate responsibility, which each man holds to himself and his God."[74] Charles Boynton, a Presbyterian pastor from Cincinnati, provides one of the most striking examples of deference to the New England heritage. "Puritanism," he said, "is but another name for Apostolic Christianity. Puritanism, Protestantism, and True Americanism are only different terms to designate the same set of principles."[75]

The Beecher clan contributed significantly to the romanticizing of New England's Protestant heritage. Lyman Beecher frequently equated Protestantism with republicanism, and in a show of affection for Congregational church polity, he compared the office of Protestant ministry to the office of an elected official. "The opinions of the Protestant clergy are congenial with liberty," he wrote, because the Protestant clergy "are chosen by the people who have been educated as freemen, and they [the ministers] are dependent on them for patronage and support."[76] Edward Beecher, Lyman Beecher's second oldest son and one time pastor of Park Street Church in Boston, also saw a relationship between Protestantism and democracy. For him, the idea of being "chosen" extended beyond the ministry to the nation as a whole. He declared that America was "chosen by God to enjoy the honor of being the receptacle of Puritan ideas." With such a "glorious birthright," the "Puritan Churches" have inherited "the power to lead this nation in the great work of education not only at the East, but at the West also."[77]

Although Edward's esteem for his New England Protestant heritage may strike some as pretentious, he appears modest when compared to his brother Henry Ward Beecher. In a lecture intended to inspire lukewarm northerners to consider taking up arms against the South, Henry Ward reminded his audience that "the North is the nation, and the South is but a fringe." "The brain of this nation," he continued, "is New England," and New England is "that part of this nation which has been the throne of God"; it "has been the source of all that is godlike in American history." Even more:

Liberty, democratic equality; Christianity; God, the only king; right, the only barrier and restraint; and then, God and right being respected, liberty to all, from top to bottom, and the more liberty the stronger and safer—that is the Northern conception. And that is the precious seed that shall pierce to State after State, rolling westward her empire.[78]

Henry Ward, like his father, brought a crusader's spirit to ministry. He held several Presbyterian pastorates in the Midwest between 1837 and 1847. In 1847, following the earlier example of his father, he left the Presbyterians for the Congregationalists and accepted a position at the Plymouth Church in Brooklyn, New York. Here he developed a reputation as a colorful and dramatic preacher and on any given Sunday commanded the attention of up to 2,500 worshipers.[79]

Henry Ward was not shy about expressing his opinions on public questions. Assimilation of immigrants, especially Irish and German Catholics, along with challenging the slaveholding aristocracy of the South topped his list. In addition, he was enthusiastic about the temperance crusade and early efforts to establish women's suffrage.[80] Henry Ward vigorously denounced the compromise measures of 1850, believing like most Whigs that too much had been conceded to the South. Also, like so many other northern evangelicals, he actively campaigned for John Fremont in 1856 and Abraham Lincoln in 1860.[81]

While Henry Ward Beecher carried the evangelical banner in Brooklyn, Lyman Beecher's son-in-law Calvin Stowe, husband of Harriet Beecher Stowe, fought to ensure that public education in the Ohio Valley was guided exclusively by Protestant commitments. Stowe was a professor of Bible at Lane Theological Seminary, the seminary founded by his father-in-law. He shared with his in-laws a deep fear of European Catholic "barbarism" transplanted to American shores.[82] He believed that if the customs and beliefs of the immigrant population remained unchecked, public morality would suffer. What was needed was a medium whereby those who were not from America could be taught how to be Americans, citizens who would at least tacitly comply with, if not fully embrace, the moral consensus of the Protestant majority.[83]

For Stowe, as for the Beechers and their evangelical allies, the mediating institution between the immigrant and Americanization would be the public school system. Public, or common, schools were to be governed by Protestant principles and dedicated to ensuring a homogenous ethical vision for the country. Stowe spoke for many evangelicals when he argued, "it is altogether essential to our national strength and peace, if not even to our national existence, that the foreigners who settle on our soil, should cease to be Europeans and become Americans."[84] The common schools would oversee the process of reconstructing the children of European immigrants. They would be a perpetual institution that could sustain "national feeling" and ensure "national assimilation" without the undue influence of local peculiarities.[85]

In many ways, the scions of the Puritans had every reason to be optimistic. Protestant evangelicalism at midcentury, due largely to the efforts of New Englanders, had seen dramatic success. Beginning in the early years of the nineteenth century, a series of sporadic and spectacular revivals captured the imaginations of young ministerial students coming out of Yale and Andover. By the late 1820s, preachers such as Joshua Leavitt, Charles Finney, Jacob Knapp, and Jabez Swan had made revivals commonplace in the Northeast and the Midwest. These seasonal "manifestations of the spirit" possessed their own internal logic, and they could be successfully produced and reproduced by "the right use of constituted means."[86]

To be sure, revivals were reproduced over and over again in upstate New York, the Western Reserve, and cities peppering the Atlantic seaboard states from Boston to Philadelphia.[87] Although revivalism was initially controversial and divisive, most Protestant leaders eventually warmed to it, with Presbyterians, Methodists, Baptists, and Congregationalists all participating. Revivals proved popular across the evangelical theological spectrum because they provided a way to minimize doctrinal and denominational distinctions in favor of a unified Christian front. In addition, they often served as a public forum for communicating the transdenominational vision of what a Protestant Christian America should look like. Revivalists were charismatic, politically active, and frequently published their own journals. They were also educated and shared with more reserved evangelicals the common cause of promoting Protestant social reform in the public square.[88]

The revivalist preacher Joshua Leavitt had been active in benevolent causes since his student days at Yale, and in 1831, he began a career as an editor of a series of religious journals dedicated to New School doctrine, antislavery, and temperance. In 1837 after selling his paper, the *Evangelist,* Leavitt took over the *Emancipator,* the journal that created such a stir in Alabama during the abolitionist postal campaign in the autumn of 1835. In 1841 Arthur Tappan's brother, Lewis, financed a trip to Washington for Leavitt so he could argue the antislavery cause before Congress. When the *Emancipator* ran into financial trouble in 1848, Leavitt devoted his talents to the *Independent,* a journal of religion and politics that actively supported the young Republican Party in the late 1850s and the presidential campaign of Abraham Lincoln in 1860.[89]

Jabez Swan served as the pastor of two Baptist churches in Connecticut and New York between 1827 and 1838. Known for his pulpit theatrics and his ability to arouse excitement in his audience, in 1841 he committed to full-time itinerant evangelism, a career he maintained into the 1870s. Swan was a strong advocate of temperance, and he insisted that all those who converted at his revivals sign a pledge that they would never again consume alcohol. The usual suspects—hyper-Calvinists, deists, Unitarians, Catholics, and Masons—were harangued from the pulpit at Swan's protracted meetings, and to this group Swan often added German pantheists and Mormons. He was also dedicated to the abolitionist cause and in 1856 made several stump speeches for John C. Fremont, the first Republican nominee for president.[90]

Jacob Knapp graduated from Hamilton Literary and Theological Institute in 1825, two years before Jabez Swan. Like Swan, he had a reputation in the pulpit for flamboyant antics mixed with sentimental pathos, and also like Swan, he took to the itinerant circuit early in his career. Unlike Swan, Knapp did not limit his social evangelism to small communities in the Northeast. Knapp carried the evangelical abolitionist cause to the South's doorstep, preaching against slavery in Baltimore, Washington, Richmond, and Louisville. He gained notoriety for claiming that "Christianity is a radical principle" and that "a Bible Christian cannot be a conservative." Radical Christianity for Knapp, in addition to supporting abolition, consisted in attacking a host of personal sins that he believed increased as Catholic immigration increased, namely, dancing, gambling, and drinking.[91]

Charles Grandison Finney was perhaps the most notable religious personality of his day, and in 1835 he took a post at the newly founded Oberlin College.[92] Oberlin was itself the product of a controversy that began at Lane Theological Seminary in 1834 when fifty students decided to hold a debate on the issue of immediate abolition. Sensing the heated controversy that was about to ensue, President Lyman Beecher and other faculty members agreed to delay the discussion. The students protested, followed through with their debate, and within a matter of weeks, formed their own chapter of the Anti-Slavery Society. This proved too much for Beecher, school administrators, and the Board of Trustees, who felt that colonization, not immediate abolition, would be the more prudent position for luring potential donors to contribute to the school. The young "Lane Rebels," as the students came to be known, ignored the appeals of the faculty, and after hearing that Charles Finney had accepted a post at a new school funded in large part by the Tappan brothers, abandoned Lane in favor of the Oberlin enterprise.[93]

The draw Finney had for the spiritually and socially idealistic Lane Rebels is understandable in light of his personal charisma and widespread reputation as a revivalist. Finney was the product of Presbyterian teaching in Oneida County, New York, and he rose to national prominence when he preached a series of revivals near his home county in 1826. Trained as a lawyer, Finney brought to the evangelistic task the skills of colloquial persuasion and emotional appeal. He convinced many other evangelical leaders that sinners would never understand the gospel message as long as religion was "some mysterious thing they cannot understand."[94] Rather, Finney adopted revival practices, or "new measures," that focused on an individual's relationship with God, including *anxious meetings,* for individuals to "take up all their errors" before God in a group setting; *protracted meetings,* held over several days "to make a more powerful impression of God upon the minds of the people"; and the *anxious seat,* where troubled individuals could be "addressed particularly, and be made subjects of prayer."[95] Hundreds of people claimed to be converted at Finney's revivals, and his success at winning people to the Christian faith brought both wanted and unwanted attention to his work. Presbyterian and Congregational stalwarts such as Lyman Beecher found themselves in conflict with Finney early in his career, but as his influence grew, even Beecher conceded that the positive effects of Finney's new measures could not be denied.[96]

Charles Finney, more than any of the northern evangelists, strove to free Christianity from the authority of learned clergy, the tangles of ecclesiastical bureaucracy, and the nuances of theological debate. In doing so, he unleashed what one historian has called a "Copernican revolution" in the world of the northern evangelicals by emphasizing the religious experience of the convert rather than the formal teachings of the church as the starting point of true Christian knowledge.[97] Furthermore, Finney taught that conversion was just the beginning of religious experience. Christianity was much more than an assent to articles of belief written long ago in Europe. Converts were encouraged to apply faith to daily life, to find practical benevolent activities that could serve both as evidence of true conversion and as steps toward remaking society in the image of God's kingdom. Christian interests were one with "the interests of God's Kingdom," and the believer was expected to "aim at being useful in the highest degree possible."[98]

The zealous emotions unleashed by Finney and his evangelical imitators formed the foundation of what would grow to be called the "benevolent empire."[99] In the middle decades of the nineteenth century, numerous religious organizations were dedicated to combating the deleterious social effects of personal and public vice. Lyman and Henry Ward Beecher, Lewis and Arthur Tappan, Albert Barnes, Joshua Leavitt, Jabez Swan, Jacob Knapp, Francis Wayland, and Charles Finney were evangelical generals in a war against both individual and social sins. Many joined them, and a few attained high positions in the ranks of evangelical leadership.[100]

Although they never achieved perfect agreement, northern evangelicals shared the lofty, if ill-defined, goal to demonstrate the harmony between Protestant theology and republican political values. They wanted to bring their religious convictions to bear on a culture increasingly hostile to inherited authority, class distinctions, and aristocratic privilege. At the same time, they did not want to sacrifice the formalities of social deference, their distrust of mass politics, and their attachment to the goal of cultivating a virtuous and still "free" society. To accomplish their goals, they set out in often uncoordinated but always earnest efforts to convince believers that the Christian life was a life of transforming activity, and that the virtuous activities of the individual believer ensured the proper balance between the potential deleterious effects of freedom and the need for social stability.[101] As the Charleston abolitionist mail campaign and the Charlestown convent burning of 1834–35 demonstrate, however, the price of social stability was high for Catholics and slaveholders who were considered a threat to northern evangelical interests.

Fault Lines in the Evangelical Front

In the 1840s and 1850s, as the possibility for real political and economic unity grew increasingly elusive for the Whig proponents of nationalism, evangelical Whigs continued to believe that the churches could at least keep up the appearance of religious unity. They had witnessed, if not helped to orchestrate, the success of a growing network of benevolent, voluntary organizations and missionary societies that incorporated almost every Protestant denomination in the country.[102] The achievements of these voluntary reform movements inspired a sense of pride and purpose in New England's evangelicals. Additionally, revivalism and social reform had a significant southern component, a fact that reinforced the hope that in spite of the all the sectional posturing there was a common Protestant ethos that bound the two regions. Religious unity, however, had its limits. Southern evangelicals never wholeheartedly embraced two unique contributions New England evangelicals made to the American religious landscape: millennialism and modified Calvinism.[103]

Much has been written about the millennial optimism that pervaded the churches in the 1830s and 1840s.[104] Scores of Protestants of every denomination believed that God intended to use the United States to usher in the reign of Christ on earth. Church leaders in both the North and the South looked upon the success of revivalism and the spread of benevolent religious organizations as proof that the kingdom of God would eventuate through the activities of the American churches. As Anne C. Loveland has noted, however, millennialism received much less emphasis in southern evangelical thought. Southerners in general did not share the same urgency and optimism that characterized so much of northern evangelical life. Furthermore, Presbyterians and Baptists in the South endorsed a more thoroughgoing Calvinism than did the same denominations in New England. Even Southern Methodists, though far from Calvinistic in their theology, did not embrace the idea that society could be perfected as did Methodists in the North.[105]

Southern Protestants believed along with northern Protestants that conversion would lead the individual to a life of moral improvement and charity. But the idea that the social activism of the churches could sooner rather than later usher in the kingdom of God never received the same kind of treatment in southern pulpits as it did in northern pulpits. Consequently, it may have been easy to find southern clergy who would agree with Charles Finney that "every truly converted man turns from selfishness to benevolence." But it would have been more difficult to find a minister or theologian in the South who would agree with Finney's claim that "if the church will do her duty, the millenium [*sic*] may come in this country in three years."[106]

Similarly, southern ministers did not endow the industrial revolution with the same eschatological significance as northern ministers did. Horace Bushnell declared that the incredible gains in technology and industrial output were a sure indication that the age in which he lived had "some holy purpose . . . which connects with the coming reign of Christ on earth."[107] Although neither unaware nor in many cases unappreciative of advances in industry, southern ministers did not share the same hopefulness that Christ would return to earth following the sufficient growth of trade and industry.[108]

In addition to millennialism, revivalism divided northern and southern evangelicals. Northern preachers frequently used revivals to spread a more palatable version of New England Calvinism. Despite their reverence for their Puritan heritage, many northern evangelicals struggled with Calvin's teaching on human depravity. For some the idea of total moral corruption proved a critical stumbling block to missionary endeavors. Lyman Beecher attacked this problem head on. Since the mid-1820s, Beecher, along with his astute theological ally Nathan W. Taylor, had championed a benign Calvinism as the orthodox answer to the spread of Unitarianism in New England. He defended the old theology by advocating a new middle ground between the heterodox Unitarians and the annoying hyper-Calvinists.[109]

Popularly known as the New Haven Theology because of its association with Taylor and Yale, Beecher's via media contained two crucial modifications of Calvinist doctrine. First, the idea that original sin was imputed through Adam to his posterity as hereditary depravity was denied. Original sin is not, as the earliest Puritan divines and later Jonathan Edwards taught, an inherited "physical quality," but rather it is a "wholly voluntary" transgression of the law of God. Where earlier Calvinists believed that humans inherited both a depraved nature and an actual guilt before God through the "federal" headship of Adam, the New Haven Calvinists believed that people were born only with the potential to sin and thus not accountable for sin until they acted willfully. This theological adjustment had clear implications for the second substantial modification of the New Haven Theology. If people are not born depraved, and in turn not guilty as the progeny of Adam, then infants are born sinless. If infants are born sinless then God does not damn infants. For Lyman Beecher and other Neo-Calvinists, this modification of Calvin's teaching removed one of the chief intellectual obstacles of Puritan theology. Modified Calvinism was not, claimed Beecher, a repudiation of orthodox theology but rather "the predominant doctrine of the ministers and churches now denominated evangelical."[110]

Beecher was only partly correct. Modified Calvinist teaching on human depravity may have been the predominant doctrine of the evangelical churches in the North. In the South, however, modified Calvinism, or New School thinking, as it came to be called, never received widespread acceptance.[111] Southern ministers, especially southern Presbyterians, joined a minority of Presbyterians in the North in condemning the

New School doctrine. The New School teaching was considered a threat to "the essential principles of Christianity." It was also an ominous portent that the "very foundation of society" was in jeopardy.[112] The gospel, argued the distinguished Presbyterian theologian James Henley Thornwell of South Carolina, was being surrendered "to the same spirit of rationalism which . . . lies at the foundation of modern speculation in relation to the rights of man."[113] Charles Hodge, of Princeton Theological Seminary, agreed. New School doctrine, he claimed, led to "anarchical opinions" about the nature of social realities, and evangelicals who held to the teachings of modified Calvinism fell victim to the modern fallacy that "[our] own light is a surer guide than the word of God."[114]

Despite attempts to present a united Protestant front, antebellum evangelicals were divided over questions of doctrine and the way doctrinal commitments shaped public opinion about social and political realities. A spirit of missiology and moral reform allowed for the appearance of unity in the midst of growing diversities of opinions regarding the proper interpretation of Scripture and the application of Christian teaching to public life. This appearance of unity was, however, ephemeral, and it quickly evaporated as the northern and southern regions positioned to defend their interests.

Both northern and southern nationalism were predicated on how each region self-consciously exploited the vices of the other. Northern nationalism defined itself in terms of how the North was unlike the South as much as southern nationalism defined the South in terms of how it was unlike the North. Northern evangelicalism played a significant role in helping to construct a positive vision of northern nationalism, one that defined itself as much in terms of what it stood for as what it stood against.[115]

Alexis de Tocqueville observed that the United States was the only country he had seen where the intimate unity of freedom and religion could peacefully work toward political ends. The unity that Tocqueville detected was, as he also noted, based on a tenuous peace at best. The meanings of both "freedom" and "religion" were contested in the middle decades of the nineteenth century, and the notion that they could be amalgamated toward nationalist ends had yet to be fully realized. It would take four years of armed conflict to achieve that goal. In the decades immediately preceding the outbreak of war, however, northern evangelical leaders were instrumental in helping New England, and the North in general, develop a powerful sectional ideology. Northern evangelical leaders contributed to the process of creating a nationalist ideology by forcefully expressing the idea that despite the regional differences characterizing the country, one factor bound Americans together: the United States was a Christian nation, specifically a Protestant Christian nation, unfettered from the burden of European religious and political history.

CHAPTER TWO

Taking Aim at Europe and the Middle Ages

Europe in the Northern Evangelical Mind

In 1840 Francis Wayland visited Paris and was not impressed. He wrote to a friend that France was a nation bowed down "in form to the Romish Ceremonial," yet without "a God in the world." "If France is a Christian nation," he continued, "what are we, then, to say of the millions and hundreds of millions of Heathendom and Mohammadeanism?" To another friend Wayland wrote that the more he saw of France the more he believed himself to be a Puritan. Catholicism, he alleged, had paralyzed all potential for progress. On the same visit and to the same friend he lamented that while palace after palace had been raised in Paris, "there is no railroad yet from Paris to the sea, nor any railroad in the kingdom, except from Paris to Versailles."[1]

After the European revolutions of 1848, Wayland's children reported that their father was hopeful for France. He was optimistic that "the overthrow of dynasties" and "the change in forms of government" would lead to "the enlargement of intelligence, the elevation of moral principles, and the increasing supremacy of the religion of Christ."[2] By the religion of Christ, he of course meant Protestantism. "Popular institutions," he declared earlier in his career, "are inseparably connected with Protestant Christianity. Both rest upon the same fundamental principle, the absolute freedom of inquiry . . . the doctrines of Protestant Christianity are the sure, nay, the only bulwark of civil freedom."[3]

Horace Bushnell sympathized with Wayland's assessment of Europe. In the spring of 1843, Bushnell and an acquaintance from Italy collaborated with other Connecticut Protestants to form the Protestant League. Bushnell told his wife that the lofty purpose of the organization was to "move on Rome itself, and to overthrow the Papacy." He later informed the League that even if Americans could not be united against Romanism, at least "we can unite Protestants in a movement to complete the Reformation in Italy."[4]

In 1845, while traveling in Italy, Bushnell wrote to his wife that Rome was impressive, but the "grandeur of human power" he saw could not erase his cynicism toward the Catholic faith. After observing the Christmas Mass at St. Peter's, he scoffed that the "exalted savior" would regard it as nothing more than a sad compliment. "I looked round upon the vast assemblage," he wrote, "asking what is the real power of this?"[5] Similarly, while passing the Coliseum, he witnessed a company of chanting monks tending various shrines around the landmark, "a contrast," he said, that highlighted "the imbecility of religious superstition and the ferocity of the old time."[6] On the same trip Bushnell went to France, where he observed that, unlike Italy, or even England, "the French character is undergoing a thorough change. Every department of life and society is improving." The French experienced such change, Bushnell believed, because in France more than in any other European country, "the masses are more" and "the aristocracy less." He credited this progressive spirit to "the Revolution and all the tremendous experiences through which France has been carried in the last fifty years." The one thing lacking, however, was a true religion.[7]

The *New Englander,* a journal dedicated to promoting the "public sentiment of New England" and "evangelical truth" and that regularly published essays by Bushnell and other northern clergy, also weighed in on the European revolutions of the 1840s.[8] The German antipapal movement was heralded by the journal as a congregational revolution. To those Germans who supported the movement the journal advised that the only way they would succeed would be "for the people to fall back upon their own natural, primitive, scriptural and inalienable sovereignty." A free people with a free Bible "will prove a solvent at once for hierarchic and ceremonial Catholicism." Even more, the people of New England "have always maintained . . . that Romanism must be modified, softened, and eventually worn away by contact with our free spirit."[9]

In 1848 New England evangelicals had reason to cheer. On March 12, after learning that King Louis Philippe had been overthrown in France, workers and students rampaged through Vienna and invaded the imperial palace. Austrian emperor Ferdinand I conceded to the demands of the rioters and quietly encouraged Prince Metternich to resign his post as state chancellor. The next day, Metternich abdicated his position and fled to England. Insurrections followed in Germany, with the most strident nationalists demanding immediate German unification.[10]

Of the Italian Revolutions of 1848, the *New Englander* predicted the final destruction of the temporal power of the pope. "That mongrel government, which has ruled for so many centuries with fatal sway over the Seven Hills, is near its end. Pius IX, we believe, is the last Pope, who will have any temporal dominion in Italy." The journal anticipated that events in Italy were also likely to result in the destruction of the monasteries. Young men who sought to take religious orders "will be turned aside to the more exciting pursuits of politics or war; and on the first occasion the property of the convents and monasteries will be seized to defray the expenses of a great struggle for Italian independence."[11] Italian independence looked promising when, between January and March of 1848, Austria's hegemony faltered and constitutions were issued in Piedmont, Tuscany, Naples, and Rome. Charles Albert, king of Piedmont-Sardinia, sensing unity for northern Italy was at hand, declared war on Austria and for a brief period, with help from the fearless Giuseppe Garibaldi, led a successful guerrilla campaign against the Austrians. When, however, Pius IX refused to declare war against Austria and subsequently fled Rome, domestic disputes coupled with military setbacks led to the defeat and abdication of Charles Albert.[12]

Even more optimism surrounded the French Revolution of 1848. The monarchy was overthrown in February and a provisional government temporarily united competing political factions. The *New Englander* declared that the provisional government's motto, "Liberty, Equality,

Fraternity," was "similar in meaning to the famous phrase in our Declaration of Independence." Also encouraging was the impression that France was beginning to achieve a sublime synthesis of republicanism and Christianity. At last the French people "seemed to possess that republican spirit of human brotherhood, which is so well taught in the New Testament, God 'hath made of one blood all men to dwell on the face of the earth.'"[13]

In the 1840s and 1850s, New England evangelicals were eager to lead Europeans toward a new understanding of religion and politics and by so desiring, instruct Americans. B. T. Kavanaugh informed the readers of Boston's *Zion's Herald* that Protestants in the Mississippi Valley need not fear the pope or the powers of Europe. Just as "New England and the East generally have been so often, and so earnestly called upon to 'come to the rescue,' and save the country from despotism," New Englanders would, yet again, respond.[14] Readers of the *New Englander* were told that Europeans facing revolutionary changes in the late 1840s needed the example of their region. "A nation is not saved by genius and wit," said one editorial, "They need the religious principle of the staid New Englander."[15] If the European countries that were corrupted by the excesses of Catholicism would adopt the "simple ecclesiastical polity of New England," they could restore "a Christianity neither dogmatic nor ceremonial, without frigidity in doctrine or practice."[16] Triumphalism aside, in the middle of the nineteenth century, New England evangelicals were stirred by the notion that their faith was good for the rest of America and the rest of the world. They genuinely believed that their understanding of Christianity offered a moral and democratic corrective to the alleged clerical and political despotism that marred European history.

This obsession with Europe and Catholicism was not new. In the early 1820s, New Englanders were convinced that the Catholic Church was entering a period of decline. The papacy hardly seemed an international threat. Rome was reeling under the revolt of the Carbonari, a secret Neapolitan political society formed in the wake of the upheavals of the French Revolution and dedicated to spreading the principle of *égalité* first to Naples and then to all of Italy. From Naples the Carbonari moved into the territories of the papal states, where they sought to overthrow the rule of the papacy.[17]

In 1817 a rebellion in Macerata was quickly suppressed by troops dispatched at the request of the Holy See, but despite the setback the Carbonari remained dogged. In 1820, inspired by the Spanish revolution, the Neapolitan Carbonari once again took up arms in Italy. This time, however, Pope Pius VII was only able to subdue the rebels with help from Austria. It was a close call for the pope, and in the United States the woes of Pius VII did not escape notice. John Pierce, speaking at Harvard's Dudleian Lecture in 1821, expressed the opinion of many New England Protestants when he dismissed Catholic aggression as a thing of the past:

> The claims of this proud hierarchy, as they have in great measure ceased to terrify, have accordingly lost much of their former interest. . . . The thunders of the Vatican have long since spent their rage; and even in its neighboring atmosphere they are regarded as artificial and harmless attempts to imitate the war of the elements.[18]

With the pope barely able to defend his territory and with democratic movements breaking out across Europe, Protestants in the United States were hopeful that Romanism would soon be subverted under the forward movement of history. Their optimism was somewhat justified, but also short lived. The papacy, due to a variety of political machinations involving Napoleon's regime, was vulnerable in the early decades of the nineteenth century. Pius VII was proclaimed pope in 1800. Within a year, he allied himself with the fortunes of Napoleon and agreed to consecrate him "Emperor of the French." He also obliged the French clergy to reveal rumors of political conspiracies to the government. In exchange for his loyalty, Pius VII successfully negotiated the Italian Concordat of 1802–3, which declared Roman Catholicism to be the official religion of Italy.[19]

Subsequent complications from these diplomatic arrangements lingered for decades, but problems in Europe did not hinder papal interest in the United States. Pius VII quietly contributed to the growth of the Catholic Church in young America. In 1808 he established the dioceses of Boston, New York, Philadelphia, and Bardstown (Kentucky). The same year he elevated the see of Baltimore to metropolitan status. Between 1820 and 1821, he added Charleston, Richmond, and Cincinnati to the episcopal ranks. These new dioceses absorbed most of the Catholic immigrants who entered the country between 1830 and 1860.[20]

Throughout the late 1820s and early 1830s, northern evangelicals learned of the activity of the Catholic Church largely through Protestant religious journals devoted to attacking Catholicism and the papacy.[21] The calumny of the Protestant press grew so virulent that in 1833 it earned a rebuke from the bishops who convened at the Second Provincial Council of Baltimore. The Council issued a pastoral letter saying that they resented being denounced "as enemies to the liberties of the republic" and that they were tired of being misrepresented and vilified in the Protestant journals.[22] At the First Provincial Council in 1829, the bishops acknowledged that the American Catholic Church had benefited from the recent "convulsions of Europe." Yet they also tried to reassure Protestant critics that the influx of Europeans meant the Church must work harder to guarantee that immigrants assume "our native character," and "become chiefly, if not altogether national, henceforth."[23] The pledge of the Council did little to assuage Protestant fears.

In the early 1830s, evangelicals identified two European Catholic missionary societies as intent on carrying out the papal conquest of America. The Society for Propagating the Faith founded at Lyons in 1822 and the Leopold Foundation founded in Vienna in 1828 were organized for the specific purpose of promoting the growth of the Catholic Church in foreign lands. Although the Society for Propagating the Faith was the more influential of the two, in the United States, the Leopold Association attracted the most attention.[24]

The Leopold Association resulted from the efforts of the bishop of Cincinnati, Edward Fenwick. In 1827 Fenwick dispatched his vicar general to Europe to secure financial support for his diocese and to recruit German-speaking priests for service in America. Fenwick's cause found sympathizers in Germany and Austria. The archbishop of Vienna, Leopold Maximilian Graf von Firmian, was so moved by the situation in Cincinnati that he brought it to the attention of Emperor Francis II. Fenwick's vicar general, Father Rese, was granted an audience with the emperor, and soon thereafter the Leopold Association was formed for the purpose of providing financial support to the Catholic Church in the United States.[25] The organization's early success at building schools and churches, especially in the Midwest, alarmed American Protestants. The Catholic Church was growing through the generosity of millions of Catholic Austro-Hungarians, committed royalists who supported the policies of the archconservative Austrian ruler Prince Klemens von Metternich.

Metternich more than any other European leader of the first half of the nineteenth century represented the worst of Old World intrigue to many in America. He was the chief architect behind the plans for rebuilding Europe after the defeat of Napoleon, and he aimed, as far as possible, to restore the rights of Europe's aristocracy as they existed prior to 1789. Metternich and his fellow conservatives were devotees of the *ancien régime.* They disdained the excess of Jacobin radicals, the violence of romantic nationalists, and the rational planning of post-revolution social theorists. Metternich's political views, and the political views of other leading European conservatives such as Russia's Tsar Alexander I, Prussia's Frederick William III, and England's Lord Castlereagh, loosely reflected the political philosophy of the British statesman Edmund Burke: social change is good, and even necessary, but proponents of change should seek to work within, rather than overturn, established customs and practices. Europe's aristocrats had seen the chaos that resulted from the French Revolution and the reign of Napoleon. At the Congress of Vienna in 1815, they determined that this would not happen again. Unfortunately, their efforts to restore social stability often resulted in policies that appeared uncompromising. In Austria, books and journals were censored, dissenters were jailed, and domestic spies were employed by the state as police informants.[26]

The conservative reaction extended to religious as well as political opinion. In the late eighteenth century, Roman Catholicism had entered a period of marked turmoil as rationalism and skepticism captured the imaginations of both laity and clergy alike. Burgeoning nationalist sentiment secured movements to establish state churches that had little, if any, relationship with Rome. At the beginning of the nineteenth century, after the convulsions of the French Revolution had run their course, the Church found its authority significantly weakened compared to its strength just a century earlier. As the Napoleonic era came to a close, however, Catholicism began to regain much of its former power both through a series of concordats with Catholic states intent on resisting any further revolutionary change and through Catholic intellectuals who eloquently articulated the political and spiritual value of orthodoxy.

Europe after the Congress of Vienna

To European liberals and most American observers, the reunion of various conservative European monarchies with Rome in the years following the Congress of Vienna appeared ominous. In Italy, six of the country's eight separate states formed alliances with Austria and the Habsburg Empire. With Metternich's backing, the loyal Italian states granted the clergy control over education. Clergy were also given authority to censor, and they exercised their power by banning the works of the French Encyclopedists and by pressing criminal charges against public critics of Catholicism. In Spain, a liberal uprising in 1820 forced Ferdinand VII to concede to a constitutional balance of power that challenged both royal autocracy and clerical influence over politics. Spanish monarchists responded by seeking the aid of Europe's Conservative Alliance. The alliance persuaded the French army to invade Spain and restore King Ferdinand VII to the throne. Backed by French arms, the Bourbons regained power in 1823. They revoked the constitution, revived clerical political authority, and at least nominally reinstituted the Inquisition.[27]

Germany, like Italy, consisted of a number of decentralized local provincial assemblies covering a vast amount of territory. The German states were loosely connected through the Diet of the Germanic Confederation, but after 1815 the confederation fell under the control of Metternich and Austria's extensive bureaucracy. German university students, however, remained committed to a democratic and unified Germany and organized patriotic societies to continue the revolutionary cause. The most conspicuous of these societies was the Burschenschaft, a student group that alarmed authorities in 1817 after a gathering at Wartburg Castle near Eisenach to celebrate the tercentenary of the Reformation ended in revelry and public denunciation of the conservative government. Metternich convinced local authorities that this upheaval was just the beginning of more serious troubles. He proved prescient when in 1819 the assassination of one outspoken critic of the Burschenschaft and the assassination attempt of another conservative leader spread panic through Germany. These events precipitated the issuance of the Karlsbad Decrees, laws that assigned proctors to monitor professors and students in the German universities for subversive activity.[28]

In France, the seat of revolutionary radicalism, the years following the Congress of Vienna were characterized by tense relations between conservative royalists (known as "Ultras" because of their ultraroyalist politics) and liberals who retained Jacobin sympathies. The Bourbon king, Louis XVIII, tried to steer a moderate course that would satisfy the competing factions, but his efforts proved fruitless as reactionaries in both camps issued measures to thwart the success of the other. When Louis XVIII died in 1824 his brother Charles X succeeded him. Charles was a conservative, a devout Catholic, and an opponent of any constitutional revisions that would limit the power of the monarchy. He made large concessions to the Church, among them restoring the convents, inviting the Jesuits to return to France (they were expelled by Louis XV under pressure from parliament in November 1764), and appointing a bishop as minister of education. He also passed a law intended to compensate the *émigrés*, nobles who fled the country after their land was confiscated in the early years of the Revolution. Charles slowly but deliberately attempted to take France back toward the ideal of royal absolutism, and his efforts prompted a strong reaction from liberals and their propagandists. By 1830 Paris was again in arms against the king, and this time the revolutionaries succeeded in forcing Charles, and with him the Bourbon legacy, into exile.[29]

Although Charles X's vision for a strong alliance between Church and Crown failed to secure the monarchy, his unwavering devotion to Catholicism was not without ideological support. French Ultras had for years relied upon the works of Catholic intellectuals who challenged the political optimism and religious skepticism of the eighteenth century *philosophes*. The Ultras argued that the *philosphes* and their Jacobin devotees had successfully undermined the divinely sanctioned relationship between religion and the state. In turn, France as well as the rest of Europe had rejected Christian political theology in favor of metaphysical speculations about possibilities of social perfection and universal equality. The Reign of Terror, the Napoleonic wars, and the Carbonari assault on the papacy all bore witness to the violent consequences of abandoning Europe's Catholic heritage. Recognizing the urgency of the times, both lay and religious Catholic intellectuals committed their energies to defending the defeated order.

Catholic apologists such as Félicité de Lamennais, Louis de Bonald, Joseph de Maistre, and François-René de Chateaubriand furnished European conservatives with sophisticated, if at times romantic, arguments supporting the rights of the monarchy and the papacy. In his *De la Religion considérée dans ses rapports avec l'ordre politique et civil,* Félicité de Lamennais resurrected a fundamental tenet of medieval political theology by declaring that all sovereignty, including social sovereignty, belongs first and foremost to God. Borrowing heavily from Augustinian political thought as it was developed in the Middle Ages, Lamennais argued that God created humans as social beings and supplied them with the proper means by which to maintain social order. Even the great minds of antiquity, especially Plato and Cicero, understood that there is a fundamental relationship between religion and law. These pre-Christian thinkers recognized that democracy contained the seed of its own type of despotism in its dismissal of religious authority. The state, said Lamennais, cannot create truth ex nihilo, and a just society will acknowledge its dependence on an independent yet universal religious authority, the Church, which serves as the guardian of divine law and public morality.[30]

Lammenais' ideas found an audience among European conservatives in the late 1820s, but the groundwork for his resuscitation of medieval political theory had been laid thirty years earlier in the works of Louis de Bonald, Joseph de Maistre, and René de Chateaubriand. Bonald's *Théorie du pouvoir politique et religieux dans la société civile* and de Maistre's *Considérations sur la France* boldly attacked eighteenth-century notions of individual rights and popular sovereignty. Against the liberal theorists they argued that the historical continuity of the community preceded the prerogatives of the individual and that any attempt at social reconstruction apart from religious considerations was a fiction of the Enlightenment. The only insurance against violent nationalism and unrestrained despotism was a return to the organic social relations of the Middle Ages where the moral authority of the Church countered and subdued the tyrannical ambitions of the nations.[31]

Louis de Bonald and Joseph de Maistre supplied Europeans with the theoretical models needed to contemplate a return to medieval social organization. The work of René de Chateaubriand, however, popularized the idea that the Catholic Church alone provided the principle bulwark against the destructive tendencies of rationalism, democracy, and "metaphysical equality."[32] Chateaubriand's prose was elegant and accessible. His writings often contained a sentimental reading of history and his apologetic for the Church was tinged with nostalgia. Nevertheless, Chateaubriand had a profound impact on French culture during the post-revolutionary restoration of the monarchy.

In particular, Chateaubriand's *Genie du Christianisme* was popular with traditionalists who refused to divide European history into a pre-Enlightenment age of despair and a post-Enlightenment age of progress. A dedicated student of antiquity, Chateaubriand argued that it is folly to try to explain history as progress because humans are incapable of being perfected. The great lie of the Enlightenment is that individuals are capable of ruling themselves (politically and spiritually) apart from the moral cultivation of the Church and the legal coercion of a monarch. Democracies are perpetually insecure, thought Chateaubriand, because the masses are ignorant and selfish; and a political system premised on the right use of freedom will always eventuate in the destructive cycle of interest competing against interest. With Aristotle and Aquinas as his guides, Chateaubriand maintained that the stability of the state depended upon a propertied aristocracy guided by the benevolence of religion.[33]

The years following the defeat of Napoleon and the Congress of Vienna did little to calm tensions between Europe's liberal nationalists and conservative aristocrats. It appeared that Metternich's Austria, Frederick William III's Prussia, and the Bourbon dynasties of France, Spain, and Italy had doomed the nationalists to defeat. Yet liberalism would not be vanquished from Europe. By the middle of the 1830s, western Europe, with the possible exception of Great Britain, was committed to either continuing the reforms set in motion by the French Revolution or returning to a semblance of medieval political arrangements. Backed by Europe's brightest Catholic intellectuals, ultraroyalists and ultramontanists (those who wanted ecclesiastical power concentrated in the papacy) were determined that the radicals be held in check.

Liberal intellectuals, however, had a different agenda. In 1845 the French historian Edgar Quinet published a work on the political climate in Spain that was widely circulated in England and America. *Ultramontanism, or The Roman Church and Modern Society* argued that political freedom would never be secure without completely eliminating the influence of the Catholic Church from politics. "The Middle Ages," alleged Quinet, was a time "when the conscience of nations was not yet formed."[34] After the Renaissance and the Reformation, however, "modern missionaries" such as Francis Bacon, René Descartes, Wilhelm Leibniz, and Martin Luther "converted the world to new life; they have been what St. Boniface and St. Patrick had been in former times."[35] The Reformation and the Enlightenment opened the possibility for a new "universal order" that refused the counsel of the Catholic Church in favor of "the counsel of Providence" and the "universal conscience of mankind." "de Maistre's Pope may be able to maintain us in communion with the Latins," wrote Quinet, "but this is not sufficient for us; we want to be in communion with all mankind."[36]

Quinet was a romantic French nationalist deeply influenced by the late eighteenth-century German philosopher Johann Gottfried von Herder (1744–1803).[37] Herder was a language theorist who introduced the concept of the *Volk* into early German nationalist movements. He believed that nationalism was part of the natural progression of all cultures toward the universal idea of "humanity." For Herder, the peculiarities of place and local customs, while necessary for national identity, ultimately have little value if they refuse to be subordinated to an impartial concern for the worth of all human beings. To realize the worth of humanity in general, certain political prerequisites are necessary. These prerequisites include a commitment to egalitarian democracy and a belief that public ethics rest on moral sentiment rather than the dogmatic creeds of the Church. Herder's political thought provided the theoretical framework for Quinet's optimistic historicism.[38]

A good friend of Quinet and an equally influential French historian, Jules Michelet, used a similar theoretical framework in his massive study, *Histoire de France*. A liberal intellectual voice of the emerging petite bourgeoisie, Michelet argued that the growth of freedom, specifically freedom from clerisy and monarchy, was the most important theme of French history. Until the French Revolution, the history of France was a history of justice denied. Prior to 1789, France, as with all of Europe, was caught between the theology of the Church and justice for the people. Michelet argued that over the course of one dramatic year, from the assembly of the Estates-General in 1789 to the Festival of the Federations in 1790, the wrongs of the Middle Ages were righted. France had become an example for the rest of the world. "The Revolution, the daughter of Christianity, has taught its lessons to the whole world, to every race, and to every religion under the sun," and the "Revolution founds fraternity on the love of man for man, on mutual duty, on Right and Justice."[39]

The French Revolution produced a model for a new kind of Christianity, a new universal order. To critics who suggested that the Reign of Terror seemed slightly less than Christian, Michelet equivocated that the Terror exterminated only twelve thousand people while the Inquisition murdered millions. "History," wrote Michelet, "will inform us that the Revolution trembled at the thought of aggravating death . . . [while] the church of the middle ages exhausted herself in inventions to augment suffering."[40] Most important for Michelet and his friend Edgar Quinet was that the Revolution ushered in a new kind of religion that could compete with and eventually surpass the ancient tyranny of the Catholic Church. The natural state of humankind is a state of fraternity, argued Michelet, and "the fundamental basis of human nature is sociability." "The old habits, familiar objects, customary signs, and revered symbols" of antiquity are disappearing, he maintained, and "no special form of worship can confer holiness on the most holy of holy things—man fraternizing in the presence of God."[41]

The Leopold Society and the Evangelical Response

As the intellectual debate over the meaning of Europe's religious and political history brewed, the Catholic missionary organization, the Leopold Society, emerged from the heart of Europe's most conservative Catholic region, the Austro-Hungarian Empire. The Leopold Society concentrated its efforts in the United States and this, along with the large influx of Catholic immigrants, generated an enormous amount of antagonism. Protestant journals and periodicals regularly included reports on religious and political developments in Europe intended to both inform and alarm American readers.

One of the earliest and most successful pieces that called attention to the alleged Catholic threat appeared as a serial of twelve letters published in the *New York Observer* in the fall of 1834. Submitted pseudonymously by "Brutus," the letters were collectively entitled *A Foreign Conspiracy against the Liberties of the United States.* In actuality, the man who believed he sensed a conspiracy was Samuel F. B. Morse, the son of a Congregationalist minister and future inventor of the telegraph.[42] Morse's articles struck a chord with many Americans, and soon after their first publication, other evangelical and nativist periodicals such as the *Downfall of Babylon,* the *Christian Spectator,* the *Christian Watchman,* and the *Protestant Banner* began reprinting them.[43] His argument had profound effect on his evangelical audience primarily because he articulately connected Catholicism, immigration, and European conservatism as imminent threats to American democracy.

According to Morse, the Leopold Society was not simply a Catholic missionary association that sought peacefully to extend the charity of the Church to the United States. Rather, the Leopold Society was as much a political organization as it was a religious organization, and its designs included promoting the despotism of Metternich and his conservative allies. "Austria," said Morse, "is now acting in this country. She has devised a grand scheme." This "scheme" included sending Jesuit missionaries into the United States supplied by the emperor of Austria with large amounts of money. The religious nature of the missions was, however, a ruse.[44]

As evidence of a conspiracy, Morse noted a series of lectures, given in Vienna a year before the Leopold Society was formed, by the Romantic writer turned Austrian governmental official Fredrick von Schlegel. Schlegel declared that Catholicism and the monarchy opposed the republicanism of the United States, and according to Morse, it was not coincidental that the Leopold Society was formed in Vienna soon after the lectures.[45] He argued that promonarchical, pro-Catholic European conservatives viewed American democracy as the fountainhead of egalitarian chaos that had spread throughout Europe for fifty years. Why? Because, "every revolution that has occurred in Europe for the last half century has been in a greater or lesser degree the consequence of our own glorious revolution."[46] America was the seedbed of liberty, said Morse, and if the European monarchies and the papacy wished to reclaim the authority that they shared in earlier days, they had to effect a political as well as religious conversion of the United States.

Catholicism, or popery, as Morse called it, "is the antipodes of Democracy. It is the same petty tyrant of people here, as in Europe."[47] True patriots, he said, will resist popery because it "is a political, a despotic system" opposed "to all that is valuable in our free institutions."[48] For Americans, however, "the Protestant religion, and Liberty are identical, and liberty keeps no terms with despotism."[49] American Protestants exercise the "natural and revealed right of private judgment," and they have demonstrated to the world the benefits of having "the spirit of the doctrines which the Bible teaches."[50] Austrians, by contrast, "are slaves, slaves in body and mind, whipped and disciplined by priests to have no opinion of their own, and taught to consider their Emperor their God."[51]

"Brutus's" articles resonated with evangelicals, and many Protestant journals wrote favorable editorials supporting his views. The encouragement inspired Morse to elaborate on the theme of a European Catholic political conspiracy, which he did in a second series of articles published in 1835, under his given name, entitled *Imminent Dangers to the Free Institutions of the United States through Foreign Immigration.*[52] In these articles, Morse enlarged upon the role that Catholic immigrants would play in changing America's political landscape.

If Americans viewed matters of faith and matters of politics as dependent upon the assent of the individual, whether in choosing a denomination or in choosing a political affiliation, then what might happen if large numbers of Americans chose to convert to Catholicism? What if they found sympathy with Metternich and his conservative allies? To the evangelical mind, the prospects were ominous. There was, of course, no direct threat of a possible European assault against the United States. President James Monroe precluded this risk when he issued his foreign policy ultimatum to Europe's Conservative Alliance in 1823.[53] But in 1835, the problem that Morse presented was in some respects more threatening than the possibility of European military intervention in Latin America.

Morse had identified a fundamental challenge to the Protestant ethos that lingered from the time of New England's colonization. America was to be a Protestant experiment that tolerated Catholics, not a Catholic country that mimicked the political structures of the Old World. If Catholicism gained a strong enough foothold in the United States it would only be a matter of time before the country would have to confront Europe's ultraroyalists and ultramontanists.

For many Americans, the threat of internal subversion by European Ultras was more frightening than open armed conflict. Morse uncovered these fears in America's evangelical churches. In addition, he established the vocabulary that would be repeated again and again in evangelical and nativist literature over the next two decades. European monarchy and popery were the despotic "manufacturers of chains for binding liberty." They created the "terrors" of the confessional and inquisition. They were the enemies of "civil rights" and "private conscience." Their power depended upon social subordination, "masters" over "slaves." They were products of the Dark Ages, the very antithesis of Protestantism and democracy.[54]

Morse's first letter had appeared in the *New York Observer* on August 30, 1834, nineteen days after the Ursuline convent was destroyed in Charlestown, Massachusetts. The remaining letters ran through the fall of that year at the same time that Lyman Beecher was traveling the Northeast to raise money for Lane Theological Seminary. On his fundraising tour, Beecher elaborated on the theme he had first put forth the Sunday before the attack on the convent: Rome and the autocratic nations of Europe intended to conquer the United States by increasing immigration and gaining control of America's schools and colleges. The conspiracy theory proved wildly popular with his Congregationalist and

Presbyterian audiences, and in 1835 Beecher published his speeches as a book titled *A Plea for the West.*

A Plea for the West expanded on Morse's concerns. Beecher maintained that Europe was full of "masses of feudal ignorance and servitude" and that without reform "despotism and revolution will arbitrate her destiny."[55] Thankfully, he continued, "the light of our republican prosperity" is "gleaming in upon their dark prison house," and America's example of freedom is creating an "earthquake" under her "tottering thrones."[56] Still, he warned, Europe's monarchs will never passively allow America to erode their authority. They will counter by sending immigrants into the country, and with large numbers of Catholic immigrants will come the political threat of the "union of church and state in the midst of us."[57] The situation was as serious as that of the Roman Empire in the sixth century, "for since the eruption of the northern barbarians, the world has never witnessed such a rush of dark-minded population from one country to another, as is now leaving Europe, and dashing upon our shores."[58]

According to Beecher, the Catholic conspiracy aimed to check the expansion of republicanism and Protestantism into the western territories of the United States, where "the religious and political destiny of our nation is to be decided."[59] The ensuing conflict would not be decided by arms but by education. Americans faced straightforward yet diametrically opposed alternatives: "superstition, or evangelical light; despotism, or liberty."[60] Beecher amplified Morse's theory by linking the idea of a Catholic conspiracy to the problem of America's national identity.

A passage from the book of Isaiah introduced *A Plea for the West*: "Shall the earth be made to bring forth in one day? Or shall a nation be born at once? For as soon as Zion travailed, she brought forth her children."[61] This text, said Beecher, was a "prediction of the rapid and universal extension of civil and religious liberty, introductory to the triumphs of universal Christianity."[62] Universal Christianity, however, could not prevail under political conditions characterized by "arbitrary despotism" and the "predominance of feudal institutions." Rather, Christianity would triumph through "the march of revolution and civil liberty," because the United States was "destined to lead the way in the moral and political emancipation of the world."[63]

By 1835 New England evangelicals were anxious. Morse's and Beecher's efforts had made anti-foreign and anti-Catholic conspiracy theories commonplace in both the Protestant press and mainstream newspapers. Fear of promonarchist, pro-Catholic subterfuge inspired sermons, editorials, and closed meetings of concerned citizens groups. The paranoia had a political face as well. As anti-Catholic rhetoric increased in the churches, so too did sporadic local attempts to form nativist political parties in New York City; Paterson, New Jersey; Cincinnati; and Germantown, Pennsylvania.[64] These early endeavors faltered due to differences in priorities between divergent local associations and to the fact that Whigs remained the preferred party of the most strident anti-Catholics, the northern evangelicals. After the financial panic of 1837, however, public confidence in both Whigs and Democrats was shaken, and in New York, nativists gained their first major political victory by winning the mayor's office and the city council.[65]

In 1838 nativists who were concerned about immigrant suffrage petitioned Congress to change naturalization laws. The petition was referred to the House Committee on the Judiciary, whose report recommended that the probationary period of naturalization be extended well beyond the five years then required. The report echoed sentiments expressed by Morse and Beecher some three years earlier. American republicanism was threatened by European despotism, and the aliens flooding America's largest cities were quietly campaigning to reverse America's democratic heritage.[66]

The House of Representatives noted the suggestions of the committee but did not act on their recommendations. They were preoccupied at the time with the proposed creation of a national bank. Nevertheless, petitions to change naturalization laws continued to drift through committee rooms of the twenty-fifth Congress. In the late 1830s, politicians at the federal level were becoming aware of a growing constituency of anti-immigrant, anti-European, and anti-Catholic voters. Still, no legislation to change naturalization law was passed. Congress failed to act on nativist demands, an indication that at least some politicians were paying attention to the voting potential of a new constituency coming to America from across the Atlantic.[67]

Assailing the Medieval Specter

Despite the fits and starts of federal anti-immigration laws, northern evangelicals remained determined in their assault on Catholicism. What could not be secured in the halls of Congress could at least be sentimentally cultivated from the pulpit and in the religious press. Time and again, evangelical ministers and editorialists contrasted the political conditions of Catholic Europe with those of Protestant America. In doing so, they assaulted not only Catholic political theology but also the place of the Catholic Church in western history.

For nineteenth-century northern evangelicals, history was both providential and millennial. God's divine plan was working itself out in the nations, chief of which was the United States. In many ways, this understanding of history mimicked the divide between European liberals and conservatives. Rome, monarchy, clerisy, and feudalism belonged to an age of darkness. Nationalism, democracy, individualism, and industry belonged to the age of light. Evangelical clergy and theologians were largely responsible for cultivating this historical dualism in the popular imagination.

The Reverend Abel Stevens of Boston, a contemporary of Samuel Morse and Lyman Beecher, preached a rather nondescript sermon in November of 1834 titled "The Political Tendencies of Popery." Intending to convince his Boston congregation of the dangers of Catholicism, Stevens linked together three historical moments separated by more than two thousand years: the Persian assault against Greece, the Protestant Reformation, and the American evangelical campaign against alcohol. He repeated the standard indictments of the pope and Rome with impressive rhetorical flourish. "The Vatican," he said, "has been for ages a political forge, where the chains of Europe have been wrought." He also provided his audience with a touchstone from ancient history that would have been familiar to every educated New Englander. Catholics, he declared, "have already got into the Thermopylae of our liberties."[68]

The Catholic surge into the United States was, argued Stevens, analogous to the Persian invasion of Greece in 480 BC. European immigration was nothing less than an overwhelming assault by a foreign culture.

Like the 300 Spartans who fought to defend mainland Greece against 310,000 Persians, America's Protestants had to make a final glorious stand against the tyranny of Charles X and the autocracy of Austria.[69] This battle would not be fought with spears and swords but instead with the "indirect operation of moral means." In order to secure victory, Protestants had to muster "the energy of another Reformation." They needed a "moral movement" to be accorded the same importance as those that "have rendered so energetic and triumphant the Temperance Reform."[70]

Compared to other evangelical literature of the time, Stevens' use of history was typical. Evangelicals borrowed liberally from Europe's past to prove that they were living at the zenith of historical development. In February of 1834, Francis Patrick Kenrick, then coadjutor to the bishop of Philadelphia, attempted to reassure Protestant detractors that American priests had no designs but to "preach to their flocks, the Gospel of peace and charity." The following year, the *Downfall of Babylon,* a vicious anti-Catholic journal, accused Kenrick of duplicity.[71] Kenrick was a liar, said one editorial, because history proved him a liar. The "Gospel of peace and charity" was not the gospel of the Catholic Church when Pope Urban II exhorted crusaders at the Council of Clermont to "exterminate all men, women, and children with fire and sword." Peace and charity did not guide Pope Innocent IV (it was actually Pope Innocent VIII) "when he sent forth his hordes to deluge the valleys of the Piedmont in the blood of the pious and inoffensive Waldenses." Nor was Pope Sixtus IV motivated by peace and charity when he launched the Papal Inquisition and put to death "millions of Infidels, Jews, and heretics." Kenrick was not to be trusted because the Catholic Church could not escape the facts: "History, without a dissenting voice, vociferates her condemnation, and paints her character with blood."[72]

In the same vein as the *Downfall of Bayblon,* Joseph Martin's book *The Influence, Bearing, and Effects of Romanism on the Civil and Religious Liberties of Our Country,* published in 1844, argued that history condemned the Catholic Church as well. "Like the barbarian hordes of the north long since emptied upon Rome," he opined, "so Rome is now emptying her surplus population upon America."[73] Catholics were a threat because they had too long relied on the teaching of the church fathers, canon law, and apostolic constitutions. The Church's confidence in tradition distorted its understanding of authority. In particular, the Church misinterpreted what Christ meant when he committed the "keys of the kingdom" to Peter and his successors.[74] Tradition taught that the word "keys" in the Greek was plural rather than singular, and that this in turn proved that the Church was given authority over both spiritual and political affairs.[75] Without elaborating on why this interpretation was wrong, Martin explained how the exegetical error spread after Pope Boniface VIII issued the bull *Unam Sanctam* in 1302.

Unam Sanctam (One Holy) refers to the papal declaration that came about amid a controversy surrounding Philip the Fair of France and his unlawful seizure of the province of Gascony from Edward I and the English. Churches in England and France were heavily taxed for revenue to fund the war between the two countries, and this disturbed Boniface VIII because the conflict was of a purely secular nature. Monies exacted from churches in support of crusades against the infidel was an acceptable practice. Monies exacted from churches to fund land disputations between quarreling monarchs was not. For his part, Philip the Fair did not like being told how to manage the financial affairs of his kingdom and he made this known by having the pope's legate, Bishop Bernard de Saisset, accused of treason, tried in Paris, and found guilty. Boniface VIII was swift to condemn the French king, and after a series of pronouncements intended to punish Philip, he issued *Unam Sanctam,* which declared that "there is but one Holy Church, outside which there is neither salvation nor remission of sins."[76]

Martin identified this moment in church history as the watershed that initiated the corruption of the medieval papacy. He noted that later Jesuit theologians such as Robert Bellarmine (1542–1621), Francisco Suarez (1548–1617), and Thyrsus Gonzalez (1624–1705) supported the position taken by Boniface VIII. They also elaborated on the original declaration by arguing that infidel monarchs may be deprived of the dominion they have over Catholic subjects. Martin failed to mention, however, that Boniface's pronouncement resulted in his arrest by Philip's agents at Anagni in 1303, his subsequent death, and the rise of the Avignon papacy. He instead emphasized that in the sixteenth century Pope Sixtus V used the authority of *Unam Sanctum* to declare Henry of Bourbon, a Protestant, heretical and thus an illegitimate heir to the crown of Navarre. Pope Sixtus released Henry's subjects from their oaths of fidelity and consequently ignited a civil war between French Protestants and Catholics.[77]

Martin's interpretation of the doctrine of *Unam Sanctam* is brief and, by necessity of his agenda, historically selective. He concluded his indictment of the threat of popery by implying that the papal power claimed in *Unam Sanctam* could, if left unchecked, "release" Catholic citizens from their commitment to democratic principles in democratic countries.[78] For Martin, the implications were nothing short of eschatological. "Had it not been for Romanism," he writes, "the world would, ages ago, have been a comparative paradise." Even more,

> Had the principles of the gospel been preserved in their original purity, and continued to have been preached with the energy which characterized the labours of the Apostles, their triumph would long since have been complete. Christianity would now have been the religion of every nation under heaven, and the days of millennialism been witnessed in all their meridian sunshine.[79]

Martin's millennial historicism was not unique. Northern evangelicals were uncompromising in their caricature of the legacy of the Middle Ages. Central to every attack against Catholic Europe was a syllogism highlighting the character and destiny of United States: Americans are a Protestant people; Protestant (specifically evangelical) theological commitments secure civil and religious freedom; as proponents of civil and religious freedom American Protestants are destined to transform European countries stunted by Catholicism and the Dark Ages.

In an address before the New Jerusalem Temple of Cincinnati, the Reverend James Park Stuart reminded his audience that "in Christian Rome, from Constantine to the fall of the Western Empire, the Church and State were united," but today "the American Republic is the first considerable government on earth, in which the Church and State are not united."[80] The separation of church and state, he continued, was inspired by Protestantism. To an American "the nonsensical parade of Catholic worship looks so much like the dull ages of the past," and Protestantism, unlike Catholicism, is not a religion of the past. Where Catholicism is dependent on the past to understand the Christian faith, "Protestantism looks to the future, consults possibilities, and inquires diligently for the road leading forward into the better times ahead."[81] Catholicism is the religion of the Old World, and for Americans the Old World is a socially repugnant place "where mobs rise in opposition to law, and in violent hatred of law," where "the individuality of individuals is crushed in the cradle," and where "the voice of the Emperor is the voice of God."[82]

In an essay titled "Church and State, or Rome's Influence upon the Civil and Religious Institutions of Our Country," the Reverend Joseph F. Berg of Philadelphia argued that a new form of church and state was necessary because the Catholic Church had successfully subverted every attempt at good government since the seventh century. Beginning with a condemnation of Pope Boniface III's decree against the Patriarch of Constantinople in 607, which declared the Bishop of Rome to be the head of all churches, Berg offered a sweeping survey of European political history. His *tour de histoire dépravé* included Gregory II's excommunication of Emperor Leo III at the height of the iconoclast controversy; Pope Zacharias I's support of Pepin and the Merovingian dynasty against Childeric; and Pope Paul I's threats against the Emperor Constantine Copronymus because of the emperor's support of the Lombards and his opposition to the veneration of images.[83] This was just the eighth century. Berg critiqued Rome's political meddling through the seventeenth century. He concluded that although there were many "enlightened and liberal" Catholics in America who supported American civil and religious institutions, their spirit of liberality was to be credited not to any modern concessions on the part of the papacy but to "the fruit of intercourse with Protestants."[84]

The Reverend John N. McLeod, speaking to the New York Protestant Reformation society in 1843, argued that the origins of enlightened and liberal American ideals, such as liberty of conscience and freedom of speech, could be found not only in Protestantism but also in certain condemned heresies of the Middle Ages. Albigenses, Waldenses, and Lollards "kept the light of the true religion, which they had received from the primitive Christian Church, burning amidst the darkness of the papal night."[85] These anathematized movements established the right of protest and reform, a right that produced the moral revolutions of the Protestant Reformation and the war of American independence. Like the Albigensian, the Waldensean, and the Lollard, "the true Protestant is pledged to be a Reformer."[86]

Five years after McLeod's address, Italian nationalists attacked the Vatican and demanded Pope Pius IX concede a constitutional government, abolish the hierarchy of the Church, and declare war against Austria. From April 1848 until November of the same year, Rome reeled under mob violence. Rioters assassinated Pius IX's prime minister, wounded a papal prelate, and forced the pope to flee to Gaeta. In the aftermath of the violence, the *New Englander* concluded that developments in Rome possibly signaled a permanent end to the temporal power of the papacy.[87] "These remarkable events," urged the journal's editors, were perhaps the consummation "of the once vanquished revolution begun by Arnold of Brescia in the twelfth century." Hopefully, they continued, the events of 1848–49 were of a more permanent nature. Arnold was put to the pyre after being captured by agents of Frederick Barbarossa in Tuscany. The present revolutionaries were unlikely to suffer the same fate. The *New Englander* even suggested that there was reason to believe that a new pope might emerge: a pope "resembling that humble monk Celestine V . . . rather than a hawking Leo X, or a Julius II at the head of his armies."[88]

The contrast of Europe's medieval past with America's democratic present extended to the common school movement controversy. Writing from Boston, the pseudonymous Rector of Oldenwold agreed that Protestantism secured American liberty, and he echoed Lyman Beecher's concerns that if the public schools were not protected from Catholic interests, Americans would soon find themselves "inthralled [*sic*] and enslaved" like the nations of Europe.[89] Thankfully, the Rector of Oldenwold added, Americans have a national glory that far exceeds the treasures of European medieval culture. Americans, he wrote,

> have no fine palaces, in which reside a race of nobles, at whose door stands a sentinel, and in whose veins courses kingly blood . . . no Vati-

can, no Basilicas, with their Madonnas and their Scala Santa . . . none of the works of Raphael, Giulio, Domenichino, Guido, Michael Angelo, and Simonetti . . . no old castles, remains of feudal times, no pageantry of military power. . . . But we have institutions to which we can point the stranger with emotions of pleasure and honest national pride. All over our land are little elementary schools.[90]

The chief threat to the common school system according to many Protestants was the Roman Church, and in the main, New England Protestants agreed with the anonymous minister from Boston that Catholic schools "cannot exist on the same soil with a liberal school system."[91]

A contributor to the *New Englander* further emphasized this point by forcefully censuring the educational system of the monasteries in the Middle Ages: "the monastic life is a life of sloth, and this is not an age for idlers. No life can be acceptable to God which is not useful to men . . . the monastery afar on top of a mountain [is] a luminary of the Middle Ages—one of those stations along which the torch of knowledge was transmitted from summit to summit, while the world beneath lay buried in darkness."[92] Several years later another article in the *New Englander* warned that "Catholics are strongest where the Protestant place of worship and Puritan school house are least known and felt—a fact suggestive of better means of proscriptive legislation to save our free institutions from the Pope of Rome."[93]

The most overt attempts at promoting proscriptive legislation against immigrant Catholics came with the rise of the American nativist and Know-Nothing movements in the 1840s and 1850s. Here too harangues against the iniquities of the Middle Ages peppered political speeches and party literature. The Philadelphia Platform, a statement of party principles adopted by the National Council of the American Party in 1855, asserted that Christianity "is considered an element of our political system," and "the Holy Bible is at once the source of Christianity, and the depository and fountain of all civil and religious freedom."[94] By Christianity, the nativists meant Protestantism, and when they published their platform for distribution, they included with it a work entitled *Young Sam,* a one-hundred-page account of the atrocities of the Catholic Church committed from the first appearance of the Donation of Constantine in the eighth century through the crisis of European liberalism in the nineteenth century.

Nativists argued that after Constantine assumed power in the early fourth century, Christian churches ceased to be private organizations, and they began to acquire property. Increased property holdings led to increased wealth, which led to the unfortunate condition of an ambitious and worldly church. This change in the public status of the Christian Church coincided with Constantine's alleged gift of western Italy and most of the transalpine territories to Pope Sylvester I. Constantine's "donation" set the stage for an uncompromising power struggle between the papacy and the emperors in the Middle Ages. In the ninth century, under the benevolent watch of Charlemagne, the strength of the Christian Church began to grow as "richly endowed churches and monasteries" converted their territorial possessions into principalities. Slowly, as wealth and status increased, the papacy claimed a temporal power independent of the emperors.[95]

According to *Young Sam,* by 1073, after Hildebrand assumed the papal chair under the name of Gregory VII and subsequently issued his *Dictatus Papae,* "the idea of a universal theocracy had grown up into a passion." Universal theocracy was given further legal legitimacy under Gratian, who launched a revival of canon law studies in the mid-twelfth century when he "collected and fecundated" the *Sentences* and *Etymologies* of Isidore of Seville (ca. 560–696). The codification of canon law paved the way for a universal tribunal at the Court of Rome from which all political and theological differences could be dispelled by the Vatican. From this point, noted the nativist writer of *Young Sam,* Rome "found itself consulted from all quarters." Bishops, abbots, monks, nobles, princes, and private individuals looked to the papacy as a civil as well as a spiritual authority.[96] The narrative continues through several more centuries with special attention given to the "influence of Frederick Barbarossa," "the audacious conduct of Becket, archbishop of Canterbury," Pope Innocent III's "celestial theory of the two powers," the zealous orders of St. Dominic and St. Francis, and the "unbounded power" of the Spanish Inquisition.[97]

There is nothing particularly unique about the nativists' historiography. Most northern evangelicals agreed with their negative assessment of the Middle Ages. What is striking, however, is that nativists believed that they needed a sweeping historical-theological narrative to reinforce their anti-immigrant, anti-European political platform. In this sense, the nativist politician, like the anti-Catholic evangelical minister, attacked Catholic immigration as a religious problem as much as an economic and social problem. The political subterfuge of Catholicism could not be dissociated from medieval political theology no matter how much Catholics protested.

Congressman Lewis D. Campbell of Ohio, a Whig who switched to the nativist American Party, advertised his religious bias on the campaign trail. "My partialities run with the Protestants," he declared before a Washington audience in 1856, "because in youth I was trained in that faith, and in manhood learned from the history of the past that the Protestant has always been the church of Freedom." He added that Americans intend no union of church and state, and "if there be any Catholic in this country who is not satisfied with this sort of religious liberty I tell him the sooner he 'packs up his duds' and goes back [to Europe] the better."[98]

Another congressman, Joseph Chandler, a Catholic convert from Philadelphia, tried to persuade his colleagues in the House of Representatives that the pope no longer exercised political power as he had in the Middle Ages. Chandler also urged that questions of Catholic loyalty to the United States should not be a topic of discussion in Congress. The Protestant press swiftly responded. Reverend Berg of Philadelphia argued that Chandler's portrayal of Catholicism hinged on his assertion that the Church recognized a "distinction between matters of opinion and articles of faith." But, Berg continued, "the system which tolerates such latitude of opinion is just as guilty before God and man as though it had enclosed them in the shrine of *its* faith."[99] Presbyterian minister Robert C. Grundy challenged Chandler's insistence that medieval compacts between emperors, kings, and popes were outdated. He said the congressman lacked historical evidence that this was the case. To prove that the Church still advocated the temporal power of the pope, Grundy strung together a series of isolated quotations on the subject of church and state from Thomas Aquinas, church historian Cardinal Cesare Baronius, Cardinal Bellarmine, and the Dutch theologian Peter Dens.[100]

In addition to the political consequences of Catholic immigration, northern evangelicals also feared that Catholics would hinder American economic expansion because their love of medieval social structures disinclined them to accept progress in any form. In 1856 the *Christian Watchman and Reflector,* a Baptist organ published in Boston, opined that "the Pope has a natural dread of railroads and the other great enterprises of modern civilization" because he is "bent on reviving the darkness and barbarism of the Middle Ages."[101] Five years earlier, Noah Porter, a respected professor of moral theology at Yale College, suggested that a careful comparison of the Jesuits and the Puritans proves which group favors technological progress. "The Jesuit lives in the past," said Porter, "he adores and reverences the men and institutions that are gone by." By contrast, the Protestant knows "what is true and useful for the present generation," and "the Protestant will be more likely to start a new theory, to invent a new method, or make a new discovery."[102] A contributor to Oberlin College's *Oberlin Quarterly Review* declared one of the primary purposes of the gospel was "to promote the *civil, social,* and *physical* interests of man." The Catholic faith failed to succeed at this mandate in Europe because the "mystery of iniquity" has "aimed to hold *free, immortal mind*[s] in perpetual vassalage" (emphasis original). True Christianity is a religion of progress:

> Hence civilization increases the facilities of the church for doing good. Let the press, the steam engine, and the telegraph, be wielded by the good for the advancement of Christianity, and Christian civilization, with energy, and all the powers of darkness can not stay the progress of reform.[103]

While the political legacy of medieval Europe was bleak, many northern evangelical leaders remained optimistic. The forward movement of history appeared to be on the side of Protestants. Reverend Thomas Brainerd, pastor of the Third Presbyterian Church in Philadelphia, agreed that the Middle Ages were "repulsive." But he also believed that Americans should be grateful for them because "they render more conspicuous the glorious result of the Reformation."[104] Still, Americans had to remain vigilant. If the "unholy alliance of Church and State" in the Middle Ages was the result of a "conspiracy of popes and kings to enslave a race," what is to prevent the same conspiracy from being enacted again?[105] Brainerd cautioned that vigilance should not result in gloom. The civil power of Romanism had steadily waned since the Reformation, and European revolutionary movements had permanently damaged the political influence of the pope. "The truth is," said Brainerd, "since the French Revolution . . . superstition has ceased to be the governing principle of the old empires of Europe. The spirit which originated the crusades, has been supplanted, among the great, by political emulation and avarice; and among the mass, by the spirit of liberty, urging on to revolution."[106] Brainerd was sanguine about the political possibilities of Protestantism because Protestantism alone guaranteed the spirit of "reform" and "revolution" necessary to secure basic democratic principles. "Democracy," reasoned Brainerd, "is political Protestantism."[107]

Catholicism and the Middle Ages as Points of Contrast

Catholicism and the Middle Ages put the American experience into relief for many northern evangelicals. Specifically, the idea of the Middle Ages as dark, corrupt, and tyrannical provided a negative reference against which northern evangelicals could articulate their political identity. Americans, they argued, were to languish under no religious authority beyond the limits of private conscience. Americans were not to fear the *Unam Sanctam* of Boniface VIII. Americans would not be victims of an Inquisition. Americans could not be coerced by the resurrected legacy of a Julius II or a Frederick Barbarossa. Catholicism and the Middle Ages provided rhetorical capital for evangelicals seeking to unify a nation of regional prerogatives (and, in the Northeast, increasingly of ethnic enclaves) around a common commitment to Protestant values.

There was, however, another more positive sense in which the idea of the Middle Ages promoted the evangelical agenda. The political and social legacy of the Middle Ages was slowly dying in nineteenth-century

Europe. American evangelicals, like liberal Europeans, believed that they were witnessing the death rattle of a centuries-long struggle between the authority of the nations and the authority of the Catholic Church. Beginning with the French Revolution and continuing with the subsequent reactions against Metternich and the Congress of Vienna, Europe in the eyes of many Americans was changing for the better. If the European revolutions of the 1840s and 1850s stayed the course, Europeans just might follow the political precedents of the United States.

Henry Ward Beecher subscribed to this American triumphalism. He declared that the "history of preaching the Gospel has been a history of the development of Christian democratic ideas." Some European countries were believed to be catching-up to these ideals. "The progress of Europe," Beecher continued, "has been from barbarism to Christian civilization; from absolute monarchies, up through constitutional monarchies and aristocracies, toward government by the people."[108] Presbyterian stalwart Albert Barnes concurred:

> Nothing can be more true than the declaration in the immortal instrument which asserts our national independence, that "all men are created equal, that they are endowed by their Creator with certain inalienable rights." . . . Nothing can be more certain than that God has implanted in the human soul a desire of liberty which is a fair expression of what he intends shall be the settled condition of the things in the world.[109]

The "settled condition" of which Barnes spoke was in reality a particular kind of political Protestantism. For all the energy spent decrying the medieval threat of uniting church and state in America, evangelical Protestants in the North never abandoned the notion that America was a Christian nation. Reverend D. F. Robertson summarized the beliefs of many northern evangelicals: "The Constitution of the United States . . . defers in many particulars to the essential Christian Church . . . All that is good in the Constitution and laws of the United States rests on the same sublime pedestal with the Church."[110] Likewise, Thomas Bayne wrote, "the American government is founded upon virtue, intelligence, and Divine Revelation," and "any system which is operating in opposition to these excellent principles, has a tendency to subvert our government."[111]

Many American evangelicals viewed the Declaration of Independence and the Constitution of the United States as products of providential design. They were the fulfillment of Protestant political ideals that championed the prerogatives of the private conscience of the individual over and against inherited authority, political or otherwise. As one historian described the American situation, "the evangelical movement shared with the traditional religious establishments of European countries the goal of a Christian society."[112] The northern evangelical commitment to a Christian political order, however, was not based upon the same assumptions that inspired European Catholic apologists René de Chateaubriand, Louis de Bonald, Félicité Lamennais, and Joseph de Maistre. European Ultras were committed to defending the universal dependence of the state on the universal moral authority of the Catholic Church. American evangelicals were committed to a different kind of universalism, a universalism that could unite people apart from the institutional control of the Catholic Church. Evangelical universalism was based more on sentiment than on dogma and, like the politics of those who advocated revolution and reform in Europe, evangelical politics sought to secure what was common to humanity without sacramental coercion. According to this universalism, the only authority to which people were required to submit was the authority of private conscience as informed by the Bible.

CHAPTER THREE

Northern Evangelicals
Define the Other

Ideological Others

In the two decades prior to the Civil War, northern evangelicals found a domestic complement to the threat of Catholic Europe in the slave system of the American South. It has been well documented that evangelicals played a significant role in the antislavery fervor that swept through northern churches in the 1840s and 1850s. Indeed, recent scholarship has served as a welcome corrective to the disproportionate attention that earlier works on the subject gave to the radical abolitionist minority.[1] Less attention has been paid, however, to the fact that the northern evangelical crusades against Catholicism and slavery emerged in the same period and in large measure shared the same premise. Northern evangelicals believed Protestantism to be a religion of progress and freedom. The same political theology that motivated them to combat Catholic immigration and European conservatism also compelled them to secure political arrangements that challenged the alleged tyrannies of the southern slaveholder.[2]

Leading northern evangelical journals used their publications to rebuke all kinds of vice. Drinking, gambling, impiety, and violence were frequently assailed. But Catholicism and slavery were particularly knotty because they were not simply socially corrosive "personal sins."[3] Catholicism and slaveholding represented deep-seated ideological threats to the northern evangelical conception of America. Catholics who criticized the common schools, or encouraged European missionary activity in the states, or feared the liberal political forces besieging Rome and Pius IX, were not, like drinking or gambling, a habit of character. Likewise, the proslavery intellectual class, who insisted that slavery was compatible with both the Bible and the Constitution, or that slavery was beneficial to the slave, or that slavery provided the only plausible economic solution to the deleterious effects of industrial capitalism, was more than simply a social threat. Slaveholders and Catholics were incompatible with the northern evangelical idea of what it meant to be an American because they challenged the unique political-theological temperament that informed that idea.

Spectacle in Babylon

The *Downfall of Babylon* ran regular pieces attacking both Catholicism and slavery. Its editor, Samuel B. Smith, a frequent speaker for the New York Protestant Association, offered one of the first defenses of the mob that burned the Ursuline convent in 1834. He suggested that the arsonists had acted properly in light of the iniquities that they believed were occurring inside the building.[4] Bawdy tales of nuns and priests filled every edition of the journal, but at times Smith opted less for the vulgar and more for the polemical. His journal, along with the *New York Observer*, took the lead in publishing Samuel Morse's *Foreign Conspiracy against the Liberties of the United States* in serial form in the spring and summer of 1835.[5] Smith's forte was scandal and spectacle, and along with persistent burlesque attacks against the evils of "Romanism," the *Downfall of Babylon* contained caricatures of slavery and slaveholders bordering on the inane.

An 1835 article in the *Downfall of Babylon* entitled "Industry" argued that "nothing is more important to your usefulness and happiness than habits of industry," because "we all cannot be '*lords*' and '*gentlemen.*'"[6] The article condemned the slaveholder who does not live by his own labor and suggested that often the slave is "a thousand times" more intelligent that his tyrannical, drunk, and foolish master. The important thing to be aware of, said the author, is that "there is slavery of several kinds; there is mental slavery as well as bodily." While the subject matter of the article is not particularly unique, its location in the journal is noteworthy, as is its use of the phrase "mental slavery." The article followed a brief autobiographical lament written by Smith in which he described the "mental slavery" of Catholicism. Here, Smith claimed that he himself was "late a Popish priest" and offered a detailed account of how he struggled to break himself from the bondage of the Catholic Church. He confessed that his judgment and all the powers of his soul "were completely held captive by the chains of Infallibility." Popery had blinded his understanding and had left him "in a very unhappy state" until the truths of Protestantism "broke through the thick clouds."[7]

An earlier edition of the *Downfall of Babylon* similarly juxtaposed articles on popery and slavery. "A Voice from the West" described horrors accompanying the consecration of a Catholic Church in St. Louis in December of 1834. Citizens who turned out to watch the procession of priests marching through the city were said to be "paying homage to the vassals of a foreign Potentate," and their actions were explained as a Catholic "spell" that "has spread over the discernment of our people." The very next article in this edition, "The Pious Negro," described "a grey headed African" in Virginia named Caesar. Caesar professed the faith of a Christian, but Caesar's beliefs were formed under the yoke of bondage. Slavery had left "this degraded son of humanity" with a pious heart but nevertheless a deficient and jaded understanding of Christianity. Common to both stories was the idea that religious conviction formed under a perverted, coercive power resulted in a deluded faith.[8]

Given the alleged appalling conditions that prevailed in both the Catholic Church and the slave system, the most wretched scenario the *Downfall of Babylon* could imagine involved priests who owned slaves. One such story came from an agent of the journal who took a trip to New Orleans where he discovered that "Popery in the south was the same as Popery in the north."[9] In the South, however, the wickedness of the priests descends "with all its pollutions, into his poor negro slave." One Sunday the writer claimed to observe an intoxicated priest shooting dice and smoking Spanish tobacco, all the time watching from his window his naked male and female slaves toiling in the hot sun. Witnessing firsthand the brutality of the priests toward their slaves, the curious northern traveler inquired about their religious beliefs. To his utter dismay, he discovered that the slaves were idolaters who had erected a temple in the remote recesses of the cypress swamps. The walls of their temple were covered with Spanish moss, serpent skins, the wings of birds, and a cross. The altar of this "church" was a rotten log, the god they worshiped was a "stuffed alligator," and the worship itself consisted of nude dancing and singing that "was concluded by rolling in the mud." This scene, said the author, "is the picture of Popery in full triumph," and if left unchecked, "such would be the condition of the whole human race, and such the worship that would be offered to the God who made us."[10]

What this northern traveler actually witnessed is difficult to say. Perhaps he uncovered a syncretism of Christianity and Voodoo, or perhaps he supplemented the reality of the slaves' existence under Catholicism with vulgarities of his imagination. Whatever the truth behind the tale, it is clear that the writer found the vision of a nation filled with Catholic slaveholders to be a dire prospect. While the source may have been marginally reliable at best since the entire purpose of the paper was to alarm readers of the dangers of Catholicism, its publication nevertheless reinforced its message. The pattern, however, of uniting the twin evils of slavery and Catholicism was not limited to lurid periodicals such as the *Downfall of Babylon.*

Heralding Zion

The mainstream northern evangelical press also ran stories haranguing the place of Catholicism and slavery in a free republic. Conservative political movements in Europe received a fair share of criticism as well. Through the late 1830s and into the 1850s, *Zion's Herald,* a Methodist organ headquartered in Boston, regularly attacked Catholics, slaveholders, and European conservatives. During the week of March 16, 1836, two separate editorials decried slaveholding as a "God-dishonoring, anti-

Christian system," as well as a "heinous sin against God and the rights of humanity." Immediate abolition, argued the writers, was the only measure that could "counteract the influence of selfish principles" of those who supported the slave system.[11]

The same edition of the journal ran a piece detailing the scandalous claims of sexual torture made by Maria Monk in her recently published *Awful Disclosures of the Hotel Dieu Nunnery of Montreal.* A rival crosstown Catholic journal, the *Boston Pilot,* had earlier claimed that Miss Monk's story was untrue and that *Zion's Herald* and other Protestant journals were irresponsible in reporting the sensational story. *Zion's Herald* retorted that Maria Monk had given a "correct representation of the moral conduct of Catholic nunneries" and that Miss Monk's story captured the "licentiousness and pollution" of the Catholic Church.[12]

The following month saw a repeat of articles on the subjects of slavery and Maria Monk. The article on slavery was a convoluted exegetical exercise attempting to show that the Greek word for slave in the New Testament, *doulos,* did not mean "slave" (as argued by many southern clergy) but rather "hired servant." The article on Maria Monk described a meeting held by the American Tract Society concerning Monk's accusations of lechery against the priests of the Montreal diocese. At this meeting, the society resolved that the nunnery from which she had allegedly escaped was in all probability a "sanctified brothel, full of all manner of uncleanness and adultery." Although two Protestant ministers from New York had examined the nunnery, these initial investigations, according to *Zion's Herald,* were insufficient because conducted by ministers who were "strongly and actively prejudiced against Maria Monk." The American Tract Society and the editors of *Zion's Herald* thought it necessary that a committee of "four gentlemen" be appointed for the purpose of reexamining the Hotel Dieu Nunnery. They also suggested that Samuel Morse be asked to accompany the inquisitors.[13]

In addition to scrutinizing local politics in Boston and New England, *Zion's Herald* also monitored Catholic participation in European and American political affairs.[14] When Catholics from New York City became involved in the 1842 New York state senate race, the journal reported that pamphlets printed with the words *in hoc signo vinces,* "by this sign conquer," were circulated among the working poor. This was the same motto said to have been adopted by Constantine as he crossed the Tiber River at the battle of the Milvian Bridge. Yet again, noted the reporter, another "ignorant band is marched to the polls under the banner of the Pope."[15]

Like most religious journals of the period, each edition of *Zion's Herald* included a section on the news from Europe. Here, a reader could find information ranging from the activities of the pope, to the status of various European monarchies, to battle statistics and military maneuvers of the Austrian, Italian, and Prussian governments as they sought to extinguish revolutionary activities in their territories.[16] Interspersed between news about Catholics and European politics were article after article describing the importance of evangelical piety in bringing an end to slavery. The Catholic threat to the Mississippi Valley and the menacing expansion of slavery into the western territories remained persistent concerns of *Zion's Herald* until the eve of the Civil War.[17]

The Burden of Evangelical History

Another religious periodical that regularly featured articles on the evils of slavery and Catholicism was the *New York Evangelist*. Founded in April 1830, the *New York Evangelist* was the product of a collaborative effort by some of the most distinguished Christian businessmen in New York City. Led by Arthur and Lewis Tappan, the men who supported the journal called themselves the Association of Gentlemen. Their vision was to create a news periodical that promoted Christian benevolence without advertising support from undesirable businesses such as theaters and breweries.[18] After an earlier attempt by the Tappan brothers to create a news journal covering both evangelical and commercial news proved unprofitable, they colluded with the Association of Gentlemen to create the *New York Evangelist*. With this effort, the Tappan brothers abandoned commercial news in favor of articles on revivals, temperance, Romanism, and slavery. Under the editorship of the Congregationalist minister Joshua Leavitt, the *New York Evangelist* grew into the leading organ of New School theology as well as the literary voice of Charles Finney and his supporters.[19]

From its inception, the *New York Evangelist* maintained that immediate abolition was the only moral solution to the problem of slavery. The journal sent correspondents to cover antislavery meetings all over the New England states, and it often featured melodramatic stories of abolitionist travels through the southern states.[20] Careful examination of the journal reveals that northern evangelicals who supported immediate abolition, at least those who subscribed to the political commitments of the *New York Evangelist,* also held strong antipathy toward Catholicism.

At the 1837 meeting of the Massachusetts Anti-Slavery Society, much discussion arose over whether evangelical abolitionism intentionally sought to stir up strife and discord. Reverend Russell from Lynn, Massachusetts, stood and announced that the principles of New England abolitionism had always been peaceful. Yet, he continued, though the Anti-Slavery Society was a peaceful body, they were indeed guilty of stirring up strife, and as long as "inhuman apathy" toward slavery prevailed, they would persist in stirring up strife. Russell did not believe that abolitionism was creating trouble simply for the sake of obstinacy. Rather, he assumed, and the applause reported indicated others assumed, that the kind of discord the abolitionists sought was a righteous discord.[21]

Strife, argued Russell, has "always been the effect, when truth has come into contact with error." Strife was the legacy of Christ after he reproved "the Pharisees, lawyers, and doctors." Strife was the inheritance of the apostles as they traversed the Mediterranean world. The apostle Paul "had the spirit of a modern Abolitionist." After the apostolic era, it was Martin Luther who "stirred up Pope, Cardinals, and all, till the church was reformed."[22] Antislavery men were admonished that troublemaking was in continuity with both Scripture and the principles of the Protestant Reformation. In this light, the evangelical abolitionists conceived of themselves as benevolent truth-tellers. Like the apostolic and reformation churches, their cause was to promote "pure" truth that corrected inherited error.

Many northern evangelicals believed slavery was a sin that justified the most damning condemnations they could muster. Slavery, they argued, violated the spirit of the New Testament. But the progress of history, especially the contributions of the Protestant Reformation and the rise of political liberalism, also condemned the practice. Evangelical abolitionists reasoned their blunt assaults were warranted because "Jesus Christ and his Apostles, and the Reformers used plain and pointed language, often with great severity." Similarly, the "framers of the Declaration of Independence used severe language" when they said "*all men are born equal*" and thus implicitly declared "every slaveholder is a manstealer."[23] "The unanimous voice of all northern Christians and Americans" favored immediate emancipation, and American Protestants should assail slavery with the courage and consistency modeled to them "since the days of the Pilgrim Fathers."[24]

Northern evangelicals believed that they were part of a glorious tradition in continuity with New Testament Christianity, the Protestant Reformation, the pilgrims, and America's founding. Their moral pedigree began with the teachings of Christ and entered the modern world through the Reformation. Jesus and the apostles proclaimed liberation for those who were held captive by sin and the law. The Reformers proclaimed liberation for those who were held captive by Romanism and the papacy. The Founding Fathers proclaimed liberation for those held captive by political tyranny. Now northern evangelicals assumed the mantle and proclaimed liberation for those in physical bondage.

The *New York Evangelist* promoted this historical-theological narrative. The struggle against slavery was an extension of Christianity's perpetual struggle against evil. Above all, abolitionists bore a special indebtedness to the Protestant Reformation and the Reformation principle of *sola scriptura*, by Scripture alone. *Sola scriptura* created a new standard for moral reasoning that freed Protestants from the oversight of a magisterium. When faced with questions of either public or private morality, the unaided Bible was the only authority to which the Protestant conscience was accountable.

This principle was to have far-reaching consequences for northern evangelicals. According to the *New York Evangelist,* the Bible "was the acknowledged standard of morals in this country," and more, "the subject of slavery is one on which the Bible has legislated."[25] The most effective way to "remove the evil" was to convince people that "slavery was contrary to the Bible."[26] Politics alone would never bring about the collapse of the slave system because political rights must "be conceded by operations of conscience, and by the principles of religion."[27] The only hope for overturning slavery lay in "bringing the principles of the Bible to bear on it." Evangelical influence over public policy could undo the "ignorance, and degradation, and corruption of morals which slavery engenders."[28] History proved the point. Slavery was not challenged in antiquity under the Tarquins, or the consuls, or the Caesars, or the patricians of the Roman Empire. It likewise survived the Middle Ages "when spiritual despotism swayed its scepter over the nations."[29]

Northern evangelicals believed they lived in the historical moment that could bring about the permanent abolition of slavery. Protestants had long heralded "freedom" as a theological distinctive that separated them from Catholics. Freedom was also the virtue that separated Americans from other nationalities. Many understood the political freedoms guaranteed by the Constitution as compliments to the spiritual freedom guaranteed by Protestant theology. "The right to worship God, to read the Bible and to pray" was "an American right as really and inalienably, as the free use of the limbs."[30] Slavery could be challenged on the grounds that Protestants had "always practically taken the side of freedom."[31] Protestants rejected inequitable hierarchies in favor of the doctrines of "human brotherhood" and the "essential equality of all men."[32] They were enemies of despotism and champions of the "rights of the many." Wherever true Christianity flourished, one would inevitably find "the growth of liberal views" and "the due recognition of human rights."[33]

The problem, argued the *New York Evangelist,* was that true Christianity was not flourishing in the United States. Southern slaveholders and Roman Catholics threatened ideals of human brotherhood and freedom so dear to northern evangelicals. In the early 1840s, some suggested that Catholics were more of a threat than the slaveholders were. One contributor argued that slavery could "be overthrown a thousand times easier than the monster with which the heroes of the Reformation contended." Catholicism was more dangerous than slavery because it "blended . . . earthly power" while at the same time shackling its "mysterious fetters on the conscience." The only thing that would save Americans from the "monster" of popery and prelacy was a sustained effort to enlighten the "free portions of the church of Christ."[34]

Lyman Beecher echoed these concerns in a letter to Albert Barnes, a part of which was published in the *New York Evangelist.* Beecher contended that Catholic immigrants under the guidance of the American hierarchy "intended to make themselves the political balance of power at the polls." He added that, once they accomplished this, they would destroy the common schools. Readers were warned that Catholics would enlist to their cause every element of "infidelity, irreligion, ignorance, and profligacy" to win the impending political struggle. Both the Protestant religion and republican institutions faced "persecution and blood" if Catholics successfully manipulated "the violence of party spirit" in the western part of the United States.[35]

The *New York Evangelist* was less concerned about the Catholic threat after the revolutions of 1848 and 1849 in Europe. With the conservative Austrian hegemony weakened and Pius IX fleeing Rome for Gaeta, popery, it seemed, was "a thing of the past—a thing that has long since ceased to hold any vital connection with the thought, the spirit, or the moving powers of the age."[36] Papists were "facing a new state of things," and their fate lay with other "old and worn out systems" slowly disappearing from Europe. The imminent threat to the nation was no longer the foreign tyranny of Rome but the domestic tyranny of slavery. In the 1830s and early 1840s, northern evangelicals feared Catholic immigrants were invading the West in the name of the pope. By the late 1840s and early 1850s, northern evangelicals were more afraid of southern political influence in the territories. Once the South succeeded in forming a "Confederacy of slaveholders," nothing but the free states of the North would be able to stop them from trying to build an empire that extended from "the Potomac to Panama."[37] Nevertheless, in 1849 the editors of the *New York Evangelist* remained hopeful that, like popery, the slave power would be checked by the "spirit of freedom moving over all the civilized world."[38]

Calvinist Observations

The *New York Evangelist* was the unapologetic voice of New School Presbyterianism and revivalism in the northern states. But Old School Presbyterians, those who did not support Charles Finney's new measures and

Lyman Beecher's modified Calvinism, were not to be outdone. Under the leadership of Sidney and Richard Morse (brothers of Samuel Morse), the *New York Observer* began in 1823 as an organ of Calvinist orthodoxy.[39] When the *New York Evangelist* published pro-Finney and pro-revivalist articles in 1832, the *Observer* promptly responded. Exchanges between the *Observer* and the *Evangelist* over the finer points of Calvinism ensued, and the argument at times grew acrimonious. Still, in spite of all the theological posturing, the *New York Observer* shared the same revulsion toward Catholicism and slavery as its crosstown rival.

Although the *Observer* and the *Evangelist* differed in their approach to Presbyterianism, one editorial in the *Observer* noted that both journals remained "in the hands of sons of sainted New England pastors!"[40] Moreover, both journals voiced hope on the subject of slavery because they spoke for "the mass of Christians and patriots in the Northern states."[41] The editorial ran in March of 1854. Within two months, the Kansas-Nebraska Act became law and, like the *Evangelist*, the *Observer* feared that the balance of political power was shifting through southern expansion into the territories.

Included in the March edition of the *Observer* was an argument against slavery by a Reverend Doctor Perkins. He was a noted expert on the subject of oppression because he had served for many years as a missionary "against the powers of darkness" in Persia. Perkins compared the abolitionists of the North to the "unprejudiced soldiers" and "common people" who heard the teachings of Christ and embraced his message. These common Christians were not like the politicians and Pharisees of "that day" whose hearts were hardened by pride. American slavery, said Perkins, was a sin, and it was also "the greatest human obstacle to the triumph of Christianity that exists at the present period."[42]

The *Observer*'s editors said they agreed with Perkins in the main but suggested that southern clergy made a compelling case from Scripture that slavery was not in and of itself sinful. Still, there was no doubt that slaveholders represented a threat to American progress. Southerners would have no problem wresting political rule from the free states because they could rally around "one interest and feeling growing out of their peculiar institution." Northerners, by contrast, were divided. The North had to contend not only with a more diversified economic system than the

South but also with more diversified political interests. In particular, the North had a factional party spirit fueled by Irish and German Catholics.[43]

According to the *Observer,* slavery was a curse and a crime and not to be advocated, but slaveholders themselves were not necessarily evil because of an economic system they inherited. If northern abolitionists were honest, they would realize that in condemning the slaveholder they equally condemned themselves. Their linens, clothes, household fabrics, coffee, sugar, and molasses betrayed just how many comforts northerners accrued through slavery. The *Observer* agreed with the *Evangelist* that slavery was a "foul blot" and a "blasting stigma" on a nation that professed "devotion to free and liberal principles." They disagreed with their rival, however, over the necessity of immediate abolition.[44]

What the South needed was the example of the superior profitability of free labor and industrialization. The North could lead the South "by the examples of the northerner's advanced wealth, commercial enterprise, and social improvement."[45] Once the South conceded to the northern economic system and subsequently weaned the region off dependence on slavery, northern evangelicals could turn their attention to solving the Catholic problem. After all, "Negro slavery is indeed a curse, but what is it compared with the curse of Popery! . . . The number of negroes imported from Africa in one hundred and fifty years, was less than 300,000—less than the number of Papists we are now importing every five years from Europe! We shall soon have more Papists in the North than they have slaves in the South."[46]

Regarding the Catholic problem, the Old School *Observer* could be just as resolute as the New School *Evangelist.* The *Observer* asserted that America owed its principles of "religion and humanity" to the pilgrims and their ideological heirs.[47] New England's Protestant political legacy captured the imaginations of the creedal Calvinists as much as it did the revivalists. America's national character, they argued, reflected the values of the Reformation, and no region of the country had more influence in shaping the national character than the people of New England.[48]

New Englanders "were among the best part of the best nation on the face of the globe," and under their direction the United States had entered an enlightened age where "a thousand authorities and prejudices connected with long established forms" were swept away.[49] Old School Calvinists were as earnest as New School Calvinists in the conviction that Protestant Christians had a duty to bring "Romish Children and youth" into Sabbath schools. Protestant schools, they urged, were the strongest counter against Catholic efforts to return to "the faith of those medieval churches."[50] Likewise, Old School devotees took as much pleasure as their New School rivals in learning that European countries were experiencing a "powerful reaction against the political supremacy of the clergy," and that Spain, France, and Belgium were seeking to establish governments "more in harmony with the liberal opinions of the nineteenth century."[51]

Cautious Watchmen

While northern Presbyterians remained optimistic about the relationship between Protestantism and political liberalism, the Baptists of New England were more conflicted. In 1834 the Boston-based *Christian Watchman and Examiner,* the largest Baptist weekly in the country, announced that the United States was the last hope for the conversion of the world to Christianity. The religious life of Great Britain was "choked and enfeebled." France was still suffering from "moral desolation." Spain and Portugal were "under the vials of divine wrath." Germany was "'twice dead' with apostasy." Italy harbored the "mother of harlots." Austria was "the sister and child of Rome." And the Orthodox Church in Russia was "bound under chains of superstition." American Christians, by contrast, were engaged in the "grand Christian enterprises of the age," and they rightly "looked upon the world as their field."[52]

That Baptists viewed Europe as a vast wasteland of moral turpitude and theological error is not surprising given the high priority they placed on the "right of individual conscience in religious matters, against all civil enactments."[53] They were proud of their commitment to the idea that Christianity should be unencumbered by political questions. They also believed that the relationship between church and state had been settled in the United States. In Europe, however, "the great moral battle between the church and state is yet to be fought."[54] The Catholic Church might be able to conceal its political ambitions for a season, but in due time it would become obvious that popery had no intention of abandoning its "anti-republican tenets."[55] Like other evangelicals, Baptists were convinced that the pope was "following the plans and instructions of the Imperial cabinet of Austria" and that Metternich intended to make Catholic "vassals" in the United States.[56]

Despite their ardor for separating religion and politics, northern Baptists had difficulty maintaining a consistent position. One reason for their inconsistency was the uneasy relationship New England Baptists shared with their Puritan ancestors. They agreed that the Puritan experiment was founded in "brotherhood of equality and affection" and that the Puritan heritage was superior to the "fruits realized by Catholicism, despotism, and slavery."[57] Yet they wrestled with the fact that the Puritans who fled England "never relinquished the principle of a national church" and that the Puritans were responsible for the exile of Baptist forefather Roger Williams.[58]

A speech by the Swiss preacher and historian Merle d'Aubigné published in an 1845 edition of the *Watchman* highlights another reason northern Baptists waffled on the church and state question. D'Aubigné warned that the revival of the Roman Church under the leadership of Pius IX was nothing less than "a war against the gospel." Protestant countries were admonished to abolish all forms of "external hierarchical theocracy" in favor of the "internal theocracy of the Holy Ghost." The interests of the church must never be left in the hands of clergy. If the zeal of the laity waned, wrote D'Aubigné, then it would be better for the state to intervene in the life of the church rather than retreat to the "exclusive domination of the clergy."[59] D'Aubigné did not address exactly how the state should intervene to ensure that the work of the Holy Ghost remained confined to the private life of the believer.[60]

Northern Baptists were well aware of the dilemma that D'Aubigné presented. Private judgment and personal responsibility were Protestant distinctives, and Baptists, more than other Protestants, took pride in the fact that they, unlike Catholics, "put no strait-jacket upon the soul."[61] A contributor to the *Watchman* noted that Christianity need not be connected with political questions because "whatever may be the form of government" the "Christian religion is designed to bless man universally" and thus "will ultimately unloose the tyrant, crumble the impure throne in the dust, and adjust every difficulty of magnitude between master and slave."[62] Still, northern Baptists, like other evangelicals of the region, could not escape the conviction that slavery was opposed to "the spirit and precept of the gospel." Also like other evangelicals, they held that both the Scriptures and the Declaration of Independence affirmed certain natural and inalienable rights.[63] For all their insistence that Baptist theology offered an alternative to the Puritan legacy of the theocratic Protestant state, New England Baptists, when confronted with the moral implications of slavery, defaulted to the same theocratic language of other Protestants. Slavery was opposed to the principles of the gospel and the principles of natural rights, both of which northern evangelicals believed to have the perfect political compliment in American democracy.[64]

Oberlin Secessionists

For many northern evangelicals, slavery forced important questions about the purpose of the church. This was especially true for those who followed the teaching of Charles Finney and the Oberlin doctrine of Christian perfectionism. Oberlin College produced the *Oberlin Quarterly Review,* a journal edited by Finney and the president of the college Asa Mahan. In 1848 the *Oberlin Quarterly Review* raised the question of whether Christians in the northern United States should secede from churches that were in fellowship with slaveholders.

In an article titled "Come-Outism and Come-Outers," William Goodell, an outspoken evangelical abolitionist from Ontario County, New York, argued that true Christians could not remain in fellowship with churches that violate "principles of equal brotherhood," or that "set up a hierarchy contrary to God's word."[65] Christian churches are "assemblies of equal brethren." Church discipline proceeds on the assumption that individuals are responsible for maintaining credible evidence of Christian character. Christ never transferred this responsibility "to a

Bishop, to a Cardinal, or even to a Pope."[66] According to Goodell, the only reason the "true Church" survived was that secessionist movements throughout church history preserved individual responsibility. The Novationists, Donatists, Albigenses, Lutherans, and Puritans were willing to leave the Catholic Church in order to maintain the principle of individual responsibility.[67] These seceding churches kept the true church alive in the face of an immoral and persecuting ecclesiastical hierarchy. For Goodell, there was a lesson to be learned. Like the "come-outers" of earlier periods in church history, antislavery Christians were right to break fellowship with proslavery Christians because "the pro-slavery churches of this country, northern and southern, are persecuting churches."[68] Christians should hold "church relations" only with those who demonstrate religious earnestness through "faith, piety, and good works." This, he argued, was the position of the Puritans and of "consistent Protestants, and of the great body of those who have withstood the Man of Sin, in past ages."[69]

Martin Luther's stand against the "corruption of morals in the Romish Church" also provided an example for northern Christians who opposed the slave system. When the hierarchy refused to address the abuses of the Church, Luther "came out" of the Church. Goodell added, "had Luther been an American Presbyterian, hating slavery as all good men do hate it," he would have "excommunicated the General Assembly, and come out from *its* Presbyterian church" (emphasis original).[70] Goodell believed there was an overt analogy between the Church in the later Middle Ages and Protestant churches that maintained communion with slaveholders. Both promoted a coercive licentiousness that could be withstood only by Christians who held to "higher and holier maxims."[71] Just as Protestants judged the Catholic Church "as a whole and condemn it as a church," so too "the 'church north,' so long as she persists resolutely in holding ecclesiastical affinity with the 'church south,' or religious cooperation and fellowship with her," must be judged as a whole.[72]

Other contributors to the *Oberlin Quarterly Review* forced a comparison between Catholicism and slavery. William Brown of Sandusky, Ohio, wrote that while slaveholding had always been a sin, the degree of guilt attached to the sin had grown incrementally since slavery originated in the Ancient Near East. "In the light of the present day," he urged, there could no longer be any doubt that slavery was "an enormous and unmingled wickedness and can no more be reconciled with the spirit of the gospel than heaven can be reconciled with hell."[73] Like William Goodell, Brown viewed slavery as a problem that Christians had to address. Also like Goodell, Brown believed that true Christians could not remain in fellowship with slaveholders. Brown, however, extended Goodell's logic to the vast network of evangelical organizations that found common cause in promoting missions and improving social conditions.

For Brown, the American Board of Commissioners for Foreign Missions, the American Home Missionary Society, the American Bible and Tract Society, and the American Sunday School Union shared the same culpability as the denominations that remained in communion with slaveholders.[74] Any attempt by these organizations to "harmonize their respective enterprises with slave-holding" gives countenance to the system and indicts them as "partakers of its guilt."[75] Brown found it particularly reprehensible that the American Bible Society was "loud and constant in denouncing the Pope for withholding the Bible from the people," while it simultaneously cooperated with a slave system that denied the Bible to almost three million slaves. As long as the voluntary societies admitted slaveholders into their activities, they were complicit in the moral crime of slavery. In fact, said Brown, "there is no more proof that Popery favors spiritual despotism, and general ignorance, than that these Institutions favor slavery."[76] The large network of Protestant benevolent agencies had no right to criticize the Catholic Church as long as they too were willing to collaborate with an oppressive and unchristian economic system.

Brown's comparison did not stop there. He believed that Christians should withdraw support from any religious organization willing to cooperate with slavery, but he recognized the objections to his position. If Christians withdraw from religious societies because they share a connection with slavery, then where does the withdrawing stop? If Christians never associate with corrupt institutions, then where do they find "pure" institutions with which they might cooperate? Rather than answer these questions directly, Brown argued that "this is precisely the objection that papists have always urged against protestants [*sic*] for withdrawing from the church of Rome."[77] If corruption alone were not a sufficient reason for withdrawing from the church, then Protestants would have to "repent of their sins and become papists." If Christians refused to admit grounds for seceding from a corrupt church, then they may as well "surrender their consciences to the keeping of a Pope, and submit to an ecclesiastical despotism." The right to sever fellowship with adulterated Christianity is a "right of conscience" that belonged to every individual believer. Only those who hold to the dictates of popery would deny this right.[78] Brown concluded his censure of the voluntary organizations with a warning to Christians who denied that the churches could ever separate from the sin of slavery:

> When we hear men denying this right, and denouncing others for its exercise we bless God that they are not Popes, holding in their hands the power which the Vatican wielded six hundred years ago. The truth is, the spirit of popery is not yet cast out of protestant [*sic*] churches, the rights of conscience in matters of religious faith and practice are not yet half recognized.[79]

Between 1835 and 1860, Methodists, Baptists, Presbyterians, and Congregationalists used their religious periodicals to promote the idea that northern evangelical political values were incompatible with slavery and Catholicism. Protestantism was portrayed as a religion that defended the rights of individuals against oppressive hierarchies, religious or secular. Protestantism, specifically New England Protestantism, furnished the theological categories that lent credence to the American political vocabulary. Protestants allegedly shared a rich heritage that emphasized universal human equality, the right to private conscience, and respect for freedom tempered by personal responsibility. According to the historical-theological narrative put forth by northern evangelicals, these traits translated easily from the religious to the political sphere, and indeed, for some, they were the religious foundation for American politics.

CHAPTER FOUR

Southern Evangelical Dilemmas

That the northern evangelical press incessantly portrayed Catholicism and slavery as irreconcilable with democracy had little to do with the reality of either Catholicism or slavery in the American South. Southern Catholics retained the political commitments of their region, and this alone indicted them by evangelical abolitionist standards. But Catholics also reflected the political diversity between the upper and lower South as well as differences between the coastal and inland states. If the northern evangelical press wished to prove a conspiracy of slaveholders and Catholics, demographics were not on their side. Between 1820 and 1860, there were simply more Catholics in the North than in the South, and there were many more Protestants in Dixie than Catholics. Still, the South was far from devoid of Catholic influence, and Protestant and Catholic southerners shared at least one common conviction: northern evangelical political agitation was the result of a defective Protestant political theology.

Southern Catholicism

The actual relationship between Catholicism, slavery, and the South was complicated. Just as there was no monolithic "southern identity" embracing the regional diversity among Protestants, so too there was no homogenous "southern Catholic" identity. As far as the region itself was concerned, Catholics were a distinct minority, yet prior to the 1830s and 1840s, the majority of bishops in the United States lived below the Mason-Dixon Line. The flagship diocese of the country was in Baltimore where John Carroll labored as the first American bishop from 1789 until his death in 1815. By the middle decades of the nineteenth century, in addition to the three archdioceses of New Orleans, St. Louis, and Baltimore, twelve other dioceses were scattered across both the upper and the lower South. In the 1830s and 1840s, immigration shifted Catholic power toward the large cities of the Northeast and the growing cities of the Midwest, but the southern church remained strong.[1]

Antebellum Catholics had deep roots in the American South. Early French and Spanish settlements along the Gulf Coast and the Atlantic Coast created pockets of Catholic influence stretching from Texas to Florida. Throughout the nineteenth century, the cultural and social influence of the Catholic Church thrived in cities such as Galveston, New Orleans, Mobile, and Pensacola.[2] In the upper South, a Catholic legacy emerged out of the English tradition of the Calvert family and Maryland Catholicism. Maryland produced a class of Catholic planting families whose descendents combined with newer immigrants to gradually populate Virginia, Kentucky, Tennessee, and Missouri. Apart from the Gulf Coast and the border states, a strong Catholic presence could be found in Charleston and Savannah. By 1860 the only southern state that did not have a diocese or vicariate apostolic was North Carolina. This was primarily because there was no concentrated Catholic populace around which a diocese could organize. Hence, the bishops of Charleston oversaw Catholic needs in North Carolina.[3]

North Carolina is characteristic of how despite a scant Catholic presence the southern states often produced accomplished Catholic political and social thinkers. The state was home to William Gaston, one of the more astute juridical minds of the early nineteenth century. A close friend of Bishop John England of Charleston, Gaston served in the state senate, the United States House of Representatives, and the supreme court of North Carolina. A lawyer and a jurist, Gaston maintained the disposition of a Federalist and yet early in his career expressed concerns about the power of majorities over minorities, similar concerns of which John C.

Calhoun would later articulate in his political works. A Catholic in a state dominated by proslavery Protestants, Gaston not only took the unpopular position of criticizing the slave system, but also worked to ensure that religious minorities had protection from state interference.[4]

Other southern Catholics exercised political and social influence in their states as well. Roger Taney, a lawyer and the scion of a wealthy Maryland planting family, served five years in the state senate as a Federalist but abandoned the Federalists in 1824 to support Andrew Jackson and the Democrats. For his loyalty and his talents, Jackson appointed him Attorney General in 1831, where he served two years before assuming the position of Secretary of the Treasury in 1833. Refused appointment to the Supreme Court by the Senate in 1835, Taney managed to gain enough senatorial votes in 1836 to be seated on the court. In time, he replaced John Marshall as Chief Justice of the United States. Taney served until his death in 1864 and is best remembered for his decision in *Dred Scott v. Sandford* (1857), where the Missouri Compromise of 1820 was in effect declared unconstitutional.

Abraham Lincoln and the Republicans detested Taney not only for endorsing the Dred Scott decision but also for challenging the actions of the president in a time of war. In 1861, after Lincoln placed Maryland under martial law and suspended the protection of the writ of habeas corpus from select citizens, Taney ruled that only Congress could take this sort of action. Despite his reputation as a narrow and contentious man who supported slavery at all costs, Taney, in the pattern of many privileged southerners, freed his slaves many years before the Dred Scott case and provided pensions for those who were too old to work.[5]

While Maryland produced Roger Taney and North Carolina, William Gaston, Virginia did not have a Catholic citizen of comparable legal acumen. Even though Catholics comprised one-fourth of Richmond's population by 1860, most were either first- or second-generation Irish and German immigrants who belonged to the laboring class.[6] Norfolk had a sizable Catholic presence, but here too Irish and German workers predominantly made up the Catholic population. One exceptional figure among Virginia's antebellum Catholics, however, was the newspaper publisher and political activist Anthony M. Keiley from Petersburg, Virginia.

Keiley began his career as editor of the *South-Side Democrat*. As the Know-Nothing movement gained strength in Virginia, he became more politically involved as the leader of one Irish political club and the founder of another in Richmond in the 1850s. In response to Know-Nothing agitation, he insisted that Catholics, like other southern democrats, did not oppose slavery. The Know Nothings, according to Keiley, were employing a campaign of misinformation to rally southerners to the anti-Catholic cause. When Virginia seceded from the Union in 1861, Keiley defended the move as well as the South in general.[7]

In Kentucky, another successful Catholic journalist, Benedict Webb, argued that both secessionists and nativists were wrong. Like Keiley, Webb opposed the Know Nothings, but unlike Keiley, he remained loyal to the Union. Appointed publisher of the Bardstown diocesan paper the *Catholic Advocate* in 1836, he moved the paper to Louisville in 1841 to combat growing anti-Catholic sentiment in that city. In the 1850s, Webb became editor of the *Louisville Courier Journal*. Here, he recorded first-hand accounts of the riots that ensued when a mob of Know-Nothing sympathizers refused to let Catholics vote in the 1855 election.

Like many citizens of the border states, Webb had little interaction with the planter class, and thus he saw few advantages in Kentucky joining the Confederate cause. At the same time, however, he believed that abolitionists were advancing a dangerous proposition based on religious principles that the government should interfere with property rights. He referred to the abolitionists as a "new sect" that sought to secure "political effect by religious motives." Although not an advocate of slavery, he warned that if the abolitionists had their way, the result would be the implementation of "wild, fanatical, and barbarous" political schemes.[8]

Benedict Webb, like most Catholics in the border states, reflected the ambivalence of that region toward slavery and abolitionism. In the lower South, especially the Gulf Coast states of Alabama, Mississippi, and Louisiana and the Atlantic Coast states of South Carolina, Georgia, and Florida, Catholics were less conflicted. Catholics in the Deep South opposed both nativism and abolitionism, and as tensions mounted with the North, they defended slavery as the only meaningful way to ensure southern interests against northern aggression. Mobile, Alabama, journalist and Mexican War hero Theodore O'Hara, future Confederate general Pierre Gustave Toutant-Beauregard, and Louisiana congressman John Perkins openly endorsed the expansion of slavery in the Caribbean and Latin America. Equally vocal about the possibilities of southern imperialism were Catholics from successful Creole planting families, such as Charles Villere, Louis and Paul Octave, and Charles Gayarre.[9]

Few Catholics from South Carolina, Georgia, and the Atlantic Coast of Florida endorsed southern expansion in Latin America. But like other parts of the Deep South, these states boasted a Catholic intellectual class wholly committed to sectional interests. Whereas Gulf Coast Catholicism had roots in Spanish and French colonialism, Catholic populations in the southeastern Atlantic region grew primarily as a result of political turmoil in Ireland, France, and Germany in the first half of the nineteenth century. Catholics who settled in and around Charleston and Savannah were more recent immigrants, but the absence of an established southern lineage did not prevent them from defending slavery and the South from northern agitation.[10]

In 1850, out of 1,140 total Catholic churches in the United States, 141 were in the eleven states that eventually formed the Confederacy. Another 178 churches could be found in the border states of Maryland, Kentucky, and Missouri.[11] New Orleans reported a Catholic population of 170,000, while the Catholic population of Texas numbered fewer than 40,000. The Diocese of Mobile, which included churches as far inland as Tuscaloosa and Montgomery as well as the westernmost part of northwest Florida, had around 10,000 parishioners in 1860.[12] Mississippi, like Alabama, was under a single diocese as well, the Diocese of Natchez, with around 10,000 Catholics, or roughly 7 percent of the state's population.[13]

Between 1840 and 1860, South Carolina absorbed over 40,000 immigrants, many of whom were Irish Catholics. The number of Catholics in Kentucky grew from an estimated 30,000 in 1845 to 80,000 in 1860. The 1860 Maryland census reported that 24 percent of the Catholic population, or 52,497 of Baltimore's total population of 212,418, were born overseas. The majority of immigrants entering Maryland were German and Irish, with almost all belonging to the Catholic Church.

Virginia boasted smaller numbers but similar ethnic and religious composition. On the eve of the war, Richmond alone claimed almost 5,000 foreign-born Irish and Germans, or 13 percent of the entire populace.[14] Southern states with fewer immigrants also had fewer Catholics. By 1860, Arkansas, Florida, Georgia, Mississippi, and Tennessee had a combined Catholic population of around 22,000.[15]

Compared to the number of Protestants in the South, these statistics were hardly overwhelming. The Catholic presence in the southern states, with perhaps the exception of Louisiana, never equaled the growth of Catholicism in individual northern cities such as Boston, New York, and Philadelphia. Still, Catholicism and immigration did not go unnoticed by the Protestant majority in the South, and in some southern states— notably Maryland, Kentucky, Louisiana, and Texas—evangelical nativists found the Catholic vote to be a substantial threat. But the response to the perceived threat of immigration and Catholicism in the South never reached the same sustained level of intensity found in the North. The contrast between the northern and southern Catholic experience underscores dramatic differences in the two regions despite their common Protestant heritage.

Political Nativism in the South

One example of how anti-Catholic sentiment was more contained in the South can be found in politics. As the Know-Nothing movement gained strength and showed potential as a national political force, northern states saw an increase in anti-Catholic attitudes and mob violence toward Catholics. The Know-Nothing Party in southern states, by contrast, and with only a few exceptions, never wholeheartedly embraced the anti-Catholic agenda.[16] Early in the movement, the party made gains in the South because southern nativists feared that the political effects of immigration would tip the balance of national power in favor of the North. Prominent southern Democrats, however, were quick to challenge this accusation.[17]

In 1855 Alexander Stephens, a Georgia congressman and future vice president of the Confederacy, argued that New England Baptists, Presbyterians, and Methodists had been championing abolition for years. But unlike northern Protestants, Catholics "have never warred against our peculiar institutions," and "of the three thousand New England clergymen who sent the anti-Nebraska memorial to the Senate, not one was a Catholic."[18] Likewise, Senator Benjamin Fitzpatrick of Alabama warned that southerners had nothing to fear from foreigners or Catholics, but instead they should be wary of nativist northern abolitionists.[19] When W. R. Smith of Alabama was nominated temporary Speaker of the House of Representatives in 1856, Congressman Preston Brooks of South Carolina refused to support him because he was an enemy of Catholics, and Catholics were "friends of the Constitution and of the South."[20] Another congressman, Representative William Barry of Mississippi, declared that Know-Nothingism was a dangerous synthesis of all "isms"—free soilism, Whigism, woman-rightism, socialism, and anti-rentism—that threatened the stability of the Union.[21]

Southerners who opposed nativism often found support from evangelical ministers who objected to overt politicization of the faith. Two Methodist journals, the *New Orleans Christian Advocate* and the *Nashville Christian Advocate,* warned against rashly and imprudently promoting Protestant principles in the political sphere. Similarly, the president of the University of Mississippi, Reverend Augustus B. Longstreet, also a Methodist, questioned the legitimacy of fellow ministers who used their office to promote a nativist agenda. Longstreet publicly censured Reverend William Winans because Winans insisted that ministers had a responsibility to protect "the well being of their country" from the Catholic threat.[22]

In Virginia, Charles Dabney, a distinguished planter, earnestly sought to convince his equally well-known brother, Presbyterian minister Robert Lewis Dabney, to avoid falling prey to nativism despite the latter's deep suspicion of Catholicism. Charles admonished his brother that "the true fanatic" is the Yankee, and the Yankee, not the southerner, seeks to persecute the foreigner.[23] Robert Dabney did not need to be persuaded of the dangers of northern evangelicalism. In a speech before the faculty and students of Union Theological Seminary (Virginia), he alleged that northern evangelicals masked a "shallow and arrogant theology." Also, in a piece entitled "Civic Ethics," he challenged the popular northern evangelical argument that American political values could be traced to the Protestant Reformation.[24]

Of particular concern for southerners, whether or not sympathetic with nativism, was the connection between New England and the Know Nothings. John Pendleton Kennedy of Maryland was a Whig who leaned toward the Know Nothings but acknowledged that the movement was faltering in the South because its New England leadership had become a "nest of pestilent abolitionists."[25] Likewise, Governor Henry Wise of Virginia lamented that the movement was "a devious act of political cunning" whose ultimate design was to subject the South to the "oligarchy of New England."[26] The editors of the *Montgomery Advertiser and Gazette* took up the matter in good southern fashion by appealing directly to the question of honor and bravery. Southern Catholics, they urged, were more faithful to America than many Protestants in New England. Why? Because "Catholic Louisiana, in the Mexican War, furnished seven regiments of 7,000 troops to fight against her brethren of the Catholic faith, while Know-Nothing Massachusetts furnished but one regiment of 930 men raised by Democrats against the prevailing sentiment of the State."[27]

Southern Democrats also exploited Know-Nothing anti-Catholicism to try to undermine southern Whigs who had bolted for the American Party. Yet many southern Whigs who joined the Know Nothings were uncomfortable with anti-Catholicism. After the passage of the Kansas-Nebraska Bill in 1854 thousands of southern Whigs who felt betrayed by their party began a last ditch effort to quiet the slavery issue by aligning with the Know-Nothing American Party. In June 1855, the American Party held their convention in Philadelphia to outline their platform. The platform ended up including a pledge of resistance "to the aggressive policy of the Roman Catholic Church in our country."[28] The northern nativist wing of the party also tried to insert a proviso that would prevent Catholics from joining the party or holding public office under the party name. Southern delegates, however, led by Maryland and Louisiana, argued that Catholics should be welcome in the party. What is more, they successfully campaigned to have the intolerant anti-Catholic language found in the eighth section of the national platform modified to appear more religiously neutral.[29]

Local chapters of the Know Nothings in the South were equally condemnatory of the exclusion of Catholics from public office. The Louisiana chapter openly considered separating from the national party because of the party's commitment to religious discrimination, and it intentionally inserted a clause in the state platform condemning the use of religious belief as a test for holding public office. Maryland Know Nothings likewise distanced themselves from the thorny question of a religious test. The editor of the *Baltimore Patriot and Commercial Gazette* endorsed the national platform but qualified his support by arguing that the party was mistaken in discriminating against Catholics simply because of their religious beliefs.[30]

Alabama Know Nothings were emphatic that they in no way supported the original eighth article of the national platform. Local party officials inserted a clause in their state platform stating that they not only disagreed with discrimination based on religion, but they also opposed the election of anyone from a religious group who claimed a "higher law" as one's reason for entering politics. At a large rally in Montgomery, party officials condemned as unacceptable the discrimination against "Catholics who are Americans by birth, education, and training."[31] Florida Know Nothings were equally condemnatory of anti-Catholicism. Three months after the national convention, they issued a resolution stating that they disagreed with the original wording of the national platform and that they did not "entertain the opinion that Roman Catholicism . . . must necessarily convert a native born American into a Benedict Arnold."[32]

In December 1855, the American Party issued a second resolution disclaiming any intention to prescribe a religious test for holding public office and insisting that they "war against no man's religious principles."[33] A leading spokesman for the party in Arkansas, Albert Pike, though no friend of immigration, suggested that the national party make it clear that the political purposes of Americanism were directed against the temporal powers of the pope, not the entire American Catholic Church. Even in Texas, where nativism found a substantial foothold, critics were decrying the Know Nothings as reactionaries. The *San Antonio Ledger* implied that the American Party suffered from both intolerance and silliness. How could Catholics possibly threaten a state with an overwhelming Protestant majority when not one Catholic held a prominent political office?[34]

In Virginia, the Know Nothings received their greatest setback. Here, the party faithful believed that they had an opportunity to "nationalize" their movement and possibly capture the presidency in 1856 if they could defeat Democratic gubernatorial candidate Henry Wise. The Know Nothings backed Thomas S. Flournoy against Wise, but in his acceptance letter for the nomination, Flournoy made a foolish error and openly referred to the Catholic Church as despotic, proscriptive, and intolerant. He also indicated that he believed that Catholics should be excluded from public office.[35] Wise, long a vocal critic of the Know Nothings and the anti-Catholic clause in the Virginia party platform, seized upon Flournoy's mistake. In the heated campaign that followed, he successfully painted his opponent and the Know Nothings as religious bigots who allied themselves with northern abolitionists. Wise won the election with slightly more than 10,000 votes, and he later suggested that his victory signaled the beginning of the end of the Know Nothings in the southern states.[36]

The Philadelphia convention and the Virginia election reveal the extent to which regional commitments weakened the national Know-Nothing alliance. Most southern Know Nothings opposed the anti-Catholic bias of section eight of the national platform. Most northern Know Nothings, by contrast, could not support the twelfth plank of the platform that required at least a tacit acceptance of the Kansas-Nebraska Act. Representatives from both regions insisted that the convention address the slavery question, and large numbers of northern delegates allied themselves with the Know Nothings precisely because they believed the party would take a firm stance against slavery.

William M. Burwell of Virginia made a speech on the floor of the convention that exposed the ideological fault line. He declared that southerners were not really interested in nativism but that they were willing to accept the northern position toward immigrants and Catholics as long as northerners could agree to a neutral position on the slavery question.[37] Because only a handful of northern Know Nothings found the terms of the Kansas-Nebraska Act acceptable, Burwell's appeal fell on deaf ears. When section twelve passed the floor of the convention, the majority of northern representatives protested by advocating the restoration of the

Missouri Compromise. Cooperation between the northern and southern factions of the American Party quickly disintegrated. By 1856 many northern Know Nothings began a rapid defection into the Republican Party, creating a political shift that culminated with the election of Abraham Lincoln in 1860.[38]

Ultimately, the go-along-to-get-along position would not work for the Know Nothings because northerners and southerners had very different reasons for aligning with the movement. Although some southerners harbored nativist sentiments, the most appealing aspect of the party was that it offered a possible compromise on the issue of slavery.[39] But in the North, and especially the Northeast, keeping Catholics out of power appeared to be just as important as preserving the Union. For over a generation northern evangelicals promoted in New England pulpits and religious periodicals the ideal of a Protestant Republic. With the formation of the American Party, they finally had a political program that strove to make the ideal a reality. While it is impossible to reduce the popularity of the Know Nothings in any region to a single factor, it is difficult to ignore the fact that the crusade against Rome had long been a central feature of the New England religious tradition. Here, even more than in the Northwest or the border states, the American Party experienced its greatest success.[40]

Southern Evangelicals Confront Catholicism and New England

Political nativism failed to succeed in the South largely because the northern evangelical nativist wing of the Know-Nothing movement was uncompromising about slavery. But another reason political nativism never gained momentum in the South is less political and more practical. In the twenty-five years leading up to the Civil War, southerners were simply not exposed to the same volume of anti-Catholic literature as published above the Mason-Dixon Line. Between 1800 and 1860, only four out of twenty-five clearly identifiable anti-Catholic newspapers and periodicals originated in southern cities.[41] Three of these, the *New Orleans Protestant*, the *Jackson* (Tennessee) *Protestant*, and the *Baltimore Weekly Pilot*, had very brief publishing lives, and their influence was negligible.[42] A fourth periodical, the *Baltimore Literary and Religious Magazine,* saw slightly more success. Founded by well-known Presbyterian pastor Robert J. Breckinridge, the monthly publication ran from 1835 to 1841. It was discontinued after local Catholics sued for libel and slander. Undeterred, Breckinridge started another anti-Catholic monthly entitled *Spirit of the XIX Century,* which lasted only a year. Both publications ended as financial failures, but together they had more longevity than any other southern anti-Catholic periodical.[43]

Although lacking an aggressive anti-Catholic press, Presbyterians, Methodists, and Baptists in the South still devoted attention to the Catholic "problem." Southern evangelicals could be as pugilistic as northern evangelicals were in their outbursts against Catholicism, but their attacks were erratic and often concerned nuanced theological questions. Only occasionally did they portray Catholics as tools of the pope determined to overthrow republicanism.[44]

Benjamin Morgan Palmer told a Presbyterian congregation in Columbia, South Carolina, that "Romanists" suffered from "ritualism." Because of their commitment to ceremony, they "thrust aside the exposition of doctrine" and impeded direct application of "divine truth upon the conscience and the heart." Protestants, by contrast, championed "individual responsibility" and rejected any human mediator between the individual and God.[45] At the behest of Baltimore's Breckinridge, the Old School Presbyterian General Assembly of 1841 adopted resolutions condemning the superstitions of popery and warning Presbyterians to avoid "patronizing or encouraging popish schools and seminaries."[46] Four years later after a lengthy debate over the question of whether or not Catholics were really Christians, the southern dominated General Assembly voted to reject the legitimacy of Catholic baptism.[47]

At times southern evangelicals could be as alarmist as northern evangelicals were about the question of Catholic loyalty to the United States. In 1855 Methodist minister William Brownlow accused then-governor of Tennessee Andrew Johnson, as well as the entire Democratic Party, of being tools of the pope and the Catholic Church.[48] Brownlow's *Americanism Contrasted with Foreignism, Romanism, and Bogus Democracy* challenged the youth of America to confront the Catholic threat to civil and religious liberties. William Sands, Baptist editor of the Richmond-based *Religious Herald*, argued that Catholics could not be "true friend[s] of Republicanism" because the pope remained an enemy of "liberalism and republican aspirations" despite the advances of the revolutions of 1848.[49]

Well into the Civil War southern ministers made the occasional reference to Catholic political infidelity. The Reverend Thomas Smyth, a noted Presbyterian minister from Charleston, suggested in 1863 that the "vindictive and persecuting clergy of the North" were responsible for the war and that the "absolute government" they endorsed from the pulpit was the same as "the Roman Church and the dark ages."[50] Also in 1863, Presbyterian minister James A. Lyon of Mississippi published an article urging southerners not to abandon the notion that there was a legitimate relationship between religion and politics. Lyon maintained that the idea that religion and politics should have nothing to do with one another was very recent. This notion resulted in an "injurious error instilled into the popular mind" because people incorrectly associated it with the union of church and state. The union of church and state, he said, was the result of "priestcraft" and "jesuitism," and these were very different things from the influence of religion on politics.[51]

The proper relationship between church and state preoccupied many southern ministers throughout the secession crisis and the war. Although critical of Catholicism and European political arrangements, southern evangelicals were much more critical of the way in which northern evangelicals promoted politics through the church. James Henley Thornwell of South Carolina was no friend of Catholicism, but he was equally hostile to the Puritan political legacy of New England. With a scathing polemical style, he denounced New England theology as a combination of "shallow and sophistical psychology" and "still shallower and more sophistical ethics." According to Thornwell, the northern evangelical church gravely erred because it carelessly undermined its spiritual task by overemphasizing social and political questions. The sole mission of the church was to preach redemption. Doing so would prove that "the salt that is to save this country is the Church of Christ, a Church that does not mix with any political party, or any issue aside from her direct mission."[52]

Many southerners agreed with Thornwell. They interpreted the crisis of the Union as stemming in large measure from the politicization of the northern pulpits and the Puritan legacy that made political preaching acceptable. Before the war began, the Virginia Historical Society asked William McDonald to prepare a chronicle of John Brown's raid at Harper's Ferry. McDonald took the opportunity to outline the moral questions surrounding the idea of rebellion in general and to demonstrate that John Brown's raid was the product of radical ideas that "had almost entirely subjugated the northern intellect." He argued that northern radicalism "began with the first Puritan sect who confounded notions of free and equal salvation with wild notions of political equality."[53] Puritanism had historically tried to hold together two contradictory doctrines. First, that "Jesus Christ died for all men . . . so all men are equal in all things"; and second, "that to the saints belong the government of the world, and, they [the Puritans] being the saints, are the divinely commissioned lords of creation." Northern pulpits, said McDonald, continued to promote these conflicting doctrines. This lingering Puritan political disposition "converted the radicalism which it helped to create into a sort of politico-religious antagonism to southern institutions."[54]

In lectures delivered at Petersburg and Richmond, the Reverend William A. Hall, a Presbyterian, declared that the war against the North was a war against the fanatical excesses of the Protestant Reformation. "Protestantism," he said, developed hand in hand with "the same essence that begat modern philosophy." While the Reformation brought about positive changes, it also introduced a dangerous deference to the authority of private conscience.[55] Hall assessed that the struggle to define the Union was the culmination of a centuries-long struggle that began with modernity's emphasis on the individual. "Modern history," he said, "has been a recession of power from the mass to the individual," largely as a result of Protestant fanaticism.[56]

According to Hall, the most excessive religious manifestation of individualism was in the congregational form of church government that grew out of New England Puritanism. Congregationalism helped foster the more radical tendencies of northern political culture because "the Puritan form of government is pure democracy." Pure democracy inevitably gave "unrestrained freedom to all individual tendencies."[57] Once northern churches embraced the cause against the South, evangelical heirs of the Puritans did not have the ability to keep proponents of "fanatical higher law" in check.[58] The South, by contrast, was leading a conservative revolution. Southerners championed the preservation of "organic law" and "republican government" against the forces of unrestrained "individual power which are to-day asserted through a lawless northern democracy."[59]

Fear of religious extremism united Southern Baptists, themselves Congregationalists, with Southern Presbyterians such as William Hall. The Baptist Association of Virginia published an address in 1863 stating that the Civil War had been "provoked by fanaticism in the name of religion" and that history teaches "a fearful lesson of the danger of spiritual pride and religious intolerance."[60] Northern churches generated the conflict, not "designing politicians . . . but ministers of reconciliation— heralds of the gospel of peace, [who] have sown the seeds of the whirlwind which is devastating the land."[61]

Francis Wayland, president of Brown University, and Richard Fuller, pastor of the Seventh Baptist Church in Baltimore, argued the point in a well-publicized correspondence debate. Fuller insisted that Wayland's understanding of slavery was political "fiction," the product of a "distempered imagination." He contended that Wayland, like northern evangelicals in general, viewed slavery and other social issues as abstractions, as if they had no basis in "real" historical conditions.[62] Fuller saw in New England a radical version of political Protestantism that assaulted an imagined southern society. Other Southern Baptists agreed. In the fallout that followed the Kansas-Nebraska Act, journals such as North Carolina's *Biblical Recorder* and Virginia's *American Baptist Memorial* condemned northern religious fanaticism and insisted that Southern Baptists were committed to the strictly religious purposes of the church.[63]

Conflicted Conservatives

Disdain for New England political theology united southern evangelicals. They did not like the Puritan legacy. They derided northern preachers who inflamed regional tensions from the pulpit. Although at times critical of

Catholicism, they shied away from the vituperative anti-Catholic rhetoric found in the North. Their condemnation of "popery" never matched that of the northern evangelical press. Still, despite an ostensible commitment to a politically neutral church, southern evangelicals proved inconsistent. With the formation of the Confederacy, many southern ministers adopted New England's habit of mixing politics and religion.[64] They too began to use the symbolic language of the Bible and the theology of postmillennialism to suit their sectional ideology. Southerners who once eschewed the Puritan-inspired "civil millennialism" of the northern churches developed their own millennial eschatology to characterize the destiny of the southern states. As historian Mitchell Snay describes it, they took "the idea of America as God's Redeemer Nation and the image of the United States as the New Israel, and reshaped them to apply exclusively to the South."[65]

With a zeal that rivaled the most energetic evangelical abolitionists, southern ministers depicted the Confederacy as the last great hope of Christian civilization. In the late eighteenth and early nineteenth centuries, southern evangelicals were willing to entertain the possibility that slavery was a temporary institution likely to be abrogated at some point in the future. After the war began, however, slavery was held to be an essential component in God's plan for the human race.[66]

The Cherokee Baptist Association of Texas announced in 1861 that "slavery is an institution of divine appointment" and Christians should pledge to perpetuate it.[67] Alabama Baptists concurred. The official report of their 1861 convention stated that the "moral strength now exhibited by our beloved land, is due, under God, in no small degree to the labors of Southern Christians."[68] The *Southern Christian Advocate,* a Methodist journal, declared that disunion and war presented a "coveted occasion for the pulpit to assert itself as a power in the land."[69] Methodist minister R. N. Sledd of Petersburg, Virginia, told an audience of soldiers that southerners were chosen by God as "His peculiar people" and that the South was "the repository of His will and the light of the world."[70] The Reverend John Wightman of Yorkville, South Carolina, also a Methodist, pointedly described the eschatological significance of the southern cause. God, he said, was "leading the South along the pathway to the highest culmination of Christian civilization."[71]

Despite their desire to distance themselves from the New England theocratic tradition, southern Presbyterians perhaps more than any other denomination used the church to advance their own theocratic ideals.[72] In April 1861, the *Princeton Theological Review* accused southern Presbyterian ministers of agitating the national crisis by advocating secession from the pulpit. The Reverend John Holt Rice of Louisville, Kentucky, countered that abolitionists instigated "utterly fruitless" attacks against slavery and the South for the last thirty years. If over the same period "the same assaults had been made upon the social system of the North by the pulpit and press of the South," and, if ministers had sought "to stir up the poor against the rich and the laborer against the capitalist," the result would have been devastating for northern society. Rice concluded that southern ministers did not assault northern social arrangements precisely because they, more than northerners, valued order and stability.[73]

Notwithstanding protestations to the contrary, hints of a not so subtle inconsistency in southern Presbyterian thought can be seen as early as 1850 in two sermons preached by James Henley Thornwell. Thornwell, in language reminiscent of the New England concept of the "national covenant," told the students of South Carolina College that Americans were "the federal representatives of the human race" and that America had a special role to play "in the progress of civilization." If the United States divided over slavery, he warned, the very missionary purpose of the church would be in jeopardy.[74] The next month Thornwell preached a sermon in Charleston entitled "The Christian Doctrine of Slavery" in which regional interests replaced the nationalism of the first sermon. Southerners and slaveholders rather than America and Americans represented the human race. The South was the "last redoubt" upholding "the principles of regulated liberty" against the "despotism of the masses on the one hand, and the supremacy of a single will on the other."[75]

Thornwell suggested that the impending crisis of the Union involved much more than a conflict between slave and free labor. Rather, the crisis represented a fundamental struggle over the question of what constitutes a civilization. To emphasize his point, Thornwell employed imagery from the political revolutions that had convulsed Europe for almost a century. Radical ideas "shaking thrones to their centres" and "upheaving the masses" were the same ideas "rocking the solid pillars of this Union."

Moreover, said Thornwell, "the parties in this conflict are not merely Abolitionists and Slaveholders":

> They are Atheists, Socialists, Communists, Red Republicans, Jacobins on the one side, and the friends of order and regulated freedom on the other. In a word, the world is the battle ground, Christianity and Atheism the combatants, and the progress of humanity at stake. One party seems to regard society . . . as the machinery of man. . . . The other party beholds in it the ordinance of God.[76]

Over the course of one month, Thornwell offered two very different pictures of evangelical Christianity and the meaning of the Union. In his first sermon, a unified American church was essential to progress, national destiny, and missiology. But in the second sermon, a more ominous note is sounded. The North and the South are portrayed as different civilizations. At stake between them was an impending crisis over the meaning of Christianity for the state. The clash of regional interests reflected a greater, almost cosmic, conflict between champions of Christian order and advocates of godless statism.

Thornwell was not the only southern Calvinist to characterize the crisis of union as a dramatic eschatological contest between radicals and conservatives, and his references to the revolutions in Europe were not simply political hyperbole. Many southern ministers compared the struggle to define the Union as the American equivalent of the struggle to define Europe from the time of the French Revolution onward. Writing in response to John Brown's raid at Harper's Ferry in 1859, Reverend George Howe of Columbia Theological Seminary in South Carolina said that Brown found his inspiration in the merciless Black Republicanism of the French Revolution. Brown, said Howe, was a ruthless radical who had hoped his insurrection would result in a similar massacre as occurred during the slave rebellion in Saint-Domingue (modern Haiti) in 1791.[77] Like the Jacobins of the French Revolution, Brown and his followers were "borne away by impracticable theories of human freedom and equality, which the government of God in His providence, does not permit to be carried out in this sinful world."[78]

In the aftermath of the presidential election of 1860, Benjamin M. Palmer preached a sermon describing the similarities between the French Revolution and the "spirit" of abolitionism. Like other evangelical ministers, Palmer insisted that the cause of the South was also the "cause of God and religion" and southerners had been assigned with the high position "of defending, before all nations, the cause of all religion and of all truth."[79] "The abolition spirit," he said, "is undeniably atheistic," and it reflects the same spirit of the "demon which erected its throne upon the guillotine in the days of Robespierre and Marat."[80] Because America is a generally religious country, however, the demon had to assume a disguise, and thus the same demon that "abolished the Sabbath and worshipped reason" in France took on the form "of the advocacy of human rights" in the United States. The American Jacobins, warned Palmer, have adopted the same decree as the French Jacobins: "every evil shall be corrected, or society become a wreck—the sun must be stricken from the heavens, if a spot is found upon his disk."[81]

Another southern Presbyterian minister, R. S. Gladney, made a similar comparison between the French Revolution and American abolitionism. Gladney's critique, however, came in the form of a moral play entitled *The Devil in America: A Dramatic Satire,* which he published under the pseudonym Lacon. Written in blank verse and intended as "a school exercise," *The Devil in America* was Gladney's account of how atheistic ideology had come to control the United States. Scene four of the play, "The Irrepressible Conflict," stages Satan addressing his demons and describing his plan for an impending war between the North and the South that will result in the "overthrow of the United States" and "arrest the progress of the gospel and civilization."[82] To this end, Satan appoints several demons to carry out his charge. The demon Delusion is assigned the task of confusing men about the true teaching of the Bible. Satan tells Delusion:

> Nowhere in the Bible is it taught
> That men are free and equal made and born
> The liberty which God prescribes for man
> Consists with government of every form,

With all relations known in social life,
With stations, ranks, pursuits of every sort,
With all diversities of human kind,
Requiring each to act within his sphere,
And duty do by moral law prescribe.[83]

Delusion's task is to convince the people of the North that the Bible in
no way endorses social hierarchy as a means of regulating freedom and
that true liberty and equality consists of a universal counterfeit freedom
that reflects the "pride and rebellion in man." After Delusion has com-
pleted his work, the demon Abolition is appointed to urge the "conflict
irrepressible," but before Abolition is commissioned, he is reminded by
Satan of his greatest historical successes:

The work to you assign'd is nothing new,—
A war in which you great experience have.
In France your deeds of valor still are known,
And liberty was then, as now, the cry.[84]

Before, during, and after the war, Presbyterian minister Robert Dabney repeated the refrain that the "true abolitionist is, of course, a Red Republican and a Jacobin" and that the first attempt at abolition in the western world was enacted by the Reign of Terror on behalf of the French
colonies.[85] In America, "the Jacobins," led by President Lincoln, "needed
a war for their own factious ends," and after the seven states of the lower
south seceded, the Jacobin Party was left with a full working majority in
Congress.[86]

Dabney maintained that, like the radicals of Europe, the Republicans adopted a political theory that "had no standard whatever of intrinsic righteousness," and that they replaced the moral precepts of religion
as a check on the absolute power of the state with the "iron logic" of the
secular social contract. Under this system, "there is no morality to enforce
duties or guarantee rights except human laws," and without a shared
moral consensus that exists independent of the state, the people will be inevitably subject to the cravings of "licentious, ruthless, and selfish wills."[87]

The result of such a government is that the will of the majority defines the purposes of the state at the expense of the minority—"*vox Populi, vox Dei*"—and this, said Dabney, was precisely the pattern that created the worst of European despotism in the nineteenth century.[88]

For Dabney, as for other southern Calvinists, the alleged crisis of European tyranny was not produced by monarchists who supported the *ancien régime* but by egalitarians who failed to make a distinction between moral equality and social equality. Social equality, such as championed by the French Jacobins and the Republican Party in America, was political fiction, whereas moral equality was the given condition of all people because "all have a rational, responsible, and immortal destiny, and all are inalienably entitled to pursue it."[89]

According to Dabney, the northern states had every intention of making social equality the governing political philosophy of the Americas and Europe. "The first step in their vast designs," he argued, "was to overwhelm the Conservative States of the South." After conquering the South, they would spread their ideology to Europe where the people of Ireland, Great Britain, France, and Germany would be inculcated into their reckless understanding of liberty. The North waged war not only against the South but against all the civilized nations of the world. Likewise, the South undertook their defense against northern aggression "in behalf not only of their own children, but of the children of all men."[90] The Confederacy, said Dabney, was the last political stand "against the licentious violence of physical power," and "the assumptions they resisted were precisely those of that radical democracy, which, deluged Europe with blood at the close of the eighteenth century, and which shook its thrones again in the convulsions of 1848." Radical democracy was an old European fiend assuming a new American form in the northern understanding of equality. This destructive ideology originated in "the old States of Europe," and upon transferring "its immediate designs across the Atlantic," it "was preparing to make the United States, after crushing all law under its brute will, the fulcrum whence they [the Northern states] should extend their lever to upheave every legitimate throne in the Old World."[91]

Like northern evangelicals, southern evangelicals compared their domestic political interests to the political strife that had beleaguered Europe since the French Revolution. In doing so, they capitalized on a vocabulary familiar to their counterparts in the North. For almost thirty years prior to the Civil War, northern evangelicals argued in their pulpits and their presses that liberal movements in Europe were unleashing positive forces of social change in countries haunted by medieval social structures. These movements were described as the providential outworking of Protestant values in the political sphere, and groups that opposed them, specifically Catholics and royalists, were chastised as ideological anachronisms. Southern evangelicals at times participated in this triumphalist rhetoric, but when faced with the grim prospects of disunion and ultimately defeat, they adopted a very different understanding of history and theology.

The southern evangelical historical-theological narrative of the 1850s and 1860s tried, in effect, to reverse the northern evangelical historical-theological narrative of the previous thirty years. Northern evangelicals had long expressed the fear that conservative European immigrants threatened the Protestant character of the country; it was now southerners who were crying foul. According to southern clergy, the northern understanding of freedom and equality challenged basic civilizing principles such as regulated liberty, enlightened aristocracy, and *noblesse oblige.* Not only were the conservative social arrangements of the South threatened, but traditional social arrangements in Europe were threatened as well. For many southern evangelicals, Catholic and ultraroyalist conservatism was not as dangerous to Americans as American liberalism was to Europe. In a strange if not ironic twist, southern evangelicals, many of whom had Whig sympathies before the war, sounded like the American Protestant equivalent of Louis de Bonald or René Chateaubriand or Joseph de Maistre — conservative Catholic European royalists who championed medieval social arrangements over and against the destructive excess of democracy.

Yet, as Eugene Genovese has argued about slaveholders as a class, southern ministers were not pining for a return to medieval social organization, nor did they believe the South to be the heirs of the feudal social conditions of the Middle Ages. Southerners, evangelical or otherwise, appreciated progress and innovation, and at least prior to their bitter defeat they anticipated, as much as northerners, a bright future for the country.[92] Moreover, as the nativist movement in the South indicates, southerners may have valued Catholics as political allies in the struggle against New England abolitionists, but they were by no means endeared to Catholic theology. Southern evangelicals did not believe that the Confederacy would eventuate in a premodern society that shunned republicanism. They did believe, however, that their conservatism offered an alternative to what they perceived as a dangerous and aggressive northern political theology that championed egalitarianism at the expense of order. Still, in trying to discern and explain their social sympathies in terms of a global struggle between radicalism and conservatism, southern evangelical ministers exposed a tension between their theological and their political commitments that could not be easily resolved.

Northern evangelicals had for years prior to the war demonstrated that they believed Christianity, Protestant Christianity, was a religion that supported social progress and democratic reform. All tyranny, either political or spiritual, had to be eradicated in order to have an authentic Christian culture. They believed Catholics and slaveholders were serious impediments toward achieving this culture, and accordingly, these groups were persistently demonized in the northern evangelical press. Any setback Catholics or slaveholders suffered was interpreted by northern evangelicals as the forward movement of Protestant Republicanism in history. Southern evangelicals at times echoed these anti-Catholic sentiments, but as tensions mounted between the North and the South, and as northern churches became more aggressive in their attack on slavery, evangelicals in the South became more convinced that progress and reform could never be dissociated from slavery and natural inequality.

In their critique of abolitionists, southern evangelicals were careful to distance themselves from an excessive reliance on private conscience when it came to drawing moral conclusions from Scripture.[93] Even so, they never abandoned the leveling theological principles of Protestantism, and they did not agree that the natural progression of Protestantism through history would eventuate in the leveling of social differences. Consequently, by the time the conflict ignited between the North and the South, southern evangelicals were touting organic, hierarchical, and elitist political and social arrangements while at the same time they defended the priesthood of the believer, the private action of God upon the conscience, and the unfailing perspicuity of an open Bible. In short, southern evangelicals were seeking to give religious justification to a conservative social vision that valued caste, aristocracy, and the natural condition of human inequality. Yet, as evangelicals, they were inevitably committed to certain Protestant religious presuppositions that championed none of these things. By recasting their Protestant political identity in terms that were amiable to southern social conditions, southern evangelicals confirmed what northern evangelicals had been arguing for years: slaveholders were a threat to their nationalist aims precisely because they offered a competing vision of what a Christian republic might look like. In this sense, southern evangelicals found themselves in a predicament remarkably similar to a group with whom they would otherwise have very little in common, American Catholics in both the North and the South.

CHAPTER FIVE

The Hierarchy Responds to Political Protestantism

As northern and southern Protestant denominations slowly divided over slavery, the American Catholic hierarchy worked hard to keep the Church out of sectional conflict. Throughout the antebellum period, differences in ethnicity and cultural habits severely separated many Catholic communities. Immigrants tended to commit to parishes that reflected their European origins. Irish Americans wanted Irish clergy and Irish customs. Germans wanted German clergy and German practices. The French wanted their native traditions preserved. The longer divisive political issues such as slavery could be avoided the better for a Church struggling through its brick-and-mortar phase in a predominately Protestant culture.[1]

Ultimately, the slavery question could not be avoided. Nor could Catholics ignore the charge that their political theology was incompatible with American republicanism. As the strain of immigration and sectional strife brought these issues to the fore, Catholic intellectuals rose to the challenges of their evangelical detractors. Luminaries of the Catholic hierarchy disputed the notion that Protestantism alone guaranteed America's republican ideals. Catholics, they insisted, had a more theologically developed understanding of politics. Long before American evangelicals, the Church had struggled with the complexities surrounding church and state relations, including the practice of slavery.

The Church on the Eve of War

On Friday, January 4, 1861, a day appointed by President James Buchanan to be set apart for "Humiliation, Fasting, and Prayer throughout the Union," Augustin Verot, bishop of St. Augustine, Florida, stood before his congregation and outlined what he believed to be the causes of the imminent crisis facing the country.[2] His sermon was soon after published in both English and French and circulated around the southern states as a propaganda piece supporting the formation of the Confederacy. Issued on the eve of the Civil War, the sermon reiterated many of the longstanding problems that Catholics, in both the North and the South, had with the abolitionists. Verot stated that abolitionist attacks against slavery and the South were "unjust, iniquitous, unscriptural, and unreasonable" because slavery had "received the sanction of God, of the Church, and of Society at all times, and in all governments." He accused the northern Protestant clergy of inciting "intolerance and bigotry," and he placed responsibility for the impending sectional conflict squarely on their shoulders.[3]

Verot came to the United States as a young French Sulpician intending to stay as a missionary for only seven years. Political circumstances in France, however, would force him to change his plans. He departed for America in July of 1830, the same month that French revolutionaries unseated Charles X and replaced him with the anticlerical Louis Philippe. Because conditions in France discouraged his return, Verot settled in Baltimore, where he became a professor of mathematics, science, and theology at St. Mary's College. He remained at St. Mary's until 1853 when he was appointed to a parish ministry in Maryland. Four years later, in 1857, Archbishop Kenrick of Baltimore nominated Verot to be the first bishop of St. Augustine, Florida, a position he held until 1861 when Pope Pius IX announced his transfer to the See of Savannah.[4]

Verot's denunciation of the northern evangelical clergy on the eve of the war was pointed, but it was not new. He took his first shots at Protestant nativism in 1843 in a piece he wrote for the Catholic Tract Society of Baltimore titled *A Just Judgment on Catholic Doctrines*. Here, he demonstrated his sardonic wit against those who believed the papacy was a political threat to the United States. "Some would scare the people," he wrote, "as if the Pope was on the point of invading the U. States at the head of an army." The whole idea was ridiculous, "when we reflect that all the dominions of the Pope would scarcely form a larger extent than a few counties of our States, and that he is at least four thousand miles from us without a navy."[5]

Verot argued that southern antagonism toward the North increased because the same "fanatical preachers" and "zealots" who drove the Know-Nothing movement had "now turned [their] weapons against the South."[6] In an 1855 piece written for the *New York Freeman's Journal,* a periodical unambiguously committed to the Catholic Church and the Democratic Party, Verot said it was the northern Protestant clergy "who have irritated and exasperated the North and poured obloquy and misrepresentation on the South." Northern Protestants, he urged, "are the true fomenters of the mischiefs which imperil this union."[7] A year later he wrote in the same journal that the Protestant clergy had "brought about this deplorable state of affairs, in which the South is arrayed against the North" and that "Protestant intolerance and bigotry" would soon demolish the "beautiful edifice" of political liberty.[8] By 1860 Verot was convinced that the damage done by the northern clergy was irreparable and that great blame lay on their shoulders for the imminent danger the country faced. "There are men in these United States, in clerical garments," he wrote in the Baltimore-based *Catholic Mirror,* "who, by neglect of their own business, and meddling in that which was not, and is not theirs, have done evils to this country which they cannot repair . . . and which may yet prove fatal to this now glorious and powerful union of states."[9]

Verot's prediction was hardly novel. The American Catholic press had noted for years that evangelical nativists viewed both Catholics and slaveholders as twin threats to a progressive Protestant America. Beginning in the 1830s, the *United States Catholic Miscellany,* an organ of the diocese of Charleston, candidly decried the errors of abolitionism.[10] Other southern Catholic journals such as Baltimore's *Catholic Mirror* and *Le Propagateur catholique* of New Orleans soon joined the *Miscellany* in denouncing both abolitionism and nativism.[11] Significantly, southern Catholics did not rail against abolitionism in isolation. The northern Catholic press was equally condemnatory of Protestant clergy who fueled the abolitionists. The *New York Metropolitan,* the *New York Freeman's Journal,* and the *Boston Pilot* all maintained there was a link between abolitionism and Protestant nativism. Even after the war began, these journals frequently defended the southern cause.[12]

Because of his editorial assaults on President Lincoln's policies toward the South, James McMaster, owner of the *Freeman's Journal,* was arrested in 1861 and confined to Fort Lafayette for almost a year. While he was in prison, his paper was suppressed and did not resume publication until his release in April 1862. Prior to McMaster's run-in with Lincoln's wartime policies toward unsympathetic northern journalists, the *Freeman's Journal* maintained there was a close relationship between the Republican Party and the Know Nothings. Both were subject to the "blind and provoking dogmatism of Abolitionism."[13] Like most southern critics, the journal decried abolitionism as another "New England *ism*" that would, if carried to its logical conclusion, benefit no one. John Brown's efforts, argued one editorialist, proved the point. Behind every madman like Brown stands the "bad dogmas and the brutal teachings" of Protestant preachers who inflame them. Referring to a group of northern evangelical ministers, the writer added that "the Sillimans, Beechers, Phillipses *et id omne,* preach treason and Brown practices it; they furnish rifles and he fires them; they are cowards, he is not."[14]

Rhetorical attacks against New England evangelicals and the Republican Party remained strong in the *Freeman's Journal* late into the war.[15] In the spring of 1864, the journal insisted that Republicans represented the political incarnation of "the canting Abolition Puritans." With a touch of apocalyptic hyperbole, the writer added that Republican political and military success signaled the end of orthodoxy because of the party's association with Protestant extremists. Under Republican rule, "the Revelation of God is replaced by the revelation of table-tipping spirit rappers," and "Christianity is replaced by Lincoln, Seward, Chase, and their generals."[16]

Farther south in Baltimore, the *Catholic Mirror* expressed similar concerns about evangelical abolitionism. As the official organ of the archbishop of Baltimore as well as of the bishops of Richmond and Wheeling, the *Mirror* enjoyed popularity in the South throughout the 1840s. Under the direction of the Reverend Dr. Charles Ignatius White, a well-known historian and a Sulpician priest, the journal gained a national reputation in the 1850s.[17] In 1852 the *Mirror* editorialized that the "fanatical spirit" of Protestant abolitionism had "arrested the progress of emancipation in Maryland, Virginia, Kentucky, and other States" and that this "genius of discord" was hurting rather than helping future prospects for the "colored race."[18] Eight years later, the journal urged that "Black Republicanism" was "obtrusive and hostile to national peace and prosperity." While the Catholic Church did not advocate human slavery, individual states "had a right to settle the question for themselves without interference from other States or the general government."[19]

Like northern Catholic periodicals, the southern-based *Mirror* insisted that Protestant zealots intensified the national division. Also, and not surprisingly, the *Mirror* agreed with the *Freeman's Journal* that fanatics like John Brown were dangerous to the Union, but "they are not a whit worse than the preachers, political and religious, who urge them to their work."[20] In an article written just days after Confederate artillery shells fell on Fort Sumter, the *Mirror* noted that "sensation preachers and sectarian papers have been whetting the appetite of the people for discord and war," and now they had the fight they had long been seeking.[21] A year after Fort Sumter, the same journal editorialized that the Catholic Church "has never fanned the flames of discord," and "her ministers have never substituted any *issues* of the day for the word of God in their mistaking the abolition of slavery for the abolition of sin."[22]

Though the Catholic press tended to side with the political and economic arguments of the South, and though it openly chastised the abolitionist preachers of New England, this did not mean that it uncritically embraced proslavery arguments. Writer and editor Orestes Brownson, a native of Vermont who eventually settled in Massachusetts, took both anti-abolitionist and pro-abolitionist positions over the course of his career. Unlike other influential Catholic apologists of the period, Brownson was a layman and a convert. His journey to the Catholic faith afforded him the unique perspective of a religious pilgrim who had sampled almost all the New England varieties of religious experience. Raised in a

Calvinist Congregationalist home, he underwent a Methodist evangelical conversion at age thirteen, embraced Presbyterianism as a young adult, abandoned the Presbyterians after three years to become a Universalist minister, gave up Universalism for Unitarianism, and finally converted to Catholicism in 1844 at the age of forty-one. He remained a Catholic the rest of his life, yet he demonstrated in his faith the same tendency toward extremes that plagued him as a Protestant.[23]

Throughout most of his Catholic years, Brownson edited *Brownson's Quarterly Review* where he argued vigorously that Protestantism perpetuated its own version of political tyranny. Protestants, he said, "raised the State over the Church" and left the individual without appeal to any authority outside of private judgment.[24] His critique of individualism and subjectivism echoed the criticisms that southern ministers leveled against northern evangelicals. Before the South seceded from the Union, Brownson agreed with many southern arguments, including the opinion that slavery was a local institution that did not concern the federal government. An admirer of the political theory of John C. Calhoun, he argued that the Wilmot Proviso of 1846, which forbade slavery in territories acquired from Mexico, was unconstitutional and that the Free Soil Party of 1848 was the American version of Red Republicanism. If the Free Soilers succeeded, anarchy would surely follow. He would later argue that slavery was wrong and that the Civil War was rightly being fought to liberate the slaves. In the 1840s and 1850s, however, Brownson was convinced that abolitionists, Free Soilers, teetotalers, and navtivists were a recrudescence of a virulent Puritanism that had plagued the Church since the Manichean heresy of the third century.[25]

Brownson demonstrates that Catholic intellectuals were not always consistent regarding the politics of slavery. Nevertheless, the Catholic hierarchy had a developed theological tradition on slavery, and this tradition not only predated the American South but also predated America as a country. The Catholic approach to slavery had origins in antiquity and the early church, and this meant that from the Catholic perspective, American evangelicals were latecomers to moral arguments surrounding the slavery controversy.[26]

In 1860 James McMaster summarized the thoughts of many American Catholics concerning the evangelical approach to the slavery debate.

While "religionists at the North have, to a great extent, been led into the meshes of error, by the narrow dogmatism of the anti-slavery preachers," the ministers of the South were equally in error when they promoted slavery as "a rule of life to be insisted upon—to be spread—to be perpetuated—to be adored where it exists, and its absence to be everywhere regretted."[27] A later edition of the *Freeman's Journal* argued that the Catholic Church had a more acceptable tradition on the issue of slavery. Though not a divine right, slavery was nevertheless a legitimate human relation that could be maintained justly.[28]

The Catholic Church and Slavery

The slavery question was never directly addressed by any of the eight provincial councils held by the American Catholic Church between 1829 and 1849 or by the First Plenary Council of Baltimore held in 1852. Yet even without an official position, Catholic intellectuals had a theologically informed opinion about slavery as a moral issue. This fact became clear after Pope Gregory XVI issued the apostolic letter *In Supremo Apostolatus Fastigio* in December 1839. Though not specifically addressed to the United States, the papal brief stated in no uncertain terms that the slave trade was to be condemned.[29] Somewhat problematic, however, was that it did not condemn the institution of slavery along with the slave trade.[30]

For Democrats looking to hold on to the presidency against the Whigs, the papal letter came at a fortuitous moment. Feeling the pressure of possibly losing the 1840 election to Whig war hero William Henry Harrison, Democrats, who had occupied the White House since 1828, decided the ambiguity of the pope's dispatch was combustible enough to catch political fire in the South. Democrats gambled they could secure the southern vote by convincing southerners that Whigs and Catholics were secretly united in the cause of abolitionism. Conveniently, so they thought, the pope had handed them a gift. Secretary of State John Forsyth of Georgia assumed the role of attack dog on behalf of Democratic presidential candidate Martin Van Buren. Forsyth warned southerners that Catholics were taking their orders from Rome and that Pope Gregory's recent address indicated that the Catholic Church was sympathetic with abolitionism.[31]

John England, bishop of Charleston, South Carolina, took offense at Forsyth's allegations. Responding in the *United States Catholic Miscellany,* England appealed to Scripture, the traditions of the Church, and principles of natural law to clarify the Catholic position on slavery:

> Slavery . . . is regarded by that church of which the Pope is the presiding officer, not to be incompatible with the natural law, to be the result of sin by Divine dispensation, to have been established by human legislation, and, when the dominion of the slave is justly acquired by the master to be lawful, not only in the sight of the human tribunal, but also in the eye of heaven.[32]

Bishop England was one of the most vocal Catholic opponents of what he characterized as "the lack of pharisaical restraint" in evangelical political activism.[33] Born in Cork, Ireland, England came to the United States in 1820 keenly aware of the price of dissent. His father was a surveyor who fled Protestant authorities because he refused to deny the doctrines of transubstantiation and penance. His grandfather was an equally obstinate Catholic who was confined to prison for over four years on similar charges. Early nineteenth-century Irish reform movements influenced his views on church and state; and his opposition to the right of British Parliament to veto the nominations of Irish Catholic bishops brought him into contact with some of the leading political thinkers of the day.[34] England's background made him a formidable opponent of nativists who claimed that Catholicism was incompatible with American political institutions. Like other prominent antebellum Catholic leaders, he saw an essential connection between republicanism and Catholicism. His essays in the *United States Catholic Miscellany* defied those evangelicals who insisted that the United States was a Christian nation. There was, he argued, no political mandate that corresponded with the mission of the Protestant church.[35]

England's appeal to natural law as well as to the tradition of the Church distinguished the Catholic argument about slavery from arguments put forward by both northern Protestants who opposed slavery and southern Protestants who supported it. Catholics used the Bible to explain their moral theology, but their moral theology also always employed evidence from patristic and medieval interpretations of biblical texts.[36]

Borrowing from St. Augustine of Hippo, England maintained that without the introduction of sin (*peccatum*) slavery (*servitudo*) would not exist. At the creation no one was made either slave or free, but "sin introduced servitude as a means by which God enjoins the preservation of the order of nature, and forbids its disruption."[37] Augustine, said England, recognized that "the origin of slavery, as of all our infirmities and afflictions, is to be found in sin," and that "for a person who believes in the fall of man, as every Catholic must," abstract speculations about the subject are fruitless.[38] Catholics, he urged, traditionally agreed with Augustine's lengthy elaboration in book 19, chapter 16 of *De Civitate Dei*. As long as the laws concerning slavery are just, "the peace and good order of society, as well as religious duty, demand that the laws of the state regulating the conduct of slaves, should be conscientiously observed."[39] England also noted that the writings of several of Augustine's contemporaries made similar arguments. St. Ambrose's "On Elias and Fasting," St. John Chrysostom's commentary on Genesis 29, and Pope Gelasius I's letter to the bishops of the Picene territory in Italy condemning the Pelagian heresy all upheld the notion that slavery was one social condition among many created by the introduction of sin.[40]

In addition to the writings of late fifth-century and early sixth-century bishops, England pointed out that the Council of Nicaea in 325 censured early Gnostic and Manichean errors concerning slavery. The Manichean teaching that circulated through much of Asia Minor in the third and fourth centuries falsely "proclaimed the *obligation on all* to enter into religious societies," denounced "the use of wine," and "decried the lawfulness of slavery" (emphasis original).[41] He added, perhaps with the northern evangelical abolitionists in mind, that these ancient "fanatics"

> denounced the slaveholders as violating equally the laws of nature and of religion; they offered to aid slaves to desert their owners; gave them exhortations, invitations, asylum and protection; and in all things assumed to be more holy, more perfect, and more spiritual than other men.[42]

According to England, the decrees of the Nicene Council on slavery were given further sanction around the year 500 under the guidance of Pope Symmachus. Symmachus declared that while many local assemblies had been formed in the early church to correct the Manichean errors on slavery and property in general, the acts of the Council of Nicaea concerning slavery were to be considered part of canon law that governs the conduct of the Catholic Church. Thus, the decrees officially provided the Church with a universal rule regarding abolition: "If anyone under the pretence of piety, teaches a slave to despise his master, and to withdraw from his service, and not to serve his master with good will and all respect. Let him be Anathema."[43] England noted that the last phrase, *Anathema sit,* "is never appended to any decree which does not contain the expression of unchangeable doctrine respecting belief or morality, and indicates that the doctrine has been revealed by God."[44]

That Catholics recognized God-ordained rules for the maintenance of slavery did not mean, as many southern Protestants were concluding after 1835, that slavery deserved to be proliferated indefinitely. England maintained that because slavery was a consequence of sin, Catholics viewed slavery in the same way they viewed "death, sickness and a large train of what are now called natural evils."[45] He understood slavery as a social institution that, like all postlapsarian social institutions, could never be made perfect, but could nevertheless be ameliorated through mercy and justice. According to the church fathers and later, Thomas Aquinas, the institution of slavery was given to the state to enact laws regulating property, and "the church was to plead for morality" and to exhort the state "to practice mercy."[46]

England's opinion about the distinct responsibilities of church and state regarding property rested largely on Aquinas's "view that the law of nations is distinct from natural law" and that "slavery belongs principally to the law of nations."[47] In his defense of the Church, England accepted the basic Thomistic principle that the natural law neither establishes nor forbids slavery but rather slavery was introduced by "the reason of man for the benefit of human life."[48] Utilizing categories introduced in Aristotle's *Politics,* Aquinas argued in the *Summa Theologiae* that the goal of politics was to establish the best form of government for a particular society based on rational reflection about human ends and human needs. Aquinas argued that every being has a mode of conduct natural to itself and by fulfilling its own nature, plays its proper part in the overall scheme of the universe. It is natural for people to live in society because of the intrinsic truth that people are by nature political and social creatures. But living in society also requires adherence to defined rules of conduct. These defined rules of conduct are natural to man in that both the need for them and the means of devising them are part of humanity's created nature. When rational persons conform their actions to the fulfillment of their nature, they are participating in the general harmony of the universe, and thus they are ordering their life according to the proper end for which they have been created. In short, natural law for Aquinas is a basic framework of moral principles inherent in the created human condition that are necessary to the coherence of human societies.

Slavery, like the concept of property in general, is not "natural" in the sense that it is neither part of the original created condition, nor is it necessary per se for the maintenance of an orderly society. It is not, however, *contra naturum,* or against nature, in that, like private property, it in no way opposes or takes away from the moral principles necessary for rightly ordering society. Slavery, for Aquinas, is *praeter naturam,* a justifiable addition to nature that, like all human law, is grounded in human reason and designed to serve the general welfare of all. This did not mean for Aquinas, or for England, that slavery was by necessity "good," or even that the practice of slavery could be exercised in such a way as to be contrary to natural law. Rather, like all relationships involving coercive power, there was a proper moral way of exercising authority (*dominium*) and an immoral or licentious way of exercising authority.[49]

Starting from both Augustinian concepts of original sin and Thomistic concepts of rightly ordered political and social life, England articulated a careful defense of the Catholic Church against charges of abolitionist sympathies. He also established the intellectual pattern that would be used by other members of the American hierarchy as they too sought to explain the Church's position on slavery. In twenty-eight letters published between September 1840 and April 1841, England provided copious examples of how the church and the state worked together to regulate and improve the conditions of slavery in the late Roman Empire and the Middle Ages. In addition to Augustine and Aquinas, his sources included the second-century epistles of Saint Ignatius and Saint Polycarp on the baptism of slaves; Constantine's decrees on manumission; Pope Gregory the Great's rules for educating slaves and his statements on the relationship between Christians, Jews, and slavery; the code of Justinian on marriage and separation of slaves; and, after the Franks conquered the Lombards, the Capitularies of Pope Adrian I to Charlemagne on the treatment of captured slaves. Beyond these references, England also alluded to local church councils held throughout Europe over the course of a millennium.[50]

Apart from John England, the most lucid analysis of slavery from the Catholic perspective came from a contemporary who lived farther north. Patrick Kenrick served as bishop of Philadelphia from 1831 to 1851, and later, archbishop of Baltimore from 1851 to 1863. Like England, Kenrick was a native of Ireland. His early years in Dublin exposed him to English penal legislation that barred Catholics from professional employment and ensured that Parliament held full control over nominations to Ireland's episcopal sees. Rather than study for ministry at Maynooth Seminary near Dublin, which was caught in the middle of a controversy over episcopal appointments, he chose the College of the Congregation of Propaganda Fide in Rome.[51]

After ordination, Kenrick was appointed to teach theology in a small diocesan seminary in Bardstown, Kentucky. Recognizing his talents as a theologian, the First Provincial Council of Baltimore nominated him for the position of coadjutor to the bishop of Philadelphia, a post he assumed in 1831. In 1842 Kenrick was named bishop of Philadelphia, and here he produced his *Theologia Moralis,* a manual of moral theology for seminary students designed specifically to "meet American social conditions."[52] Following principles derived from Augustine, Thomas Aquinas, and Alphonsus Ligouri, Kenrick proposed that his moral theology was intended to address difficulties arising from a society of citizens "with no religious bond in common," who are free "to follow each his own conscience."[53]

A significant part of the *Theologia Moralis* was devoted to the slavery controversy. Like Bishop England, Kenrick's opinion of slavery rested largely on categories drawn from medieval theology. Slavery was a consequence of sin and the disorder generated by sin. Because sin altered the original state of freedom in which people were created, perfect freedom could never again be attained through either political or social manipulation.[54] The work proved popular, and a later edition published on the eve of the Civil War elaborated on the theme by excoriating abolitionist societies. The same edition also explained how Constitutional prohibitions forbade the federal government from intervening in the affairs of particular states.[55]

Kenrick's analysis of slavery utilized Aquinas's distinction between the natural law and the laws of nations. According to the natural law, all men are indeed morally equal. But slavery did not rest on principles of natural law. The "*dominium* of jurisdiction," or lawful oversight of slavery, like the lawful oversight of private property, belonged to the *jus gentium,* or law of nations. Specifically, the jurisdiction of slavery belonged to the *jus gentium voluntarium,* or the laws of social regulations that nations observe out of a sense of equity or justice.[56]

Because slavery, like all relations between capital and labor, involved questions of morality, the *dominium* of the state could never be considered absolute. The state could not dispense with the ethical demands of the natural law, nor could it abrogate them through human legislation. If the state tried to dispense with the ethical demands of the natural law, it lost its legitimate "*dominium* of jurisdiction" over slavery. Kenrick explained that the state had a warranted yet imperfect relationship with the natural law. The purposes of the *jus gentium* with regard to slavery were not unlike the ways in which nations regulated other social conditions. According to the natural law, people have equal access to common resources that can be used to meet individual needs. By general agreement and consent, however, nations regulate the rules surrounding the acquisition and ownership of property in an effort to protect the general welfare of all. Likewise, under the natural law, people are born free, but again, by general agreement and consent in times of crises, the state can abrogate freedom to fulfill its obligation to the common good.[57]

Kenrick's argument also appealed to the canonical legislation of the Church. In the *Theologia Moralis,* he noted that the Synod of Gangra, which met in 340 to condemn the extreme asceticism of Eustathius of Sebaste and his followers, pronounced anathema on "any one who teaches a slave, under the pretext of piety, to despise his master, to forsake his service, or not to serve with good will and entire respect."[58] He emphasized that through the centuries the Church encouraged masters to manumit their slaves and to reform unfavorable conditions in which a slave might be held. Kenrick noted the Third Lateran Council held in Rome in 1179, which, in addition to condemning the heresies of the Cathars and the Waldensians, also decreed that neither Jews nor Saracens could possess Christian slaves. In a later edition of *Theologia Moralis,* he added that in *De Civitate Dei* Augustine outlined the proper boundaries of both ecclesiastical and political authority. According to Augustine, slavery was a social institution under the legal authority of the state yet subject to the moral oversight of the Church.[59]

Though Kenrick's knowledge of theology and history shaped his position toward slavery, his concerns were much more than academic. In the mid-1840s, he found himself at the center of a controversy in Philadelphia over the use of the King James version of the Bible in public schools. What started as a minor hullabaloo escalated into several days of riots culminating with the torching of three parish churches.[60] Kenrick's Philadelphia experience allowed him to witness firsthand the excesses of political Protestantism, and the lessons were not forgotten. As evangelical abolitionist activity increased in the wake of the 1857 Dred Scott decision, Kenrick urged the American Catholic Church to maintain its "peaceful and conservative character." The clergy, he reminded, should remain "free on all questions of polity and social order" and only oversee those issues that fall "within the limits of the doctrine and the law of Christ." He further exhorted that the Church should "not, in any way, identify the interests of our holy faith with the fortunes of any party."[61]

Challenging Political Protestantism

Keeping faith out of politics proved easier said than done precisely because so many Protestants believed Catholicism to be a threat to their political values. For decades prior to the Civil War, evangelical presses and pulpits scorned Catholics as nemeses of republicanism. As a result, Catholic leaders found themselves defending their place in the republic by attempting to right the theological and historical record.

In October 1822, the *Gospel Advocate,* a monthly periodical published in Boston, printed an article titled "The Dispensing Power of the Pope." Using examples from the Middle Ages, the article suggested that because the pope could "dispense with the obligations of oaths, contracts, and agreements," Catholic fidelity to the United States could not be trusted.[62] John England was incensed. He responded that the *Advocate* was wrong to try to prove a doctrine of the Church from isolated papal acts conditioned by historical circumstances. American Protestants, moreover, were naïve if they thought that they were the first Christians to wrestle with questions about political rights and responsibilities. Long before Protestants, Catholics were concerned with protecting the general welfare of all from the tyranny of a few (or one). American political conditions, he concluded, actually had some precedent in the medieval system of checks and balances, which included the power of the pope to dispense with certain kinds of contracts and oaths of fealty.

The *Advocate* cited Gregory VII's deposition of Emperor Henry IV as an example of papal abuse. England argued that, under the political conditions of the eleventh century, what Gregory did in Germany was no different in substance from what the American colonists did in declaring independence from Great Britain. The emperor of Germany "ceased to have a claim upon the allegiance of his vassals, by having violated the conditions of his compact." Thus, according to the "law of nations" current at that time, Gregory VII had the same power to free Henry's subjects as eighteenth-century Americans had to declare themselves free from British rule.[63] England noted that one of Henry IV's "first acts upon coming of age, was to impose taxes which were not usual," and this action created an arbitrary burden on the people of Germany. When the editors of the *Gospel Advocate* criticized the pope for taking action against Henry IV, they were in effect "lecturing the founders of American liberty, and defending the King of England."[64] Circumstances dictated:

the Pope had a right to interfere in the election and confirmation, and to judge whether allegiance was or was not due to the claimants of the imperial crown. Not by divine right, but by human and temporary institution; and his exercise of this right is no part of the Roman Catholic religion.[65]

According to England, history proved that many others besides Catholics had exercised the power of absolving oaths of allegiance. After all, he wrote, "Did not General Washington take an oath of allegiance to King George the Third of England, and to his heirs and successors? Did not Mr. Monroe himself take this same oath? . . . And shall we say that all the fathers of church and state in America were perjurers who violated their oath?"[66]

England applied the same argument to other historical cases raised by the *Advocate*. When Pope Urban II reinforced Gregory VII's earlier declaration on Henry IV at the Council of Clermont in 1095, England insisted that once again the pope acted because the political arrangements of that time obligated him to provide a check on the power grab that was taking place in Germany. Catholics, he asserted, never believed that subjects could at all times and in all places declare themselves free from the authority of an immoral or unchristian monarch. In fact, "the Catholic Church condemned this doctrine as heretical when it was taught by Wickliffe, and Huss, and the German boors, and some of the Puritans in England and Scotland."[67]

Likewise, in 1215 when Pope Innocent III deposed Otto IV for neglecting "to purge his territory from heretical filth" and pronounced Frederick II to be emperor, he acted under temporal law not ecclesiastical law. The power given to the pope at that time was delegated by "the whole of Christendom" for the purpose of controlling the "unnatural consequences of Manicheism." It was no more a usurpation for the pope to exercise this power "than it would be for the President of the United States to use the power given to him by the Congress."[68]

In 1825 Bishop England again found himself defending the Church against charges of anti-Americanism. The Reverend William Hawley, an Episcopal minister from Washington, D.C., published a series of articles in the *Theological Repertory* alleging that Catholics could never be faithful to a Protestant government because historically the Church claimed political coequality with the state. England objected to what he believed to be a gross misrepresentation of Catholic history and theology. Not only was Hawley wrong "in styling America as a Protestant country," he was also wrong to equate the pope's ecclesiastical jurisdiction and spiritual power with "magisterial rights in the state."[69] "Roman Catholics," insisted England, "believe that as political power is derived from the people—so spiritual and ecclesiastical power is derived from God." "The Pope is Christ's Vicar on earth," and the general councils of the Church are "infallible in doctrinal decisions." Nevertheless, Catholics deny to the pope and to the councils "any power to interfere with one tittle of our political rights, as firmly as we deny the power of interfering with one tittle of our spiritual rights to the President and Congress."[70] Furthermore, when Protestants argued that "spiritual obedience to a foreigner is a violation of allegiance to the state," they carelessly gave sanction to the kind of state persecution endorsed against the martyrs of the early church. The first martyrs "adhered to foreign claimants of spiritual power," and they openly "disobeyed kings and emperors in matters of religion."[71]

England defended the Catholic Church again in 1826 after the works of Blanco White, an apostate Spanish priest, began circulating in the United States. Like other allegations England encountered early in his tenure as bishop of Charleston, White's accusations charged the pope of meddling in civil affairs and promoting political absolutism.[72] Again, England reiterated that while there were very specific historic conditions where the pope "did upon special grounds interfere with the civil allegiance of some of his spiritual subjects," these instances never constituted the doctrine of the Church. White, he said, was guilty of arguing "*a dicto secundum quid, ad dictum simpliciter,*" from particular premises to universal conclusions.[73]

Against the "calumnies" of White, England claimed that Catholics never believed the Church had a universal right to regulate civil concerns. "The Church," he explained, "is a society established by God himself for spiritual purposes," and it functioned as "a body established for spiritual objects, [just] as a kingdom, an empire, a republic are bodies for political objects."[74] By arguing that the purposes of the Church were distinct from political purposes, England could be interpreted as promoting the same argument for the spirituality of the church that would later be made by southern Protestants in the 1850s and 1860s. Conspicuously absent from the southern argument, however, was England's belief that "the great Creator" of the Church "did not form or sanction the formation of conflicting ecclesiastical bodies, but made his Church one in her government and doctrines."[75]

As with his later argument on slavery, England made use of Thomas Aquinas's distinctions between natural, divine, and human law to explain the scope and the limits of both ecclesiastical authority and political authority. "God," he argued, "has bound man to the observance of certain great principles, which are discoverable by the natural exercise of his reason, and the collection of those principles, is called the natural law." Yet God "has also by means of revelation, given certain precepts for man's conduct," and these the Church recognizes as the divine law. The divine law includes two divisions: the negative law, which prohibits certain acts "at all times and under all circumstances," and the positive law, which commands certain acts to be performed under the auspices of the Church "according to circumstances of time and place."[76]

Besides the natural and divine law, "man is bound by the laws of society, that is, . . . by the laws of that particular nation in which the individual resides." Contrary to the claims of Blanco White and others, the pope, acting as the vicar of Christ on earth, cannot "dispense in any obligation of the natural law, nor in any obligation of the divine negative law." Likewise, the pope cannot "dispense with the divine positive law" but can only regulate the ordinances that the divine law requires. Regarding the laws of society, or human law, England argued that "the delegation of the particular nation must also precede the power to dispense in any one of its enactments." In other words, while individual nations have sovereignty over their laws, they may also, due to the vicissitude of historical circumstance, delegate their power to other authoritative bodies. Thus at various points throughout the Middle Ages

the Bishop of Rome was by the act and assent of the princes and States of Christendom, the President of the temporal confederation of those powers; and by their consent and act, he was frequently not only authorized but required to enforce by spiritual power the moral obligation of observing their compact.[77]

England used Thomist principles to convince American Protestants that the Catholic understanding of the state by necessity did not reject republicanism and that Enlightenment political ideas, such as the social contract, were not inimical to the teaching of the Church. As one historian explained, Catholics could accept republican political conditions because "according to Bishop England one's political theory was not a matter of revelation," and through the centuries Catholic theologians "had constructed a variety of theories of the state—but they did so on the basis of natural reason, not on the basis of faith."[78]

Bishop England frustrated his Protestant detractors largely because of his ability to turn their arguments back on them. Where evangelicals borrowed freely from medieval history to demonstrate Catholicism's incompatibility with "Americanism," England used the Middle Ages to establish Catholicism's contributions to republican political conditions. Other antebellum Catholic thinkers, including Francis Kenrick, followed his lead.

Kenrick recognized that Catholicism was both misunderstood and misrepresented in the Protestant press. He also knew that zealous evangelicals exacerbated the domestic crisis surrounding slavery. He sparred with Protestants throughout his career, with one of the more memorable debates occurring with B. B. Smith, the Episcopal bishop of Kentucky. Smith, in an instance of ecumenical idealism, challenged Protestants to give up their doctrinal divisions in favor of reuniting around the beliefs of the early church. Kenrick took the occasion to write an open letter to Smith where he tersely but politely reminded the bishop that the standard of the Catholic Church had always been the early church.[79] Smith did not reply, but another Episcopal bishop, the Reverend John Henry Hopkins of Vermont, did. Hopkins published a book entitled *The Church of Rome, in Her Primitive Purity, Compared with the Church of Rome, at the Present Day.* Here, in response to Kenrick, he outlined in detail the errors of the papacy and the medieval church. Kenrick was swift to offer a rejoinder against Hopkins and entered into a series of published exchanges with the bishop in an effort to defend the church.

In particular, Hopkins attacked the practice of monasticism. He referred to it as "primitive," and he boasted that Protestants were not "tied fast by vows of human institution, and secured by bolts and bars, and wrapped carefully up in secrecy and seclusion." Kenrick viewed Hopkins' characterization of monasticism as a classic example of how American Protestants grossly twisted the history of the Church. He argued that far from repressive the monasteries of the "primitive age" were "a refuge of Christian piety and holiness when the increasing spread of religion made the Church more secular." Moreover, "in Protestant countries, where monastic orders are unknown," the "more serious and anxious" have no provision for serving in the institutional church, and thus they "run into separatism."[80]

Hopkins bragged that Protestants have "no orders of the sexes who stand aloof from the social community around them, invested with the suspicious mantle of mystery and gloom." Kenrick replied that Hopkins failed to understand the purpose of female monasticism in Late Antiquity and the Middle Ages. Unmarried women were often left desolate and oppressed, and one function of female monasticism was to provide "religious sisterhoods . . . in the model of Christian charity" that could offer sanctuary for such women. "I know not any more distressing development of the cruel spirit of Protestantism," Kenrick added, "than the determined, bitter, and scoffing spirit in which it has set itself against institutions which give dignity and independence to the position of women in society."[81]

Hopkins declared that Protestantism was superior to Catholicism because Protestants were "under no oaths to a foreign prelate," nor were they "entangled in doubtful constructions, in order to settle the boundary line between conflicting rights and duties." Kenrick retorted that, yet again, Hopkins mischaracterized the Church. Catholics did not recognize the pope as a "foreign prelate" but rather acknowledged him as "the chief pastor of the Church," a "Father, according to the relations which Christ has constituted between members of his family." Echoing John England, Kenrick underscored that "in all things temporal we obey civil rulers: in matters of faith and religious communion we obey the chief pastor of the Church."[82]

Hopkins believed that the legacy of medieval Catholicism was one of violence and papal aggression and that not just the church but society as a whole had been improved through the Reformation. "Where," Hopkins asked, "was our peace before the Reformation" when "every weapon of state, fire, and sword, crusades and inquisitions, racks and gibbets, the actual torture of the body, and the threatened torture of the soul, were unceasingly employed for successive centuries, to secure peace and unity to the papal dominions, and all in vain?" Kenrick replied that before "the catastrophe which is misnamed the Reformation," Christian peace was found in the "maintenance of truth by the public authorities of the church against all the ravings of infidelity." Faith, he argued, was the basis of the Church in the Middle Ages and "faith was spread by the preaching of the gospel, not by edicts of kings, or civil laws." When the state did act to support the Church, "the severity of the Christian princes was directed against apostates, and chiefly restricted to such as in the name of Religion, disturbed public order, despoiled and profaned the churched, massacred the priests of God, violated the consecrated virgins, and shook society to its basis."[83]

Archbishop Kenrick's successor, Martin John Spalding, continued to defend Catholicism against Protestant detractors. A native of Bardstown, Kentucky, Spalding served as bishop of Louisville from 1850 to 1864 before assuming the See of Baltimore upon Kenrick's death. A gifted intellectual, as a fourteen-year-old he taught mathematics at St. Mary's College, Lebanon, Kentucky, and was a star student at the Propaganda in Rome, where he was ordained and received his doctorate.[84] While serving the Church in Kentucky, Spalding produced a number of essays and apologetic pieces defending Catholicism. In addition, he published a two-volume history of the Reformation in which he challenged Protestant claims to be the progenitors of political liberty.[85]

Politically, Spalding was a committed Whig until 1855 when the Know-Nothing Party and their anti-Catholic agenda captured the loyalties of Louisville's Whig dissidents. On election day, August 6, 1855, the Know Nothings refused to let Catholic immigrants vote, and after a series of violent exchanges, one of which included gunshots, Louisville erupted into a day of riots and murders.[86] "Bloody Monday," as it came to be called, culminated in the burning of the immigrant district around St. Patrick's Church. Several other Catholic churches were searched for allegedly hiding weapons. The incident forever changed Bishop Spalding, and thereafter he abandoned the Whigs for the Democrats. In the aftermath of the violence, Spalding wrote to Archbishop Kenrick,

> We have just passed through a reign of terror, surpassed only by the Philadelphia riots. Nearly an hundred poor Irish and Germans have been butchered or burned, and some twenty houses have been consumed in the flames. The city authorities—all Know-Nothings— looked calmly on, and they are now endeavoring to lay the blame on the Catholics.[87]

Although the Louisville riots deeply affected Bishop Spalding, he was no stranger to the dilemmas American Catholics faced in a country dominated by Protestants. Long before witnessing violence against Catholics firsthand, he was challenging the nativist historical narrative that emphasized a radical dualism between the Catholic "Dark Ages" and the Protestant age of "Enlightenment." In 1853, almost two years before the horrors of "Bloody Monday," Spalding published the first edition of a collection of popular essays entitled *Miscellanea*. Here, he attempted to correct what he believed to be a misrepresentation of Catholic history by emphasizing that Protestantism, far from being a religion of progress, had actually had a negative impact on western society. Where Protestants vilified the power of papal deposition in the Middle Ages, he responded that the extent of that power had been grossly distorted. Americans, he said, claimed the same right "when we deposed George III, and declared ourselves 'absolved' from our oath of allegiance to him." Instead of criticizing the medieval papacy, "we should rather applaud them, for thus keeping alive, amidst political darkness and confusion, that spark of popular liberty, which was destined, a little later to illumine the political horizon of Europe."[88]

Spalding singled out as particularly erroneous the claim that the eleventh-century struggle between Gregory VII and Henry IV was an irrefutable example of the papacy exceeding its sphere of authority. "Gregory," he argued, "had a two-fold obligation to the world: the one spiritual, to the Church, of which he was the visible head; the other temporal, to civil society, in the framework of which he was an important part."[89] Whenever the medieval papacy exercised the power to depose a prince, it did so "almost without exception" as a means "for checking tyranny, and maintaining the rights of the people" because the prince "had broken his solemn engagement to his people—to govern them in accordance with justice." Spalding noted that the practice of deposing a ruler "greatly contributed to the unfolding of the democratic principle," because it rested entirely upon "the doctrine of a contract, expressed or implied, between a king and his people; the former binding himself to protect their rights, and to govern them justly, and the latter, *under this condition only*, pledging to him their allegiance" (emphasis original).[90]

While Spalding conceded that Protestantism had on occasion provided some benefit to the development of civilization, on the whole its influence was negligible when compared to Catholicism. The very idea of a civilization rested on the implication that something had been rescued from barbarism. What, he asked, "has Protestantism ever reclaimed from a barbarous to a civilized condition?"[91] Catholicism, by contrast, had a civilizing influence on Europe "beginning with the conversion of the peoples making up the Roman Empire, and concluding with the conversion of the Hungarians in the early part of the eleventh century."[92] The so-called Dark Ages were actually a time when the Church almost singlehandedly preserved the elements of learning that were necessary for a cultured society.

"The usual device of Protestant writers," he wrote in the mid-1840s, "is to accuse the Catholic Church of promoting ignorance, especially during the Middle Ages." Yet "it is not true, that the epoch in question was so *dark* as it is often represented" (emphasis original).[93] "From the earliest ages, schools and colleges grew up under the fostering care of the Church" in such prominent ancient cities as "Rome, Alexandria, Milan, Carthage, and Nisbis." These institutions survived the persecutions of the emperors Decius (249–51), Valerian (253–60), and Diocletian (284–305). Their efforts preserved "the Latin language in the public service," and set the educational pattern "for the monks of the '*Dark*' Ages."[94]

Monasticism, Spalding argued, provided "sacred retreats and holy sanctuaries for learning, while the rude storm of war was sweeping over the world, destroying in mankind all relish for letters, and desolating the proudest monuments of literature and the arts."[95] The monks' efforts combined with the efforts of patrician laity to safeguard ancient "works of grammar, music, [and] arithmetic," as well as "precious treasures of ancient classic literature." In the sixth century, Cassiodorus and Boethius, "both of noble family and senatorial rank, but more illustrious by far by their piety," reestablished Greek learning in Italy. Likewise, in the seventh century, Theodorus of England (seventh archbishop of Canterbury), St. Gregory the Great of Italy, and St. Isidore of Seville kept learning alive in those countries.[96] At the close of the eighth century and into the ninth century, the efforts of Charlemagne and Alfred the Great stayed the "downward tendency of letters" and infused "a new literary energy into Europe." Both recognized the value of monastic schools. Charlemagne in particular extended these efforts by ordering "that seminaries of learning should be opened at every cathedral church throughout his vast empire."[97]

According to Spalding, the Church did more than preserve literate civilization. It also protected and unified Europe when that continent was threatened to become "a mere degraded province of a colossal Mohammedan empire." The Church and, specifically, the papacy persuaded Christians "to rally in their united strength for the defense of the cross against the invading hosts marshaled under the crescent." Protestants, he noted, failed to do the same when the Ottomans launched their campaigns into Europe in the late fifteenth and early sixteenth centuries. "If we are still free, if we bow to the cross instead of the crescent; we certainly owe no gratitude for these results to the Protestant party."[98]

For Spalding, the most detrimental consequence of Protestantism, however, was not its cultural desolation but rather the exalted privilege it afforded the idea of individualism. Spalding agreed with Kenrick and England that liberty and freedom were necessary components of a healthy republic. With them, he passionately maintained that Protestantism did not invent these civic ideals. The unfortunate complement of political freedom as defined by Protestants was a tendency to reject, or at least to minimize, the importance of tradition, community, and inherited religious authority. In place of these, Protestants favored abstract principles of enlightened liberalism such as promoted by the *philosophes* of Europe less than a century earlier. Spalding alleged that "the sectarian" celebrated "the emancipation of the human mind" as much as "the infidel philosopher":

> Voltaire and Rousseau did but seize up and re-echo through the world the self-same shout of LIBERTY, which Luther and Calvin had sent forth two and a half centuries before. . . . The infidels did but carry out the leading doctrine of the reformers, and all the world saw and felt the awful results of that principle, when it was fully developed.[99]

Protestants premised both their intellectual and social ideals on "the distracting and disorganizing principle of individuality." Consequently, they postured themselves "against the conservative principle of authority, based on antiquity, and secured from error by Divine promise." For Spalding, a narrow gap separated the principles of individualism and freedom as inaugurated by the Reformation and those same principles as championed during the Enlightenment. Both movements maintained that the idea of freedom contained its own justification that need not be tempered by the moral teachings of the Church. Thus, "the same demoniacal shout of LIBERTY" that first sounded "the battle cry of freedom from the tyranny of the papacy" became "liberty as excluding, and in deadly opposition to all restraint and authority."[100] Protestant individualism exalted the exercise of "private reason," and where "private reason first undertook to judge for itself in matters of religion . . . it has ended in rejecting religion altogether!" Catholics, he concluded, must perceive that the "great struggle in our own republic will, at no distant day, be not so much between Catholicity and Protestantism, as between Catholicity and infidelity."[101]

Almost a half a century before Max Weber proposed his now famous thesis, Spalding suggested that Protestant values contributed to the more detrimental effects of capitalism. Protestantism "sets up every man for himself . . . it leads to isolation, to selfishness," and results in an "[economic] system strongly anti-social in its tendency."[102] As a result of Protestant influence, Americans lived in a "degenerate age of Mammonism, enlightened in material interests and in the matter of dollars and cents."[103] Catholicism, by contrast, was a "religion eminently social in its very character." Spalding quipped, "if Rome were in the hands of New Yorkers for but half a century . . . mammon would riot over the ruin of all that is most beautiful, magnificent, and precious in the 'eternal city.'"[104]

Spalding believed that when Protestants promoted their religion as a religion of material progress they distorted the message of Christianity. Prosperity was not, he urged, a measure of true religion. Jesus did not "promote mere worldly comforts" but rather taught a "sublime and supernatural system . . . intended to raise mankind above this world." "We do not read" that Christ "either directly or indirectly alluded in His discourses to any of those great improvements which distinguish modern from ancient society." Nor can it be established that certain people are "wealthy because they are true Christians."[105]

Spalding's attack against Protestantism extended to his interpretation of how and why the Union collapsed into war. In May 1863, he wrote a "Dissertation on the American Civil War." Written in Italian and submitted to the Cardinal Prefect of the Congregation of Propaganda, the essay was published anonymously in the papal newspaper *Osservatore Romano.*[106] In his "Dissertation," Spalding argued that what started as a war to restore the Union had "become a war of confiscation of property" and "of destruction and desolation of the vast and fair territory of the South." He cited industrialists' support of the Tariff of Abominations and President Lincoln's duplicity as critical factors inciting the conflict. He also emphasized the unrelenting agitation of the Protestant abolitionists as one of the "principal causes of our unfortunate Civil War." "The dominant Protestant religion," he wrote, "with its principles founded on private judgement as opposed to authority . . . had already divided on political questions many years before the disastrous political division."[107] Northern preachers who "denounce—almost every Sunday—slavery as the greatest and most atrocious sin of all" demonstrate "none of that wise moderation which looks in the face all the practical difficulties of the situation and strives to adapt the means to the end." He concluded:

Some of these blind fanatics openly proposed their program of modern progress as embracing two principle points: namely "the violent destruction of those two relics of a barbarous age—slavery and Catholicism!!" Their shout was—"Down with slavery and popery!!"[108]

Six months after the publication of his "Dissertation" the Congregation for the Propagation of the Faith named Martin John Spalding archbishop of Baltimore.[109]

In the years leading up to the Civil War, many coreligionists in the North sympathized with John England, Francis Kenrick, and Martin Spalding. Bishop John Hughes of New York shared their belief that northern evangelicals distorted both Catholicism and slavery to advance their own political interests. Like so many members of the American hierarchy, Hughes was born and raised in Ireland. He immigrated to Pennsylvania in 1817 at the age of twenty. In 1820 he enrolled in Mt. St. Mary's Seminary in Emmitsburg, Maryland, and in 1826 he was ordained a priest. Following ordination, Hughes spent ten years in Philadelphia before becoming first the coadjutor to the bishop of New York and then, in 1842, bishop of New York. While bishop of New York he played a critical role in the controversy over public funding for parochial schools in the late 1830s and early 1840s. He was appointed archbishop in 1850 and held this position until his death in 1864.[110]

Hughes was not a systematic thinker like Bishop England or Archbishop Kenrick. Even so, he made significant contributions to the antebellum Catholic understanding of church-state relations. After the revolutions of 1848, as many American evangelicals cheered the demise of the papal states, Hughes vehemently defended papal political power. At the same time, he insisted that Catholicism was compatible with republican government. Never a friend of slavery and an unreserved opponent of secession, he nonetheless detested the exaggerations of the abolitionists. They erred, he said, in their insistence that slavery was an "absolute and unmitigated evil."[111] Hughes shared Spalding's frustration with the growing spirit of excessive capitalism and unrestrained individualism. Likewise, he argued that the Protestant Reformation and the breakdown of medieval Christendom successfully divorced religion from the moral questions surrounding political economy.[112]

In December 1843, Bishop Hughes addressed the Irish Emigrant Society on the subject of civil and ecclesiastical power in the Middle Ages. He reminded his audience that Protestant critics of Catholicism tended "to judge the past by the present." Using their logic, historians might as well "criticize Columbus and his associates, for not having made the discovery of America in steamers."[113] This was, of course, an "absurd approach to history," and it revealed a profound misunderstanding of actual church and state relations in the medieval period. "There was then, as there is now," argued Hughes, "a singular mixture of good and evil," and "it is quite possible that the five-and-twentieth century, looking back to the nineteenth, will perceive how different from the straight line were the leading impulses and directions of our age."[114]

Hughes described the profound impact the Church had on political and social life throughout the Middle Ages. Beginning with Constantine and continuing through the reign of Theodosius the Younger, "new and more humane elements, derived from the Christian religion" were "infused into the ancient legislative code." The "absolute and despotic" powers of the emperor were mitigated by "a new code of moral law." From this period onward the influence of the Church was "entirely of a moral nature," and "the highest penalty known to the Church, then, or at any other time was excommunication."

As the influence of Christianity spread "Christian emperors, either from a zeal of religion, or, with a desire to promote the welfare of the people [incorporated] portions of this ecclesiastical discipline [into] the jurisprudence of the state." Thus, "in a gradual and almost imperceptible manner . . . the union of the two powers seems to have occurred."[115] This union culminated in the "imperial code of public jurisprudence" compiled by the Emperor Justinian. But even this code "perished with the fallen power of the Empire." Hughes observed that after the barbarian invasions the "civil power [was] everywhere paralyzed and rendered impotent by the turbulent independence of chieftains." The Church, however, "rushed to the rescue of humanity" and salvaged both the "ancient jurisprudence" and "the religion of Christ."[116]

Hughes believed that in the chaos that followed the collapse of the Roman Empire the Church alone brought order to Europe. "Religion," he urged, "was the only social bond of communion, on which those nations could be rallied." The Church provided an early model of "well-regulated democratic jurisprudence" in a society increasingly controlled by "iron-hearted warriors" whose only law was "the law of the strong against the weak." Ancient and medieval church councils were "models of deliberative and representative assemblies," and frequently the clergy and even the pope were "taken from the ranks of the people . . . by the principle of election."[117]

What Protestants characterized as papal interference in the affairs of the state was at that time "the only means by which limits could be put to regal and imperial despotism." Society needed protection from political absolutism and "thus the Church, or rather the people, vindicating their rights through the head of the Church, tolerated no despot, no tyrant, on the thrones of Europe." "It is to this power, rightly or wrongly exercised," proclaimed Hughes, "that we are indebted for the advantage of responsible governments in modern times."[118]

In 1844, a year after his speech to the Irish Emigrant Society, the American Protestant Society of New York City issued a tract titled "Romanism Incompatible with Republican Institutions." The pamphlet charged that allegiance to Rome impeded the ability of Catholics to be good citizens in a free country.[119] Hughes responded with his own tract, "Catholicism Compatible with Republican Government." He queried his readers, "Does Christianity, in the inspired volumes of its records, any where teach that this or that form of civil government is to be adopted by its followers?" The answer was no, but nevertheless, "in view of the declaration of our divine Lord, 'my kingdom is not of this world,' it cannot be but considered remarkable that such a point of controversy should be made at the present."[120]

"Catholicism Compatible with Republican Government" repeated the argument made by many other American prelates. Hughes insisted that "the Pope's sovereignty is wholly, entirely, and exclusively a spiritual attribute" and that Catholic obedience to Rome is a "moral, not a civil or political obedience." He added that Protestants, not Catholics, were the ones "who are ever and ever convulsing the country with some measure or other at variance with the constitution or the established order of things."

"Are they Catholics," he asked, "who to-day are moving on to rebellion it-self, in the furthering of Abolitionism?" Were Catholics the ones "who have raised a banner on which is inscribed 'Abolition or Separation?' "[121]

Hughes argued that it was absurd for Protestants to pretend as if their faith had always promoted principles of republicanism and democracy. "Go to Geneva," he wrote,

> and read of . . . that spiritual autocrat, who allowed no liberty of conscience in his usurped dominion. . . . Did John Knox allow [liberty of conscience] in Scotland? Was liberty of conscience conceded to the Anabaptists in Germany? . . . Has it not been shown that the colony of Plymouth was a spiritual despotism, as severe as any ever known?[122]

If these examples were insufficient, "other and stronger evidences of a disposition on the part of certain Protestants to withdraw themselves from a full and entire allegiance to the liberal institutions of the country" could be found in an overture of the General Synod of the Reformed Presbyterian Church from October 1834. Here, "a branch of the Presbyterian Church" charged that the Constitution of the United States was an "infidel and anti-Christian" document because it "does not recognize the revealed will of God," and it "acknowledges no subjection to the Lord Jesus Christ." Hughes posed the rhetorical question, "What, if the Pope had said this, in one of his Bulls or letters, would have been the consequence, what the fate, not only of all the churches of Catholics in the United States, but of every man, woman and child among them?"[123]

Hughes maintained that Protestant exaltation of the individual had devastating consequences for both the Christian faith and American society. "Catholics," he argued, "do not believe that God has vouchsafed the promise of the Holy Spirit to every individual, but that He has given His Spirit to teach the Church collectively." Protestantism, by contrast, assumes the primacy of the individual when it comes to matters of faith, and thus, "they interpret the Bible by the standard of reason" and end up with a "Christianity of reason."[124] Hughes referred to "private judgment" as the "first principle of Protestantism," and, he added, "this principle has followed Protestantism into every department of its quasi religious life." Furthermore, "all those persons who go in the direction of rationalism, go on the first principle of Protestantism."[125]

Protestant emphasis on individualism and rationalism had led many Americans to associate wrongly the advancement of their religion with material and technological progress. He said of the age in which he lived that "there perhaps never was a period, when men entered on the pursuit of wealth, with so much of what might be called almost desperate determination to succeed."[126] Protestantism encouraged this situation because in economics as in politics it "failed to extend the obligation of duties, in exact proportion with the extension of rights."[127] In contrast with American Protestants' uncritical embrace of both political and economic freedom, the Catholic Church had "no special doctrine, no theory" regarding politics, and it likewise had no theory "on commerce or manufacturing."[128] From the time of the Reformation, Catholicism alone "created an interest not to be estimated by acquisition or exchange of material wealth, but by the consideration of advantages in the spiritual order and in the life to come."[129]

Reading History Aright

For over thirty years prior to the Civil War, evangelical nativists charged that the Catholic Church was an institution inimical to freedom. Catholic apologists countered that their religion actually provided security for American values. Protestantism, they argued, could not in the long run guard against extremism and excessive individualism. The Catholic defense rested in large part on demonstrating the contributions the pre-Reformation Church made toward checking the coercive power of the state. Catholic apologists selected examples from the history of Europe and the papacy for support, and they took care to point out inconsistencies in the American Protestant vision of church and state. Protestants, they argued, misread history. They claimed to sustain religious freedom by elevating a progressive interpretation of western history above all competing narratives.

In making their case against nativism, abolitionism, and aggressive evangelicalism, Catholic apologists often sounded like proslavery Protestant apologists in the South. Both groups criticized unrestrained individualism, impersonal expansive capitalism, and Jacobin egalitarianism. Likewise, both groups tended to be suspicious of the Whigs, opposed to Federalism, and contemptuous of the Republican Party. Catholic apologists did, however, differ from the evangelical southern apologists in one important way. They believed that history proved that the Church was not hostile to republicanism and that Catholicism, unlike Protestantism, had a moral tradition that could serve as a barrier against the excesses of evangelical nationalism.

Few historians of American Christianity have tackled the relationship between Catholicism and slavery. When the subject has been attempted, the argument tends to run that the Catholic hierarchy was "too conservative" to deal with the social implications of slavery and that the conservative tradition of the Church "contributed in some measure to influence the tenor of Catholic opinion." Moreover, the American Catholic hierarchy dodged the moral question of slavery because the traditions of the Church and the uniquely American condition of the separation of church and state excused the hierarchy from formulating a positive approach to the issue.[130] While the antebellum hierarchy indeed faced unique political conditions that required careful reflection about the relationship between church and state, there is a great deal of evidence suggesting that the hierarchy was directly engaged in slavery and abolitionism. More pointedly, in contrast with their evangelical contemporaries, the hierarchy's approach to slavery was inseparable from the tradition of moral theology that guided the Church from its earliest encounters with the Roman Empire.

If antebellum Catholicism was in fact "conservative," conceivably it was because, when compared with the political and theological emphases of northern evangelicalism, the Church inevitably appeared so. Catholics, in general, opposed abolitionism and the theology that motivated it. Catholics, in general, sympathized with the political arguments of southerners. Catholics, in general, rejected the policies of the Lincoln administration. Most significantly, Catholics refused to consent to a historical narrative exalting American Protestantism as the apex of social and moral development.[131]

Catholic opinion about slavery was conservative if "conservative" means opposing the social vision of northern evangelicals. This does not mean that the American Catholic Church lacked a social vision. Rather, it suggests that any attempt to understand the American Catholic social vision in the decades leading up to the Civil War must wrestle with what the contours of a conservative tradition look like. The fact that many twentieth-century historians have chosen to dismiss antebellum Catholicism as conservative, and therefore hostile to democratic reform, is an indication of just how successful northern evangelicals were in encouraging the notion that Catholicism stood outside the boundaries of political liberalism.

Epilogue

Evangelicals, the Bible, and Politics

Nineteenth-century Americans were the first modern westerners to live in the absence of an established church. Religious nonestablishment proved a remarkable inheritance for evangelicals. Evangelicalism, which at one time flourished outside of religious establishments, slowly became a kind of establishment itself. By the middle decades of the nineteenth century, many Protestant church traditions that valued creeds, liturgy, and discipline found themselves overwhelmed by evangelical sentiment. Doctrine was less important than an individual's personal relationship with God. Confessional boundaries receded as conversion and denominational affiliation became gradually matters of choice. Behavior and public virtue were more important marks of "genuine" Christianity than were baptism, catechesis, hearing the Word preached, and receiving communion. How one worshiped and where one worshiped mattered less than one's commitment to personal and social improvement.

These changes in theological emphases made evangelicalism valuable to the growing country. Virtue and morality were important to national life, and Christianity provided a code of behavior that could benefit everyone. But for Christianity to be useful it had to be contained. If disputes over theology and doctrine spilled into public life, then Christianity could become divisive and socially destabilizing. If, however, theological and doctrinal differences could be minimized in favor of a generic consensus form of Christianity that was adaptable to changes in public life and concerned about public virtue, then such a Christianity could prove beneficial. Evangelicalism fit the bill perfectly. Doctrinally minimalist, without liturgical commitment, and free from creedal subscription, evangelicalism was malleable. It could find expression in a variety of forms across denominational lines, and it could harness populist individualism in the name of advancing Christ's kingdom. Because American evangelicals in general and northern evangelicals in particular favored unity in the abstract over theological precision, they made theological concerns secondary to social concerns. The problem was that northern and southern evangelicals disagreed over what constituted legitimate social concerns. Where theology could be either ignored or debated without real public consequence, politics could not. Antebellum politics betrayed the unity evangelicals so desperately desired and in consequence exposed the dilemma of American evangelicalism.

Throughout the first half of the nineteenth century, northern evangelicals were outraged at the conservative insurgence that characterized post-Napoleonic Europe. They detested Metternich's reactionary policies and watched with trepidation the machinations of the ultraroyalists and ultramontanists. They feared European Catholic missionary societies that were created under absolutist governments and that sought to aid the Catholic Church in the United States. To thwart any chance European-inspired conservatism might find success in the young republic, northern evangelicals crafted a history of the Middle Ages that emphasized despotic cruelties of church and state. They also heavily propagandized their adherents with the opinion that both American politics and American Christianity represented a decisive break with history. In doing so, northern evangelicals determined that what it meant to be Protestant and American depended in large part on who controlled the narrative of Europe and the Catholic Church. At stake was whether their new narrative would triumph along with the liberal European governments allegedly patterning themselves on American ideals.

Yet, for all their outrage toward the Dark Ages, all their anxiety about the dangers of uniting church and state, and all their denunciations of Catholic political arrangements, northern evangelicals held fast to the notion that there was, in fact, a relationship between Protestant Christianity and good government. This relationship, though never explicitly defined, manifested itself through the efforts of dozens of Christian reform agencies that sought to rectify the social effects of sin. Their goal was an evangelical republic. The goal proved futile, however, as millions of evangelicals hopelessly divided over the question of how their faith applied to the problem of slavery. Northern evangelicals believed slavery to be as incompatible with American virtues as Catholicism, and thus denunciations of both groups could be found in sermons, speeches, and journal articles intended to bolster the idea that America was a country committed to theological and political liberty. A consequence of this campaign was that slaveholders, like Catholics, shared the position of the northern evangelical ideological other—the outsider who had to be assimilated or reconstructed in order for political Protestantism to reach full maturity.

In the tumultuous years leading up to the Civil War, both Catholic and southern evangelical theologians responded to what they perceived to be immoderate and aggressive northern evangelical nationalism. The southern critique of northern evangelicalism, however, was seriously handicapped by the fact that southerners accepted the moral implications of a biblical hermeneutic shared by Protestants across the country. Evangelicals in both the North and the South viewed the Bible as an instrumental means to ethical ends. They trusted individual believers could come to similar, "common sense" moral conclusions through serious intellectual engagement with the authoritative Scriptures. The difference between the two groups could be found in where they viewed the locus of scriptural authority, the spirit or the letter.[1]

Southern evangelicals argued that northern evangelicals compromised both the Bible and the received doctrines of Protestantism to fit their ideal of a good society. Northern evangelicals exaggerated human potential for moral improvement and overemphasized social perfection at the expense of sound theology. Consequently, they erred in their antislavery antisouthern agenda because they placed more confidence in the progressive character of biblical interpretation as dictated by their cultural situation rather than in the normative character of biblical interpretation true for all times and all places.[2] Northern evangelicals countered that southerners missed both the progressive spirit of the gospel and the centrality of the Golden Rule to the Christian life because they insisted on collapsing the newer dispensation of Christ with the older dispensation of God's covenant with Israel.[3] Because southerners misread the Bible, they misread the spirit of the age.

Although working from different ends of the same theological spectrum, both groups premised their moral arguments about slavery and the future of republicanism on the significance of the Bible for public life. Indeed, the idea that America was a Christian nation whose public virtue rested on an intense commitment to Protestant biblical ethics provided the two regions with a common cultural touchstone. This shared cultural touchstone, however, also proved to be a serious liability when sectional interpretations of Scripture and history conflicted over moral questions concerning the future of the Union. The result was a breakdown of moral dialogue as the controversy surrounding slavery, American political economy, and nationalism divided Christians who used the Bible to make political and social declarations.

Here, the contrast between the Catholic Church and both northern and southern evangelicalism is striking. The hierarchy insisted that the Church's social vision be grounded in vigorous political realism that took seriously both the history of church-state relations and the development of moral doctrine over time. Historical development did not mean that the political theology of the Church was progressing toward a triumphant finality. For the Church, the lessons of Late Antiquity and the Middle Ages were too hard learned. American political conditions were to be valued and protected, but contra the evangelical narrative, they were not to be interpreted as the outworking of the kingdom of God on earth. Political liberalism was as subject to admonition and correction as imperialism was under Charlemagne or throughout the Investiture Contest. According to the hierarchy, the grievous error of evangelical nationalism was its commitment to a type of political Protestantism that viewed Christian moral teaching as culminating in the American experiment rather than serving as a corrective and a counterbalance to the coercive power of the state. To prove their point, Catholics appealed to the historical and theological precedents of Late Antiquity and the Middle Ages at a time when popular conceptions of progress, Christianity, and nationalism stemmed more from an optimistic American future rather than an archaic European past.

Slavery and Catholicism revealed the American evangelical dilemma in stark terms. Evangelicals wanted to be the Christian conscience of the country, but Christian conscience could not be divorced from biblical interpretation and theology. Evangelical theology, which had always been pliant, proved incapable of formulating a coherent political theology as elastic doctrinal commitments expanded to accommodate the demands of political liberalism. While the rhetoric of Protestant values retained a place in the public imagination, the substance of Protestant theology suffered. Northern evangelicals increasingly allowed their understanding of the church to be defined as much by the American experiment as by historical theology. They happily set about transforming the country into their image, and they demonized all who challenged their vision of religion and politics, most especially conservative challenges from Catholics and southerners.

The idea that evangelicalism could function as a de facto established religion in a nation that had no established religion was promising in the 1830s. By the 1860s, sectional strife, slavery, immigration, and the place of Catholicism in the republic exposed that evangelicals were terribly divided. Neither northerners nor southerners, or any single denomination, could legitimately claim to be the representative voice of American evangelicalism. In trying to be all things to all people—liberal and conservative, populist and elitist, progressive and traditional—northern evangelicals failed to attain what they most desired, a national theological and political consensus. Southern evangelicals attempted consistency by defending a conservative social vision premised on human inequality. But as evangelicals they failed to achieve a stable conservatism because, as much as they tried, they could not escape the democratizing tendencies of American Protestantism.

These failures signaled an incoherency in evangelicalism that would have consequences well into the twentieth century. Lacking a viable political theology, evangelicals have had to constantly reinvent themselves to find relevance amid always fluid cultural, political, and social circumstances. As was the case in the antebellum period, twentieth-century evangelicals found their common identity shaped more by their political loyalties than by their theology. Alexis de Tocqueville noted in 1835 that American clergy "readily adopt the general opinions of their country and their age, and allow themselves to be borne away without opposition in the current of feeling and opinion by which everything around them is carried along."[4] For evangelicalism, this tendency proved no less true in the twentieth century than in the nineteenth century. Although Darwinism, industrial capitalism, theological modernism, fundamentalism, and the charismatic movement reshaped the post–Civil War evangelical landscape, one constant remained: evangelicals still desired a national character shaped in their own image. The incessant quest for political and cultural relevance that began in northern evangelical churches before the Civil War spread incrementally into the temperament of American evangelicalism in general. In this sense, although antebellum northern evangelicals never entirely succeeded in defining the national narrative or in ridding the country of Catholicism, they did succeed in changing the way all subsequent evangelicals appropriated the meaning of their faith for American public life.

Notes

Introduction

1. The best study to date outlining the relationship between religion and politics in the antebellum period is Richard J. Carwardine's *Evangelicals and Politics in Antebellum America* (New Haven, CT: Yale University Press, 1993). "Evangelical" is a fluid term that can have many applications depending on the period and group to which it refers. For the purposes of this book, the chief characteristics of antebellum evangelicalism include the belief that the Bible possesses moral authority as the word of God, and that this moral authority includes both proscriptions and prescriptions for private and public behavior; that salvation is between the individual and God, and true salvation manifests in transformed personal behavior; that the public declaration of the gospel is the principle duty of the church; that the traditions of the church are secondary to the authority of Scripture and the individual's relationship with God; and that the Christian life includes commitments to both personal and social improvement.

2. See James Oscar Farmer, *The Metaphysical Confederacy: James Henley Thornwell and the Synthesis of Southern Values* (Macon, GA: Mercer University Press, 1986), 66, 133, 190–92.

3. The belief that America was a unique yet precarious experiment in self-government was not limited to any particular region in the national period. Important studies suggesting that political and social instability was a common fear in the national period include: Richard Hofstadter, *The Paranoid Style in American Politics, and other Essays* (New York: Knopf, 1965), 3–23; Paul Boyer, *Urban Masses and Moral Order in America, 1820–1920* (Cambridge,

MA: Harvard University Press, 1978); Gordon S. Wood, *The Radicalism of the American Revolution* (New York: A. A. Knopf, 1992); and Steven Mintz, *Moralists and Modernizers: America's Pre–Civil War Reformers* (Baltimore: Johns Hopkins University Press, 1995), 3–15.

4. See Anne C. Loveland, *Southern Evangelicals and the Social Order, 1800–1860* (Baton Rouge: Louisiana State University Press, 1980), chaps. 5 and 6; Edward R. Crowther, *Southern Evangelicals and the Coming of the Civil War* (Lewiston, NY: Edwin Mellen Press, 2000); and Robert M. Calhoon, *Evangelicals and Conservatives in the Early South, 1740–1861* (Columbia: University of South Carolina Press, 1988).

ONE. New England Sets a Pattern

1. William W. Freehling, *The Road to Disunion: Secessionists at Bay* (New York: Oxford University Press, 1990), 291; Louis Filler, *The Crusade against Slavery, 1830–1860* (New York: Harper & Brothers, 1960), 97; and Frank Otto Gattell, ed., "Postmaster Huger and the Incendiary Publications," *South Carolina Historical Magazine* 64 (October 1963): 193–201.

2. Bertram Wyatt-Brown, *Lewis Tappan and the Evangelical War against Slavery* (Baton Rouge: Louisiana State University Press, 1997), 149; and Bertram Wyatt-Brown, "The Abolitionists' Postal Campaign of 1835," *Journal of Negro History* 50, no. 4 (October 1965): 230.

3. Wyatt-Brown, *Lewis Tappan,* 150–51.

4. John C. Calhoun, *Southern Patriot,* August 4, 1835, September 30, 1835; and Clement Eaton, *The Freedom-of-Thought Struggle in the Old South* (New York: Harper & Row, 1964), chap. 8.

5. *Flag of the Union,* August 22, 1835, quoted in Eaton, *Freedom-of-Thought Struggle,* 199.

6. Wyatt-Brown, "Abolitionists' Postal Campaign," 231.

7. Jackson to Kendall, August 9, 1835, *Correspondence of Andrew Jackson,* ed. John Spencer Bassett, 7 vols. (Washington, DC: Carnegie Institute of Washington, 1926–35), 5:360–61.

8. Ray Allen Billington, *The Protestant Crusade: A Study of the Origins of American Nativism* (New York: Holt, Rinehart & Winston, 1963), 68–69.

9. Ibid., 69–71.

10. Rebecca Reed, *Six Months in a Convent* (Boston: Russell N. Hall, 1835).

11. Billington, *Protestant Crusade,* 71–72.

12. Nancy Lusignan Schultz, *Fire and Roses: The Burning of the Charlestown Convent, 1834* (New York: Free Press, 2000), 165–67. Ray Billington notes that it is possible, but not certain, that a conspiracy to destroy the convent was afoot prior to Beecher's sermons. See Billington, *Protestant Crusade,* 73.

13. Billington, *Protestant Crusade,* 84.

14. Lyman Beecher, *The Autobiography of Lyman Beecher,* 2 vols. (Cambridge, MA: Harvard University Press, 1901), 2:251.

15. Ibid., 2:251–52. Five years before he gave his anti-Catholic sermons in Boston, Beecher declared that Catholicism was a threat to the future of the country. In July 1830, in a letter to his daughter Catherine, he stated that the "moral destiny of the nation" hinged on the development of a Protestant educational network in the West that could combat "Catholics and infidels." In 1832 Beecher accepted the presidency of Lane Theological Seminary in Cincinnati, and his trip to Boston during the summer of the riots was organized in large part to raise money for the young seminary. See ibid., 1:167.

16. Both David Brion Davis and Richard Hofstadter offer excellent studies of the fear of conspiracy during the middle period. See David Brion Davis, "Some Themes in Counter-Subversion: An Analysis of Anti-Masonic, Anti-Catholic, and Anti-Mormon Literature," *Mississippi Valley Historical Review* 47 (September 1960); and Richard Hofstadter, *The Paranoid Style in American Politics, and Other Essays* (New York: Knopf, 1965), chap. 1.

17. See Charles C. Cole Jr., *The Social Ideas of the Northern Evangelists, 1826–1860* (New York: Octagon Books, 1966), 5–7; Sidney E. Ahlstrom, *A Religious History of the American People* (New Haven, CT: Yale University Press, 1972), pt. 4; and Timothy L. Smith, *Revivalism and Social Reform in Mid-Nineteenth-Century America* (Nashville, TN: Abingdon Press, 1957), chap. 1.

18. See Ahlstrom, *Religious History,* 415–28; and Smith, *Revivalism,* chap. 1.

19. Gilbert Hobbs Barnes, *The Antislavery Impulse: 1830–1844* (New York: D. Appleton-Century Co., 1933), 17–37. Tappan, a wealthy New York silk merchant originally from New England, applied his crusading spirit to the antislavery cause, beginning in 1831 when he financed a convention in Philadelphia to address the need for a Negro college. He was instrumental in the formation of the American Anti-Slavery Society in 1833, and when the mail campaign began in 1834, he was president of the society and chief financier of the cause. Tappan was never short of critics, and when southern reaction against the merchant developed into a planned economic boycott of New York, business leaders began to worry. The Chamber of Commerce tried to persuade Tappan to cease his agitation of the southern states, but he was unmoved, saying that he would "be

hung first." A friend who witnessed the exchange noted with approbation, "That man has the spirit of a martyr!" See Lewis Tappan, *The Life of Arthur Tappan* (New York: Hurd and Houghton, 1871), 269, 270.

20. For a helpful picture of how the idea of social regeneration in the nineteenth century compared and contrasted with the social implications of evangelicalism during and after the Second Great Awakening, see Edwin Scott Gaustad, *The Great Awakening in New England* (New York: Harper & Row, 1965); Rhys Isaac, *The Transformation of Virginia: 1740–1790* (Chapel Hill: University of North Carolina Press, 1982); and Nathan O. Hatch, *The Sacred Cause of Liberty: Republican Thought and the Millennium in Revolutionary New England* (New Haven, CT: Yale University Press, 1977).

21. Lyman Beecher, *A Reformation of Morals Practicable and Indispensable: A Sermon Delivered at New Haven on the Evening of October 27, 1812* (Andover, MA: Flagg and Gould, 1814).

22. Billington argues that the mob in Charlestown consisted primarily of laborers from the lower classes who were possibly incited by some of Boston's more prominent citizens. Billington, *Protestant Crusade*, 73.

23. Ray Allen Billington, *Protestant Crusade, 1800–1860* (New York: Macmillan, 1938), repr., *Protestant Crusade: A Study of the Origins of American Nativism* (New York: Holt, Rinehart & Winston, 1963). Citations in this volume are to the reprint edition.

24. Glyndon G. Van Deusen, *The Jacksonian Era, 1828–1848* (Prospect Heights, IL: Waveland Press, 1992), 4, 6, 8; George R. Taylor, *The Transportation Revolution, 1815–1860* (Armonk, NY: M. E. Sharpe, 1989); and Daniel J. Boorstin, *The Americans: The National Experience* (New York: Vintage Books, 1965), 98–107.

25. J. D. B. Debow, *Statistical View of the United States* (Washington: A. O. P. Nicholson, 1854).

26. Setting parameters around what constitutes a "region" in America is not easy, and scholars are careful to note that regional definitions are determined as much by cultural and political distinctions as they are by geography. By lower South, I mean to include Louisiana, Arkansas, sections of Tennessee, Mississippi, Alabama, Georgia, Florida, South Carolina, and sections of North Carolina; "upper South" includes sections of Tennessee, sections of North Carolina, Kentucky, Virginia, Maryland, and sections of Delaware. The New England region includes Maine, New Hampshire, Vermont, Massachusetts, Rhode Island, Connecticut, and New York. Helpful studies that have guided these delineations include Edward L. Ayers, Patricia Nelson Limerick, Stephen Nissenbaum, and Peter S. Onuf, *All Over the Map: Rethinking American Regions* (Baltimore: Johns Hopkins University Press, 1996.); Merrill Jensen, ed., *Regionalism in America*

(Madison: University of Wisconsin Press, 1951), chaps. 1 and 4; and Howard W. Odum and Harry Estill Moore, *American Regionalism: A Cultural-Historical Approach to National Integration* (New York: Henry Holt and Company, 1938), chaps. 1, 20, and 21.

27. Freehling, *Road to Disunion,* 19.

28. *Historical Statistics of the United States* (Washington, DC: Government Printing Office, 1960), 57.

29. Marcus Lee Hansen, *The Immigrant in American History* (New York: Harper & Row, 1940), 53–76.

30. Jay P. Dolan, *The American Catholic Experience: A History from Colonial Times to the Present* (New York: Doubleday, 1985), 127–57; Billington, *Protestant Crusade,* 34–35; and Mustafa Kemal Emirbayer, "Moral Education in America, 1830–1990: A Contribution to the Sociology of Moral Education" (PhD diss., Harvard University, 1989), 109–11.

31. On the ideological heritage of the Whigs, see Daniel Walker Howe, *The Political Culture of the American Whigs* (Chicago: University of Chicago Press, 1979); Eber Malcolm Carroll, *Origins of the Whig Party* (Gloucester, MA: Peter Smith, 1964); and Michael F. Holt, *The Rise and Fall of the American Whig Party: Jacksonian Politics and the Onset of the Civil War* (New York: Oxford University Press, 1999).

32. Robert Kelley, *The Cultural Pattern in American Politics: The First Century* (New York: Alfred A. Knopf, 1979); Michael Holt, *Political Parties and American Political Development from the Age of Jackson to the Age of Lincoln* (Baton Rouge: Louisiana State University Press, 1992); Joel H. Silbey, *The Transformation of American Politics, 1840–1860* (Englewood Cliffs, NJ: Prentice-Hall, 1967); Lee Benson, *The Concept of Jacksonian Democracy: New York as a Test Case* (Princeton, NJ: Princeton University Press, 1961); and Samuel P. Hays, "Political Parties and the Community-Society Continuum," in *The American Party Systems: Stages of Political Development,* ed. William Nisbet Chambers and Walter Dean Burnham, 152–81 (New York: Oxford University Press, 1967).

33. Billington, *Protestant Crusade,* 22–24; Van Deusen, *Jacksonian Era,* 16–18; and William G. Bean, "Puritan versus Celt: 1850–1860," *New England Quarterly* 7 (March 1934): 70–89.

34. Arthur Alphonse Ekirch Jr., *The Idea of Progress in America, 1815–1860* (New York: Columbia University Press, 1944), chap. 2.

35. Alexis de Tocqueville, *Democracy in America,* ed. Harvey C. Mansfield and Delba Winthrop (Chicago: University Chicago Press, 2000), 282, 280.

36. Rector of Oldenwold, *The Cloven Foot, or Popery Aiming at Political Supremacy in the United States* (Boston: A. Wentworth and Company, 1855), 116–17.

37. William Adams, "The Law of Progress in Its Application to Christianity," *Biblical Repository,* 3rd ser., 3 (April 1847): 200.

38. Henry Ward Beecher, *A Discourse Delivered at the Plymouth Church* (New York: Cady & Burgess, 1848), 12, 20.

39. Albert Barnes, "The Position of the Evangelical Party in the Episcopal Church," in *Miscellaneous Essays and Reviews,* vol. 1 (New York: Ivison & Phinney, 1855), 371.

40. Tocqueville, *Democracy in America,* 268–69.

41. Horace Bushnell, *Barbarism the First Danger: A Discourse for Home Missions* (New York: American Home Missionary Society, 1847), 4–5.

42. Horace Bushnell, *God in Christ: Three Discourses, Delivered at New Haven, Cambridge, and Andover, with a Preliminary Dissertation on Language* (Hartford: Brown and Parsons, 1849), 72.

43. Horace Bushnell, *Politics under the Law of God: A Discourse, Delivered in the North Congregational Church, Hartford, on the Annual Fast of 1844* (Hartford: Edwin Hunt, 1844), 5.

44. Ibid., 6.

45. Arthur S. Hoyt, *The Pulpit and American Life* (New York: Macmillan, 1921), 220; and Cole, *Social Ideas,* 45.

46. Albert Barnes, *The Way of Salvation* (New York: Leavitt, Lord, 1836), 27–28.

47. His controversial theological stand eventually drew a charge of heresy. After the schism of 1837, Barnes was restored to his office and all charges of heresy were dropped.

48. Albert Barnes, *An Address Delivered July 4, 1827, at the Presbyterian Church in Morristown* (Morristown, NJ, 1827), 11.

49. Albert Barnes, *The Immorality of the Traffic in Ardent Spirits* (Philadelphia: George Latimer, 1835), 3; and Barnes, "Revivals of Religion in Cities and Large Towns," *American National Preacher* 15, no. 1 (1841): 23.

50. Francis Wayland, *The Duties of an American Citizen: Two Discourses Delivered in the First Baptist Meeting House in Boston on Thursday April 7, 1825, the Day of Public Fast* (Boston: James Loring, 1825); and Wayland, *The Elements of Political Economy* (New York: Gould, Kendall, and Lincoln, 1837). See also Richard J. Carwardine, *Evangelicals and Politics in Antebellum America* (Knoxville: University of Tennessee Press, 1933), 24.

51. Francis Wayland, *Francis Wayland on the Moral and Religious Aspects of the Nebraska Bill: Speech at Providence, R.I., March 7* (Rochester, NY: W. N. Sage, 1854).

52. Cole, *Social Ideas,* 179. See also Henry F. May, *Protestant Churches and Industrial America* (New York: Harper, 1949).

53. Francis Wayland, *Elements of Political Economy* (New York: Leavitt, Lord & Co., 1837), 111; and Wayland, *The Moral Law of Accumulation: The Substance of Two Discourses* (Providence, RI: John E. Brown, 1837), 9–10.

54. Francis Wayland, *Elements of Moral Science* (New York: Cooke & Co., 1835), 239.

55. The dioceses in the upper South include Baltimore, Richmond, Wheeling, and Louisville. See Richard R. Duncan, "Catholics and the Church in the Antebellum Upper South," in *Catholics in the Old South,* ed. Randall M. Miller and Jon L. Wakelyn, 77–98 (Macon, GA: Mercer University Press, 1983), 95.

56. This argument finds its most articulate expression in the work of Eugene Genovese. See, for example, Eugene D. Genovese, *The World the Slaveholder's Made: Two Essays in Interpretation* (Hanover, NH: University Press of New England, 1969, repr., 1988); and Genovese, *The Southern Tradition: The Achievement and Limitations of an American Conservatism* (Cambridge, MA: Harvard University Press, 1994). Some scholars, however, argue that slaveholders, whether they liked it or not, were just as committed to liberal-capitalist values as northern industrialists were. See James Oakes, *Slavery and Freedom: An Interpretation of the Old South* (New York: Vintage, 1990).

57. Alice Felt Tyler, *Freedom's Ferment: Phases of American Social History to 1860* (Minneapolis: University of Minnesota Press, 1944); Bray Hammond, *Banks and Politics in America from the Revolution to the Civil War* (Princeton, NJ: Princeton University Press, 1957); Richard Hofstadter, "Andrew Jackson and the Rise of Liberal Capitalism," in *The American Political Tradition and the Men Who Made It,* 44–66 (New York: Alfred A. Knopf, 1948); and Van Deusen, *Jacksonian Era*. For a description of which states constitute the New England region, which states constitute the southern region, and a list of scholarship that helped to determine these delineations, see note 26 above. See also William R. Taylor, *Cavalier and Yankee: The Old South and the American National Character* (New York: George Braziller, 1961); John McCardell, *The Idea of a Southern Nation: Southern Nationalists and Southern Nationalism, 1830–1860* (New York: W. W. Norton, 1979); and Paul C. Nagel, *One Nation Indivisible: The Union in American Thought, 1776–1861* (New York: Oxford University Press, 1964).

58. See Forrest McDonald, *States' Rights and the Union: Imperium in Imperio, 1776–1876* (Lawrence: University Press of Kansas, 2000), chaps. 2–5; David Hackett Fischer, *The Revolution of American Conservatism: The Federalist Party in the Era of Jeffersonian Democracy* (New York: Harper & Row, 1965); James M. Banner, *To the Hartford Convention: The Federalists and the Origins of Party Politics in Massachusetts, 1789–1815* (New York: Knopf, 1970); and George Dangerfield, *The Awakening of American Nationalism, 1815–1828* (New York: Harper & Row, 1965).

59. Peter S. Onuf, "Federalism, Republicanism, and the Origins of American Sectionalism," in Ayers et al., *All Over the Map,* 15–24; and Freehling, *Road to Disunion,* pt. 1.

60. Eugene D. Genovese, *The Political Economy of Slavery* (New York: Pantheon Books, 1965); and Eric Foner, *Free Soil, Free Labor, Free Men: The Ideology of the Republican Party on the Eve of the Civil War* (New York: Oxford University Press, 1970).

61. Clifford Geertz, *The Interpretation of Cultures* (New York: Basic Books, 1973), 89.

62. Allan Nevins and Milton Halsey Thomas, *The Diary of George Templeton Strong,* vol. 3, *The Turbulent Fifties, 1850–1859* (New York: Macmillan, 1952), 197.

63. Ralph Waldo Emerson, "The American Scholar," in *Anthology of American Literature,* vol. 1, *Colonial through Romantic,* ed. George McMichael (New York: Macmillan, 1985), 1078–79.

64. Susan-Mary Grant, *North over South: Northern Nationalism and American Identity in the Antebellum Era* (Lawrence: University of Kansas Press, 2000), 31–32.

65. On the pattern of ethnic settlement in the New World, see Marcus Lee Hansen, *The Atlantic Migration, 1607–1860: A History of the Continuing Settlement of the United States* (Cambridge, MA: Harvard University Press, 1940); and David Hackett Fischer, *Albion's Seed: Four British Folkways in America* (New York: Oxford University Press, 1989), 31–36, 219, 227, 438–45, 618–21.

66. *New York Times,* July 25, 1855.

67. John Gorham Palfrey, *Papers on the Slave Power,* no. 1, *Its Foundation* (Boston: Merrill, Cobb & Co. 1846), 1.

68. See William R. Taylor, *Cavalier and Yankee: The Old South and American National Character* (Cambridge, MA: Harvard University Press, 1979).

69. Numerous studies have attempted to explain the ways in which the North and South tried to make their particular interests the governing interests of the nation. Three very helpful modern works are David M. Potter, *The Impending Crisis, 1848–1861* (New York: Harper & Row, 1976); Freehling, *Road to Disunion*; and Foner, *Free Soil.*

70. In this regard, nineteenth-century northern evangelicals were the heirs of what Perry Miller has labeled the "New England Mind"—a self-conscious desire to unite the spiritual ends of Christian eschatology with the cause of American exceptionalism. See Perry Miller, *The New England Mind: From Colony to Province* (Cambridge, MA: Harvard University Press, 1953); and Miller, *The Life of the Mind in America: From the Revolution to the Civil War* (New York: Harcourt, Brace & World, 1965).

71. D. F. Robertson, *National Destiny and Our Country* (New York: E. French, 1851), 23.

72. Bushnell, *Barbarism,* 16.

73. James P. Stuart, *America and the Americans versus the Papacy and the Catholics* (Cincinnati: Mendenhall, 1853), 12, 20.

74. Noah Porter, *The Educational Systems of the Puritans and Jesuits Compared* (New York: M. W. Dodd, 1851), 16.

75. Charles B. Boynton, *Oration Delivered on the Fifth of July, 1847* (Cincinnati: Tagart & Gardner, 1847), 10.

76. Lyman Beecher, *A Plea for the West* (Cincinnati: Truman & Smith, 1835), 60–61.

77. Edward Beecher, *The Question at Issue: A Sermon Delivered at Brooklyn, New York, before the Society for the Promotion of Collegiate and Theological Education at the West* (Boston: T. R. Marvin, 1850), 18, 32.

78. Henry Ward Beecher, *Freedom and War: Discourses on Topics Suggested by the Times* (Boston: Ticknor and Fields, 1863), 267.

79. Cole, *Social Ideas,* 56.

80. William G. McLoughlin, *The Meaning of Henry Ward Beecher: An Essay on the Shifting Values of Mid-Victorian America, 1840–1870* (New York: Alfred A. Knopf, 1970), 26.

81. Paxton Hibben, *Henry Ward Beecher: An American Portrait* (New York: G. H. Doran, 1927), 191.

82. James W. Fraser, *Between Church and State: Religion and Public Education in Multicultural America* (New York: St. Martin's Press, 1999), 34.

83. For elaboration on the nature of the Protestant moral agenda, see Smith, *Revivalism,* 34–44, 148–62.

84. Calvin Stowe, "On the Education of Emigrants," in *Transactions of the Fifth Annual Meeting of the Western Literary Institute and College of Professional Teachers* (Cincinnati: Josiah Drake, 1835), 68–69.

85. Ibid. The notion that common schools could unite Protestant moral imperatives with national assimilation was not unique to Stowe. Indeed, one of the leading advocates of the common school movement from whom Stowe and others borrowed many of their ideas for public education was Horace Mann, the secretary of the Massachusetts State Board of Education from 1836 to 1848. A Unitarian who had experience as an educator, a lawyer, and a state senator, Mann brought to the position of secretary of education a vision of how religion divorced from sectarianism could be used in public or "common" schools to build a consensus of good citizenship. He developed his argument around three themes. First, he believed in the "absolute right of every human being that comes into the world to an education." Second, based on the conviction that

people had a right to an education, he argued that it was the "correlative duty of every government to see that the means of that education are provided for all." Finally, Mann suggested that schools could use religion to teach people how to be good only if religious principles were extracted from denominational propaganda. He reasoned that religious education was not to be used to persuade a child to "join this or that denomination, when he arrives at the age of discretion." Instead, religious training could be used in schools to help the child "judge for himself, according to the dictates of his own reason and conscience, what his religious obligations are, and whither they lead" (Massachusetts Board of Education, *Tenth Annual Report* [1847], cited in Robert H. Bremmer, ed., *Children and Youth in America: A Documentary History,* vol. 1 [Cambridge, MA: Harvard University Press, 1971], 456). See also Horace Mann, "Twelfth Annual Report (1848)" in *The Republic and the School: Horace Mann on the Education of Free Men,* ed. Lawrence A. Cremin, 79–112 (New York: Columbia Teachers College, 1957); Carl F. Kaestle, *Pillars of the Republic: Common Schools and American Society, 1780–1860* (New York: Hill and Wang, 1983), 77–103; and Lawrence A. Cremin, *American Education: The National Experience, 1783–1876* (New York: Harper & Row, 1980), 133–37.

86. This is the language of Finney and his imitators. See Charles Grandison Finney, *Lectures on Revivals of Religion,* ed. William G. McLoughlin (1868; Cambridge, MA: Belknap Press of Harvard University Press, 1960).

87. See Whitney R. Cross, *The Burned-over District: The Social and Intellectual History of Enthusiastic Religion in Western New York, 1800–1850* (Ithaca, NY: Cornell University Press, 1950); and Timothy L. Smith, *Revivalism and Social Reform: American Protestantism on the Eve of the Civil War* (Baltimore: Johns Hopkins University Press, 1957).

88. Cross, *Burned-over District*; and Smith, *Revivalism.* See also William G. McLoughlin, *Modern Revivalism: Charles Grandison Finney to Billy Graham* (New York: Ronald Press Company, 1959).

89. Cole, *Social Ideas,* 41.

90. McLoughlin, *Modern Revivalism,* 139.

91. Ibid. See also Jacob Knapp, *Autobiography of Elder Jacob Knapp* (New York: 1868), 323 ff.

92. Vincent Harding, *A Certain Magnificence: Lyman Beecher and the Transformation of American Protestantism, 1775–1863* (New York: Carlson Publishing, 1991), 348–49; and Keith J. Hardman, *Charles Grandison Finney, 1792–1875: Revivalist and Reformer* (Syracuse, NY: Syracuse University Press, 1987), 293–96.

93. Hardman, *Charles Grandison Finney,* 296.

94. Finney, *Lectures on Revivals,* 208.

95. Ibid., 262, 267.

96. See Harding, *Charles Grandison Finney,* 290–300.

97. Nathan O. Hatch, *The Democratization of American Christianity* (New Haven, CT: Yale University Press, 1989), 197. No doubt Finney was not the first Christian evangelist to emphasize the experience of conversion. Note the contributions of John Wesley in the eighteenth century.

98. Finney, *Lectures on Revivals,* 374–375.

99. Gilbert Barnes is often credited with his use of this phrase in *The Antislavery Impulse.* See also John R. McKivigan, *The War against Proslavery Religion: Abolitionism and the Northern Churches, 1830–1865* (Ithaca, NY: Cornell University Press, 1984), 19–21; C. S. Griffin, *Their Brother's Keeper: Moral Stewardship in the United States, 1800–1865* (New Brunswick, NJ: Rutgers University Press, 1960); and Charles I. Foster, *An Errand of Mercy: The Evangelical United Front, 1790–1837* (Chapel Hill: University of North Carolina Press, 1960).

100. For example, Theodore Weld, Theodore Parker, and Sarah and Angeline Grimke.

101. General introductions to the characteristics of republican political values include Bernard Bailyn, *The Ideological Origins of the American Revolution* (Cambridge, MA: Belknap Press of Harvard University Press, 1967), 344–79; McDonald, *States' Rights and the Union,* chaps. 2–4; and Joyce Appleby, *Inheriting the Revolution: The First Generation of Americans* (Cambridge, MA: Belknap Press of Harvard University Press, 2000), chaps. 2 and 8.

102. See Clifford S. Griffin, *Their Brother's Keeper: Moral Stewardship in the United States, 1800–1865* (New Brunswick, NJ: Rutgers University Press, 1960).

103. It is important to note that revivalism met a good deal of resistance in the South, especially from southern Presbyterians. The conservative theologian R. L. Dabney lamented that local pastors toil for "wearisome months and years" with their congregations only to have the revival preacher show up at "harvest time." See Thomas Carey Johnson, *The Life and Letters of Robert Lewis Dabney* (Richmond: Presbyterian Committee of Publication, 1903), 112–13.

104. Important studies include Ernest Lee Tuveson, *Redeemer Nation: The Idea of America's Millennial Role* (Chicago: University of Chicago Press, 1968); and Ernest R. Sandeen, *The Roots of Fundamentalism: British and American Millenarianism, 1800–1930* (Chicago: University of Chicago Press, 1970).

105. Anne C. Loveland, *Southern Evangelicals and the Social Order, 1800–1860* (Baton Rouge: Louisiana State University Press, 1980), 162.

106. Charles G. Finney, *Sermons on Gospel Themes* (Oberlin, OH: E. J. Goodrich, 1876), 344; and Finney, *Lectures on Revivals,* 282.

107. Horace Bushnell, *Work and Play, or, Literary Varieties* (New York: C. Scribner, 1864), 434–35.

108. Loveland, *Southern Evangelicals,* 159–63; and E. Brooks Holifield, *The Gentleman Theologians: American Theology in Southern Culture, 1795–1860* (Durham, NC: Duke University Press, 1978), chap. 6.

109. Stuart C. Henry, *Unvanquished Puritan: A Portrait of Lyman Beecher* (Grand Rapids, MI: W. B. Eerdmans, 1973), 117–26; Harding, *Certain Magnificence,* 274–78; Beecher, *Autobiography,* 104–6; and Sidney E. Mead, "Lyman Beecher and Connecticut Orthodoxy's Campaign against the Unitarians, 1819–1826," *Church History* 9 (September 1940): 218–34.

110. Beecher, *Autobiography,* 105.

111. Holifield, *Gentleman Theologians,* 196–98.

112. A comment from the *Southern Christian Herald,* quoted in the *New York Emancipator,* August, 17, 1837.

113. B. M. Palmer, *The Life and Letters of James Henley Thornwell* (Edinburgh: Banner of Truth Trust, 1875).

114. Charles Hodge, "West India Emancipation," *Biblical Repertory and Princeton Review* 10 [Philadelphia] (October 1838): 604.

115. See Hugh Seton-Watson, *Nations and States: An Inquiry into the Origins of Nations and Political Nationalism* (London: Methuen, 1977); Hans Kohn, *American Nationalism: An Interpretive Essay* (New York: Macmillan, 1957); Patrick Gerster and Nicholas Cords, "The Northern Origins of the Southern Myth," in *Myth and Southern History,* vol. 2, *The New South,* 2nd ed., ed. Patrick Gerster and Nicolas Cords, 43–58 (Urbana: University of Illinois Press, 1989); and Foner, *Free Soil.*

TWO. **Taking Aim at Europe and the Middle Ages**

1. Francis Wayland and H. L. Wayland, *A Memoir of the Life and Labors of Francis Wayland, D.D., L.L.D.,* 2 vols. (New York: Arno Press, 1972), 2:16, 23

2. Wayland and Wayland, *Memoir,* 1:173.

3. Francis Wayland, *The Duties of an American Citizen* (Boston: James Loring, 1825), 5.

4. Mary Bushnell Cheney, *Life and Letters of Horace Bushnell* (New York: Arno Press, 1969), 106.

5. Ibid., 157.

6. Ibid., 158.

7. Ibid., 161.

8. *New Englander* 1, no. 1 (January 1843): 3. It is noteworthy that the *New Englander* criticized Bushnell later in his career for his tendency to overemphasize "natural" theology.

9. *New Englander* 5, no. 18 (April 1847): 303, 305.

10. See Barbara Jelavich, *Modern Austria: Empire and Republic, 1815–1986* (Cambridge: Cambridge University Press, 1987); Peter N. Stearns, *1848: The Revolutionary Tide in Europe* (New York: Norton, 1974); James J. Sheehan, *German Liberalism in the Nineteenth Century* (London: Methuen, 1982); and Theodore S. Hamerow, *Restoration, Revolution, Reaction: Economics and Politics in Germany, 1815–1871* (Princeton, NJ: Princeton University Press, 1966).

11. *New Englander* 7, no. 25 (February 1849): 89, 90.

12. See E. E. Y. Hales, *Pio Nono: A Study in European Politics and Religion in the Nineteenth Century* (New York: P. J. Kennedy & Sons, 1954), chaps. 3 and 5.

13. *New Englander* 6, no. 3 (July 1848): 432–33.

14. *Zion's Herald,* March 16, 1836, 42.

15. *New Englander* 5, no. 25 (February 1849): 93.

16. *New Englander* 7, no. 18 (April 1847): 303.

17. On the Carbonari, see R. John Rath "The Carbonari: Their Origins, Initiation Rites, and Aims," *American Historical Review* 69, no. 2 (January 1964): 353–70; Kent Roberts Greenfield, "The Austrian Government and the Italian Conspiracy, 1831–1835," *American Historical Review* 29, no. 4 (July 1924): 716–21; Bertoldi, *Memoirs of the Secret Societies of the South of Italy, Particularly the Carbonari* (London: J. Murray, 1821); and Alan Barrie Spitzer, *Old Hatreds and Young Hopes: The French Carbonari against the Bourbon Restoration* (Cambridge, MA: Harvard University Press, 1971).

18. John Pierce, *The Right of Private Judgment in Religion, Vindicated against the Claims of Romish Church and All Kindred Usurpations* (Cambridge, MA: Hillard and Metcalf, 1821), 4. The Dudleian Lecture was endowed by Judge Paul Dudley in 1750. Every third lecture was to be used for exposing the "idolatry of the Romish Church." See Mary A. Ray, *American Opinion of Roman Catholicism in the Eighteenth Century* (New York: Columbia University Press, 1936), 64.

19. In as much as the title Holy Roman Emperor ever existed, it refers to the monarch of the Roman Empire made up of German and Central European states. Napoleon never actually held this office. In fact, he abolished it when he destroyed the ancient Reich. The Austrian emperor then inherited the rights of the Roman emperor (e.g., the veto in papal elections). See Margaret M. O'Dwyer, *The Papacy in the Age of Napoleon and the Restoration: Pius VII, 1800–1823* (Lanham, MD: University Press of America, 1985); and Owen Chadwick, *The Popes and European Revolution* (Oxford: Oxford University Press, 1981), 492–508.

20. James J. Hennesey, *American Catholics: A History of the Roman Catholic Community in the United States* (New York: Oxford University Press, 1981), chap. 8.

21. Mainstream newspapers also drew attention to the growing Church. The trustee controversy in Philadelphia and New York between Catholic laity and the hierarchy over control of parish property garnered a fair amount of press in the 1820s. See Hennesey, *American Catholics,* chap. 8; and Patrick W. Carey, *People, Priests, and Prelates: Ecclesiastical Democracy and the Tensions of Trusteeism* (Notre Dame, IN: University of Notre Dame Press, 1987).

22. Second Provincial Council of Baltimore,"The Pastoral Letter of 1833," in *The National Pastorals of the American Hierarchy, 1729–1919,* ed. Peter K. Guilday (Westminster, MD: Newman Press, 1954), 78.

23. First Provincial Council of Baltimore, "The Pastoral Letter to the Laity (1829)," in *National Pastorals,* 22.

24. Joseph Fréri, *The Society for the Propagation of the Faith and Catholic Missions, 1822–1900* (New York: Press of the Society for the Propagation of the Faith, 1912), 27–28, 58.

25. V. F. O'Daniel, *The Right Reverend Edward Dominic Fenwick, O.P., Founder of the Dominicans in the United States* (Washington, DC: Dominicana, 1920).

26. Arthur J. May, *The Age of Metternich, 1814–1848* (New York: Henry Holt and Company, 1933), 33–34. See also Alan Warwick Palmer, *Metternich* (New York: Harper & Row, 1972).

27. May, *Age of Metternich,* 30, 36–38; Alan Reinerman, "Metternich, Italy and the Congress of Verona, 1821–1822," *Historical Journal* 14, no. 2 (June 1971): 263–87; and John D. Bergamini, *The Spanish Bourbons: The History of a Tenacious Dynasty* (New York: Putnam, 1974).

28. May, *Age of Metternich,* 60–63. On conditions in Germany, see Michael B. Gross, *The War against Catholicism: Liberalism and the Anti-Catholic Imagination in Nineteenth-Century Germany* (Ann Arbor: University of Michigan Press, 2004).

29. May, *Age of Metternich,* 63–71; and Pamela Pilbeam, "The Growth of Liberalism and the Crisis of the Bourbon Restoration, 1827–1830," *Historical Journal* 25, no. 2 (June 1982): 351–66.

30. Félicité de Lamennais, *De la Religion considérée dans ses rapports avec l'ordre politique et civil* (Paris: Au Bureau du Memorial Catholique, 1826), 167–94; and John J. Oldfield, *The Problem of Tolerance and Social Existence in the Writings of Félicité Lamennais, 1809–1831* (Leiden: E. J. Brill, 1973), 120–32.

31. Louis de Bonald, *Théorie du pouvoir politique et religieux dans la société civile* (Paris: A. Le Clère, 1854); David Klinck, *The French Counterrevolution-*

ary Theorist: Louis de Bonald (1754–1840) (New York: P. Lang, 1996); Joseph Marie de Maistre, *Considerations on France,* trans. Richard Lebrun (New York: Cambridge University Press, 1994); and Richard A. Lebrun, *Joseph de Maistre: An Intellectual Militant* (Kingston: McGill-Queen's University Press, 1988).

32. Friedrich Sieburg, *Chateaubriand,* trans. Violet M. Macdonald (New York: St. Martin's Press, 1962); Harry W. Paul, "In Quest of Kerygma: Catholic Intellectual Life in Nineteenth-Century France," *American Historical Review* 75, no. 2 (December 1969): 390–91; and Richard Switzer, *Chateaubriand* (New York: Twayne Publishers, 1971).

33. François-René de Chateaubriand, *Genie du Christianisme* (Paris: P. Pourrat, 1839). Chateaubriand's argument in *Genie du Christianisme* is an extension of his argument in *Essai historique sur les révolutions anciennes et moderns,* which he wrote while in exile following the Reign of Terror: "il faut une religion ou la société perit."

34. Edgar Quinet, *Ultramontanism, or, The Roman Church and Modern Society,* trans. C. Cocks (London: John Chapman, 1845), 135.

35. Ibid., 16.

36. Ibid., 134–35.

37. On Quinet and Herder, see François Furet, *La gauche et la Révolution francaise au milieu du XIXe siècle: Edgar Quinet et la question du jacobinisme, 1865–1870* (Paris: Hachette, 1986).

38. F. M. Barnard, *J. G. Herder on Social and Political Culture* (Cambridge: Cambridge University Press, 1969); Barnard, *Herder's Social and Political Thought: From Enlightenment to Nationalism* (Oxford: Clarendon Press, 1965), chaps. 3–5; and Robert Reinhold Ergang, *Herder and the Foundations of German Nationalism* (New York: Octagon Books, 1931).

39. Jules Michelet, *History of the French Revolution,* trans. Charles Cocks (Chicago: University of Chicago Press, 1967), 22.

40. Ibid., 32–33.

41. Ibid., 442, 444.

42. Ray Allen Billington, *The Protestant Crusade: A Study of the Origins of American Nativism* (New York: Holt, Rinehart & Winston, 1963), 122–23; and Paul J. Staiti, *Samuel F. B. Morse* (New York: Cambridge University Press, 1989).

43. *Downfall of Babylon,* May 30, 1834, and ff; *Christian Spectator* 8 (June 1835); *Christian Watchman,* September 19, 1834, and ff; *Protestant Banner,* January 28, 1842.

44. Brutus [Samuel F. B. Morse], *Foreign Conspiracy against the Liberties of the United States* (New York: Leavitt, Lord, & Co., 1835), 21.

45. Ibid., 15–17.

46. Ibid., 20.

47. Ibid., 107.

48. Ibid., 106, 110.

49. Ibid., 111.

50. Ibid., 138.

51. Ibid., 27.

52. Samuel F. B. Morse, *Imminent Dangers to the Free Institutions of the United States through Foreign Immigration* (New York: E. B. Clayton, 1835). Journals in support of Morse's views included the *Downfall of Babylon* (March 7, 1835); the *Christian Spectator* (June 1835); the *Protestant Magazine* (vol. 1, July 1834); *American Protestant Vindicator* (September 3, 1834, September 19, 1834); and the *New York Observer* (April 11, 1835).

53. Metternich referred to the Monroe Doctrine as the most audacious American act since the American Revolution. See May, *Age of Metternich,* 29.

54. See Morse, *Foreign Conspiracy,* 20, 21, 23, 27, 110, 129.

55. Lyman Beecher, *A Plea for the West* (Cincinnati: Truman & Smith, 1835), 39.

56. Ibid., 53.

57. Ibid., 57.

58. Ibid., 72.

59. Ibid., 11.

60. Ibid., 12.

61. Isaiah 66:8.

62. Beecher, *Plea for the West,* 9.

63. Ibid., 10, 11.

64. Louis Dow Scisco, *Political Nativism in New York State* (New York: AMS Press, 1901), 27–30; John Hancock Lee, *The Origin and Progress of the American Party in Politics* (1855; Freeport, NY: Books for Libraries Press, 1970), 16. At this time, the only major nativist political faction in the South could be found in New Orleans. See *Address of the Louisiana Native American Association* (New Orleans: D. Felt & Co., 1839). See also Billington, *Protestant Crusade,* 131–32.

65. Scisco, *Political Nativism,* 30–31.

66. *Congressional Globe,* 25th Cong., 2nd sess., January 15, 1838, 100–101; U.S. Congress, House, *Reports of Committees,* 25th Cong., 2nd sess., no. 1040, 12–16.

67. David Russell, U.S. Congress, House, *Report from the Select Committee on Foreign Paupers and Naturalization Laws,* 25th Cong., 2nd sess., no. 1040, in *Laws of the United States Relative to Naturalization* (Washington: A. O. P. Nicholson, 1854).

68. Abel Stevens, *A Sermon on the Political Tendencies of Popery Considered in Respect to the Institutions of the United States* (Boston: David H. Ela, 1835), 8, 13.

69. Ibid., 10, 14.

70. Ibid., 18.

71. The *Downfall of Babylon* was first published in Philadelphia in 1834 and later, as readership increased, published in New York.

72. *Downfall of Babylon*, June 6, 1835, 64.

73. Joseph H. Martin, *The Influence, Bearing, and Effects of Romanism on the Civil and Religious Liberties of Our Country* (New York: H. Ludwig, 1844).

74. The biblical text believed to support this position is found in Matthew 16:19.

75. Martin, *Influence, Bearing, and Effects of Romanism,* 11.

76. The story is more complicated than space admits. Prior to *Unam Sanctam,* Boniface VIII issued the bull *Salvator Mundi,* which denied the French king the right to collect ecclesiastical revenue in defense of the kingdom. He also issued *Ausculta Fili,* which admonished the king to respect the moral authority of the pope as the vicar of Christ placed over all temporal kingdoms. Philip responded by producing his own forged bull, which exaggerated the claims of the papacy over the French in an effort to spur resentment from local bishops and clergy. See Brian Tierney, *The Crisis of Church and State, 1050–1300* (Englewood Cliffs, NJ: Prentice Hall, 1964), 180–85; Charles T. Wood, ed., *Philip the Fair and Boniface VIII: State vs. Papacy* (New York: Holt, Rinehart and Winston, 1967); and T. S. R. Boase, *Boniface VIII* (London: Constable, 1933).

77. Martin, *Influence, Bearing, and Effects of Romanism,* 13.

78. Ibid., 13–14.

79. Ibid., 14.

80. James P. Stuart, *America and the Americans versus the Papacy and the Catholics* (Cincinnati: Mendenhall, 1853), 18.

81. Ibid., 6–7.

82. Ibid., 6, 8, 15.

83. Joseph F. Berg, *Church and State, or Rome's Influence upon the Civil and Religious Institutions of Our Country* (Philadelphia: E. S. Jones & Co., 1851), 20.

84. Ibid., 25.

85. John N. McLeod, *Protestantism, the Parent and Guardian of Civil and Religious Liberty* (New York: Robert Carter, 1843), 4.

86. Ibid., 37.

87. The riots in Rome were precipitated by Pius IX's refusal to meet the demands of the radical society, Circolo Romano. In his allocution of April 28, 1848, Pius IX argued that as the Father of Christendom he could never war against Catholic Austria. Ironically, many of the leaders who led the insurrection

against the Vatican were former political prisoners pardoned by Pius IX under his early reform efforts.

88. *New Englander* 7, no. 26 (May 1849): 190, 191. The clever reference is to the election to the Holy See and subsequent resignation six months later of the hermit Peter Murrone to the Holy See in 1294. Celestine V was not a learned man, and he was not prepared for the complicated political situation he inherited. Leo X was the sixteenth-century spendthrift pope who held the office at the height of the Reformation. He is remembered for his reducing Jubilees and indulgences to simple financial transactions. His predecessor, Julius II, was a crafty soldier and diplomat who reestablished the security of the papal states after a series of Italian wars with France.

89. Rector of Oldenwold, *The Cloven Foot, or Popery Aiming at Political Supremacy in the United States* (Boston: A. Wentworth & Company, 1855), 117.

90. Ibid., 148–49.

91. Ibid., 151.

92. *New Englander* 7, no. 25 (February 1849): 90. Literature on the formation of common schools and the determination of many evangelicals to keep common schools safe from Catholicism is extensive. Essential literature on the subject includes Lawrence A. Cremin, *American Education: The National Experience, 1783–1876* (New York: Harper & Row, 1980); Rush Welter, *Popular Education and Democratic Thought in America* (New York: Columbia University Press, 1962); and James W. Fraser, *Between Church and State: Religion and Public Education in Multicultural America* (New York: St. Martin's Press, 1999), chaps. 2–3.

93. *New Englander* 13, no. 50 (May 1855): 268.

94. "American (Know Nothing) Platform of 1855," in appendix to Michael F. Holt, "The Antimasonic and Know Nothing Parties," in *History of U.S. Political Parties*, vol. 1., *1789–1860, From Factions to Parties*, ed. Arthur M. Schlesinger Jr. (New York: Chelsea House Publishers, 1973), 704.

95. Native American [E. Hutchison], *"Young Sam," or Native Americans' Own Book!* (New York: American Family Publication Establishment, 1855), 11–13.

96. Ibid., 14, 15, 17, 18.

97. Ibid., 18, 19, 25, 32.

98. Lewis D. Campbell, *Americanism: Speech of Hon. Lewis D. Campbell, of Ohio delivered at the American Mass Meeting, held in Washington City, February 29th, 1856, as reported in the "American Organ"* (Washington, DC: Buell & Blanchard, [1856]).

99. Joseph F. Berg, *Papal Usurpation: A Review of the Speech of the Hon. Jos. R. Chandler, of Pennsylvania, in the House of Representatives of the United States* (Philadelphia: J. W. Bradley, 1855), 10. Emphasis original.

100. Robert C. Grundy, *The Temporal Power of the Pope Dangerous to the Religious and Civil Liberties of the American Republic: A Review* (Maysville, KY: Maysville Eagle Office, 1855), 4–5. Cardinal Baronius was a sixteenth-century historian who wrote the twelve-volume *Annales Ecclesiatici*, a detailed history of the Church to the Reformation. Peter Dens was an influential eighteenth-century theologian who taught at the seminary of Mechlin.

101. Quoted in Richard J. Carwardine, *Evangelicals and Politics in Antebellum America* (New Haven, CT: Yale University Press, 1993), 201.

102. Noah Porter, *The Educational Systems of the Puritans and Jesuits Compared* (New York: M. W. Dodd, 1851), 63–64.

103. S. H. Waldo, "The Evidence of the World's Ultimate Reform," *Oberlin Quarterly Review* (July 1849): 287–89.

104. Thomas Brainerd, *Our Country Safe from Romanism* (Philadelphia: L. R. Bailey, 1843), 31.

105. Ibid., 32–33.

106. Ibid., 11–12.

107. Ibid., 25.

108. Henry Ward Beecher, *Freedom and War: Discourses on Topics Suggested by the Times* (Boston: Ticknor and Fields, 1863), 260.

109. Albert Barnes, *The Church and Slavery* (Philadelphia: Parry & McMillan, 1857), 37.

110. D. F. Robertson, *National Destiny and Our Country* (New York: E. French, 1851), 24.

111. Thomas M. Bayne, *Popery Subversive of American Institutions, and the Designed Destruction of This Republic by the Papal Church* (Pittsburgh: J. M'Millin, 1855), viii.

112. Daniel Walker Howe, "The Evangelical Movement and Political Culture in the North during the Second Party System," *Journal of American History* 77, no. 4 (March 1991): 1222.

THREE. Northern Evangelicals Define the Other

1. Charles C. Cole, *The Social Ideas of the Northern Evangelists 1826–1860* (New York: Octagon Books, 1966); Lawrence J. Freidman, *Gregarious Saints: Self and Community in American Abolitionism 1830–1870* (Cambridge: Cambridge University Press, 1982); and John R. McKivigan, *The War against Proslavery Religion: Abolitionism and the Northern Churches, 1830–1865* (Ithaca, NY: Cornell University Press, 1984).

2. The best work to date on northern abolitionist animosity toward both Catholics and slaveholders can be found in John T. McGreevy's, *Catholicism and American Freedom: A History* (New York: W. W. Norton, 2003), 60–66.

3. The journals under consideration in this chapter are the *Downfall of Babylon* (Independent); *Zion's Herald* (Methodist); the *New York Evangelist* (Presbyterian/Congregationalist); the *New York Observer* (Presbyterian); the *Christian Watchman and Examiner* (Baptist); and the *Oberlin Quarterly Review* (Independent).

4. *Downfall of Babylon,* August 14, 1834.

5. Ray Allen Billington, *The Protestant Crusade: A Study of the Origins of American Nativism* (New York: Holt, Rinehart & Winston, 1963), 123, 137.

6. *Downfall of Babylon,* January 10, 1835, 36.

7. Ibid.

8. Ibid., December 27, 1834, 27.

9. Ibid., February 14, 1835, 53.

10. Ibid., 54.

11. *Zion's Herald,* March 16, 1836, 42.

12. Ibid.

13. Ibid., April 20, 1836, 62.

14. On the Catholic threat to the Mississippi Valley, see *Zion's Herald,* January 24, 1838, 12; on the right relationship between New England Methodism and abolitionism, see *Zion's Herald,* September 16, 1840, 149–51.

15. *Zion's Herald,* December 21, 1842, 197.

16. Ibid., June 26, 1848.

17. See, for example, "Methodist Abolition in New England," *Zion's Herald,* September 16, 1840; and "Consistency," *Zion's Herald,* December 1842.

18. Bertram Wyatt-Brown, *Lewis Tappan and the Evangelical War against Slavery* (Cleveland: Press of Case Western Reserve University, 1969), 54–55; and Keith Hardman, *Charles Grandison Finney, 1792–1875: Revivalist and Reformer* (Syracuse, NY: Syracuse University Press, 1987), 186.

19. Wyatt-Brown, *Lewis Tappan,* 64; and Cole, *Social Ideas,* 40.

20. In particular, see *New York Evangelist,* February 4, 1837, February 11, 1837, and January 1844.

21. *New York Evangelist,* February 11, 1837.

22. Ibid.

23. Ibid., February 4, 1837. Emphasis original.

24. Ibid., October 21, 1837.

25. Ibid., January 1844.

26. Ibid.

27. Ibid.

28. Ibid.

29. Ibid.

30. Ibid., January 31, 1850.

31. Ibid., December 4, 1851.

32. Ibid.

33. Ibid.

34. Ibid., November 10, 1842.

35. Ibid., February 9, 1843.

36. Ibid., January 18, 1849.

37. Ibid.

38. Ibid.

39. Frank Luther Mott, *A History of American Magazines,* vol. 1, *1741–1850* (Cambridge, MA: Harvard University Press, 1966), 373.

40. *New York Observer,* March 23, 1854, 94.

41. Ibid.

42. Ibid.

43. Ibid.

44. Ibid., March 9, 1854.

45. Ibid.

46. Ibid., December 27, 1834.

47. Ibid., February 22, 1840.

48. Ibid., April 18, 1840.

49. Ibid.

50. Ibid., January, 29, 1857.

51. Ibid., February 22, 1840.

52. *Christian Watchman and Examiner,* November 21, 1834, 185.

53. Ibid., April 2, 1841, 54.

54. Ibid., June 8, 1848, 90.

55. Ibid., October 10, 1834, 162.

56. Ibid.

57. Ibid., January 15, 1847, 9.

58. Ibid., April 2, 1841, 54.

59. Ibid., July 11, 1845, 109.

60. D'Aubigné is also noteworthy because he wrote a very popular four-volume history describing the degeneracy of the papacy and the Catholic Church in the Middle Ages. See J. H. Merle D'Aubigné, *History of the Reformation in the Sixteenth Century* (New York: Robert Carter, 1846).

61. *Christian Watchman and Examiner,* April 2, 1841, 55.

62. Ibid., October 9, 1835, 161.

63. Ibid., June 19, 1835, 98.

64. Ibid.

65. William Goodell, "Come-Outism and Come-Outers," *Oberlin Quarterly Review* (May 1848): 421.

66. Ibid., 424.

67. Ibid., 427.

68. Ibid., 438.

69. Ibid., 423–24.

70. Ibid., 436–37.

71. Ibid., 436.

72. Ibid., 437.

73. William B. Brown, "Religious Organizations and Slavery," *Oberlin Quarterly Review* (October 1849): 415.

74. Ibid., 416.

75. Ibid.

76. Ibid., 430.

77. Ibid., 434–35.

78. Ibid., 435.

79. Ibid.

FOUR. Southern Evangelical Dilemmas

1. Randall M. Miller and Jon L. Wakelyn, *Catholics in the Old South: Essays on Church and Culture* (Macon, GA: Mercer University Press, 1983), 54. The other dioceses were Bardstown, Kentucky; Richmond, Virginia; Charleston, South Carolina; Mobile, Alabama; Natchez, Mississippi; Nashville, Tennessee; Little Rock, Arkansas; Galveston, Texas; Savannah, Georgia; Wheeling, Virginia (later West Virginia); Natchitoches, Mississippi; and Covington, Louisiana.

2. Sydney E. Ahlstrom, *A Religious History of the American People* (New Haven, CT: Yale University Press, 1972), 36–69. One of the overlooked if not forgotten ironies of southern history is that the first "southerners" were of French and Spanish descent, and the first "southern Christians" were Catholic Christians. See James J. Thompson, *The Church, the South, and the Future* (Westminster, MD: Christian Classics, 1988), 25.

3. Miller and Wakelyn, *Catholics in the Old South,* 68, 78; and Matthew Page Andrews, "Separation of Church and State in Maryland," *Catholic Historical Review* 21 (July 1935): 164–76. On the influence of the Calvert family in

early Maryland, see Thomas O. Hanley, *Their Rights and Liberties: The Beginnings of Religious and Political Freedom in Maryland* (Westminster, MD: Newman Press, 1959).

4. Joseph H. Schauinger, *William Gaston, Carolinian* (Milwaukee: Bruce Publishing Co., 1949), 200–209; and William Gaston, *Proceedings and Debates of the Convention of North Carolina, Called to Amend the Constitution of the State, Which Assembled at Raleigh, June 4, 1835* (Raleigh: Joseph Gale and Son, 1836), 264–65, 283–85, 292.

5. Carl B. Swisher, *The Taney Period, 1836–64* (New York: Macmillan, 1974), 67–70; Dan E. Fehrenbacher, "Roger B. Taney and the Sectional Crisis," *Journal of Southern History* 43, no. 4 (November 1977), 555–66; and William M. Wiecek, "Slavery and Abolition before the United States Supreme Court, 1820–1860," *Journal of American History* 65, no. 1 (June 1978), 34–59. Senator Charles Sumner of Massachusetts said of Taney, "He administered justice, at last, wickedly, and degraded the judiciary of the country, and degraded the age" (quoted in David M. Potter, *The Impending Crisis, 1848–1861* [New York: Harper & Row, 1976], 290).

6. F. Joseph Magri, *The Catholic Church in the City and Diocese of Richmond* (Richmond: Whittet & Shepperson, 1906), 46–61.

7. Gerald Fogarty, S.J., *Commonwealth Catholicism: A History of the Catholic Church in Virginia* (Notre Dame, IN: University of Notre Dame Press, 2001), 115–18.

8. Benedict Webb, quoted in Madeleine Hooke Rice, *American Catholic Opinion in the Slavery Controversy* (New York: Columbia University Press, 1944), 74–75. See also Benedict J. Webb, *The Catholic Question in Politics* (Louisville: Webb, Gill & Levering, 1856); and Miller and Wakelyn, *Catholics in the Old South*, 218.

9. Michael Kenny, S.J., *Catholic Culture in Alabama: Centenary Story of Spring Hill College, 1830–1930* (New York: America Press, 1931), 49, 98, 201; T. Harry Williams, *P. G. T. Beauregard: Napoleon in Gray* (Baton Rouge: Louisiana State University Press, 1955); and John Perkins, *The Results of Two Years of Democratic Rule in the Country* (Washington, 1855); and Miller and Wakelyn, *Catholics in the Old South*, 229–32.

10. John I. Cosgrave, "The Hibernian Society of Charleston, South Carolina," *Journal of the American-Irish Historical Society* 25 (1926): 150–58; Christopher Silver, "A New Look at Old South Urbanization: The Irish Worker in Charleston, South Carolina, 1840–1860," in Samuel M. Hines and George W. Hopkins, eds., *South Atlantic Urban Studies*, vol. 3 (Columbia: University of South Carolina Press, 1979), 141–71; Ella Lonn, *Foreigners in the Confederacy*

(Gloucester, MA: P. Smith, 1965); and Jeremiah Joseph O'Connell, *Catholicity in the Carolinas and Georgia: Leaves of Its History, AD 1820–AD 1878* (New York: D. J. Sadlier, 1879).

11. U.S. Bureau of the Census, *United States Census for 1850* (Washington, 1851).

12. Wakelyn and Miller, *Catholics in the Old South*, 202.

13. Michael V. Namorato, *The Catholic Church in Mississippi, 1911–1984* (Westport, CT: Greenwood Press, 1998), 8.

14. W. Darrell Overdyke, *The Know-Nothing Party in the South* (Baton Rouge: Louisiana State University Press, 1950), 19, 32.

15. Michael V. Gannon, *Rebel Bishop: The Life and Era of Augustin Verot* (Milwaukee: Bruce Publishing Co., 1964), 25, 63; and Miller and Wakelyn, *Catholics in the Old South*, 66, 226, 227.

16. Scholars who emphasize the limits of southern anti-Catholicism include Arthur C. Cole, "Nativism in the lower Mississippi Valley," *Proceedings of the Mississippi Valley Historical Association,* vol. 6, ed. Benjamin F. Shambaugh (Cedar Rapids, IA: Torch Press, 1913), 272; Clement Eaton, *The Freedom-of-Thought Struggle in the Old South* (New York: Harper & Row, 1964), 322; Arthur W. Thompson, "Political Nativism in Florida, 1848–1860: A Phase of Anti-Secessionism," *Journal of Southern History* 15 (February 1949): 49–53; Overdyke, *Know-Nothing Party in the South*; James H. Broussard, "Some Determinates of Know-Nothing Electoral Strength in the South, 1856," *Louisiana History* 7 (Winter 1966): 5; and Jenny Franchot, *Roads to Rome: The Antebellum Protestant Encounter with Catholicism* (Berkeley: University of California Press, 1994), xix. Scholars who suggest that southern anti-Catholicism could at times be as intense as that found in the North include Randall M. Miller, "The Enemy Within: Some Effects of Foreign Immigrants on Antebellum Southern Cities," *Southern Studies* 24 (Spring 1985): 30–53; and Richard J. Carwardine, *Evangelicals and Politics in Antebellum America* (New Haven, CT: Yale University Press, 1993).

17. This apprehension was due in part to an exaggerated fear that Irish Catholic immigrants had been unduly influenced by the ideas of Ireland's Daniel O'Connell, a political activist who had the reputation of a radical because of his support, albeit measured support, of the French Revolution and his commitment to progressive reform movements. See the *Lexington Gazette* [Virgina], March 29, 1855, and June 5, 1855; Speech of Senator Adams of Mississippi, *Congressional Globe,* 34th Cong., 1st sess., 1413; and S. F. Rice, *Speech of S.F. Rice at Talladega, Alabama, September 6, 1855,* Curry Collection of Pamphlets, Alabama State Library.

18. James Pinkney Hambleton, *A History of the Political Campaign in Virginia in 1855* (Richmond, VA: J. W. Randolph, 1856), 312.

19. *Montgomery Advertiser and Gazette,* July 7, 1855.

20. *Congressional Globe,* 33rd Cong., 1st sess., 189.

21. *Appendix to Congressional Globe,* 33rd Cong., 2nd sess., no. 59, December 18, 1854.

22. Overdyke, *Know-Knothing Party in the South,* 236; William Winans to the editor of the *Vicksburg Sentinel,* December 5, 1844, quoted in Anne C. Loveland, *Southern Evangelicals and the Social Order, 1800–1860* (Baton Rouge: Louisiana State University Press, 1980), 116.

23. Charles Dabney to Robert Dabney, March 1856, quoted in Carwardine, *Evangelicals and Politics,* 272.

24. Robert L. Dabney, "Uses and Results of Church History," in *Discussions, Vol. 2: Evangelical and Theological* (Edinburgh: Banner of Truth Trust, 1891), 14; and Dabney, "Civic Ethics," in *Discussions, Vol. 3: Philosophical* (Edinburgh: Banner of Truth Trust, 1892), 326.

25. John Pendleton Kennedy to Robert C. Winthrop, quoted in Tyler Anbinder, *Nativism and Slavery: The Northern Know Nothings & the Politics of the 1850s* (New York: Oxford University Press, 1992), 187.

26. Wise to J. L. M. Curry of Alabama, J. L. M. Curry Collection, State Department of Archives and History, Montgomery, Alabama.

27. *Montgomery Advertiser and Gazette,* July, 25, 1855.

28. The platform can be found in the appendix to Michael F. Holt, "The Antimasonic and Know Nothing Parties," in *History of United States Political Parties,* ed. Arthur Schlesinger Jr., vol. 1 (New York: Chelsea House Publishers, 1973), 575–620. The Know Nothings formally referred to themselves as the American Party, and their convention was the American National Council.

29. Overdyke, *Know-Knothing Party in the South,* 218; Leon C. Soulé, *The Know Nothing Party in New Orleans* (New Orleans: Louisiana Historical Association, 1961), 65–70; and Jean H. Baker, *Ambivalent Americans: The Know-Nothing Party in Maryland* (Baltimore: Johns Hopkins University Press, 1977).

30. Eaton, *Freedom-of-Thought Struggle,* 323–24.

31. *Dallas Gazette,* August 24, 1855, quoted in Overdyke, *Know-Knothing Party in the South,* 224.

32. Quoted in Michael V. Gannon, *The Cross in the Sand: The Early Catholic Church in Florida, 1513–1870* (Gainesville: University Presses of Florida), 153.

33. Quoted in Overdyke, *Know-Knothing Party in the South,* 227.

34. Ibid., 230.

35. Fogarty, *Commonwealth Catholicism,* 123; and Anbinder, *Nativism and Slavery,* 164.

36. Fogarty, *Commonwealth Catholicism,* 124.

37. Anbinder, *Nativism and Slavery,* 168.

38. Ibid., 168–72, 246. Scholars are conflicted over the exact relationship between nativism and the Republican Party. Works that support the notion that the Republicans courted the nativist vote include William G. Gienapp, "Nativism and the Creation of a Republican Majority in the North before the Civil War," *Journal of American History* 72, no. 3 (December 1985): 529–59; Joel H. Silbey, "[TS]'The Undisguised Connection,' Know Nothings into Republicans: New York as a Test Case," in *The Partisan Imperative: The Dynamics of American Politics before the Civil War* (New York: Oxford University Press, 1985), 127–65; and Michael F. Holt, *Forging a Majority: The Formation of the Republican Party in Pittsburgh, 1848–1860* (New Haven, CT: Yale University Press, 1969), 222. Scholars who believe nativism played a very small role in Republican politics include Eric Foner, *Free Soil, Free Labor, Free Men: The Ideology of the Republican Party before the Civil War* (New York: Oxford University Press, 1970), chap. 7.

39. Presbyterian stalwart James Henley Thornwell of South Carolina secretly commiserated with the movement. He wrote to a friend in 1855, "There is not one principle of the American party, so far as its principles are known, which does not command my most cordial approbation. Its appearance and success is the most remarkable phenomenon of these remarkable times; and if it fails our last hope for the Union is gone" (Thornwell to Alexander Pegues, July 26, 1855, quoted in B. M. Palmer, *The Life and Letters of James Henley Thornwell* [Edinburgh: Banner of Truth Trust, 1875], 479).

40. See Anbinder, *Nativism and Slavery,* 194–95; Stephen E. Maizlish, "The Meaning of Nativism and the Crisis of the Union: The Know-Nothing Movement in the Antebellum North," in *Essays on American Antebellum Politics, 1840–1860,* ed. Stephen E. Maizlish and John J. Kushma (College Station: Texas A&M University Press, 1982), 166–98; and Alice Felt Tyler, *Freedom's Ferment: Phases of American Social History to 1860* (Minneapolis: University of Minnesota Press, 1944), 391–92.

41. Ray Allen Billington, "Tentative Bibliography of Anti-Catholic Propaganda in the United States, 1800–1860," *Catholic Historical Review* 18 (January 1933): 492–513.

42. The *New Orleans Protestant* lasted just under two years, 1844–1846; the *Baltimore Weekly Pilot* lasted a year, 1840–1841; and the *Jackson Protestant* did not last a year.

43. Ray Allen Billington, *The Protestant Crusade: A Study of the Origins of American Nativism* (New York: Holt, Rinehart & Winston, 1963), 169.

44. See James Henley Thornwell, *Arguments of Romanists from the Infallibility of the Church and the Testimony of the Fathers in Behalf of the Apocrypha, Discussed and Refuted* (New York: Leavitt, Trow & Co., 1845); and Richard

Furman, *Guicciardini and the Popes: An Address Delivered before the Adelphian Society of the Furman Institution at the Commencement on Monday, June 16, 1851* (Greenville, SC: Office of the Southern Patriot, 1851).

45. Benjamin Morgan Palmer, "Warrant and the Nature of Public Service," in Thomas Carey Johnson, *The Life and Letters of Benjamin Morgan Palmer* (Edinburgh: Banner of Truth Trust, 1906), 121.

46. Reported in the *New York Observer,* June 12, 1841.

47. Palmer, *Life and Letters of Thornwell,* 285.

48. E. Merton Coulter, *William G. Brownlow: Fighting Parson of the Southern Highlands* (Knoxville: University of Tennessee Press, 1971), 122.

49. Quoted in Edward R. Crowther, *Southern Evangelicals and the Coming of the Civil War* (Lewiston, NY: Edwin Mellen Press, 2000), 90–91.

50. Thomas Smyth, "The War of the South Vindicated," *Southern Presbyterian Review* 15 (April 1863): 507.

51. James A. Lyon, "Religion and Politics," *Southern Presbyterian Review* 15 (April 1863): 570.

52. Palmer, *Life and Letters of Thornwell,* 436–37.

53. William McDonald, *The Two Rebellions; or, Treason Unmasked* (Richmond: Smith, Bailey & Co., 1865), 9.

54. Ibid., 10, 13.

55. William A. Hall, *The Historic Significance of the Southern Revolution: A Lecture Delivered by Invitation in Petersburg, Va., March 14th and April 29th, 1864, and in Richmond, Va., April 7th and April 21st, 1864* (Petersburg, VA: A. F. Crutchfield, 1864), 12.

56. Ibid.

57. Ibid., 33.

58. Ibid., 35, 44.

59. Ibid., 35, 37.

60. Baptist General Association of Virginia, *Address of the Baptist General Association [of] Virginia June 4th, 1863* [Virginia?: The Association? 1863?], 1–2, http://docsouth.unc.edu/imls/baptist/baptist.html.

61. Ibid., 2.

62. Richard Fuller and Francis Wayland, *Domestic Slavery Considered as a Scriptural Institution* (New York: Sheldon Lamport & Blakeman, 1856).

63. *Biblical Recorder,* February 10, 1854, March 21, 24, 31, 1854, April 21, 1854, May 25, 1854; and Henry Smith Stroupe, *The Religious Press in the South Atlantic States, 1802–1865* (Durham, NC: Duke University Press, 1956), 40.

64. Drew Gilpin Faust, *The Creation of Confederate Nationalism: Ideology and Identity in the Civil War South* (Baton Rouge: Louisiana State University Press, 1988), 22–23; Jack Maddex, "From Theocracy to Spirituality: The Southern

Presbyterian Reversal on Church and State," *Journal of Presbyterian History* 14 (Winter 1970): 438–57; and Eugene D. Genovese, *A Consuming Fire: The Fall of the Confederacy in the Mind of the White Christian South* (Athens: University of Georgia Press, 1998), chap. 2.

65. Mitchell Snay, *Gospel of Disunion: Religion and Separatism in the Antebellum South* (Chapel Hill: University of North Carolina Press, 1997), 192.

66. H. Shelton Smith, *In His Image But . . . Racism in Southern Religion, 1780–1910* (Durham, NC: Duke University Press, 1972), 32–73.

67. Quoted in Genovese, *Consuming Fire,* 16.

68. *Minutes of the Thirty-Ninth Annual Session of the Ala. Baptist State Convention,* November 1861, quoted in Snay, *Gospel of Disunion,* 150.

69. *Southern Christian Advocate,* April 2, 1863, quoted in Faust, *Creation of Confederate Nationalism,* 23.

70. R. N. Sledd, *A Sermon Delivered in the Market Street, M.E. Church, Petersburg, VA. before the Confederate Cadets, on the Occasion of Their Departure for the Seat of War, Sunday, September 22, 1861* (Petersburg, VA: A. F. Crutchfield & Co., 1861), 20.

71. John T. Wightman, *The Glory of God, the Defense of the South. A Discourse Delivered in the Methodist Episcopal Church, South, Yorkville, S.C., July 28, 1861, the Day of National Thanksgiving for the Victory at Manassas* (Portland, ME: B. Thurston & Co., 1871), 10.

72. Maddex, "From Theocracy to Spirituality."

73. John Holt Rice, "The Princeton Review on the State of the Country," *Southern Presbyterian Review* 14 (April 1861): 11.

74. James Henley Thornwell, *Thoughts Suited to the Present Crisis: A Sermon on the Occasion of the Death of the Hon. John C. Calhoun* (Columbia, SC: A. S. Johnson, 1850), 4–5.

75. James Henley Thornwell, "The Christian Doctrine of Slavery," in *The Collected Writings of James Henley Thornwell,* vol. 4 (Edinburgh: Banner of Truth Trust, 1875), 404.

76. Ibid., 407–8.

77. George Howe, "The Raid of John Brown and the Progress of Abolition," *Southern Presbyterian Review* 12 (January 1860): 808.

78. Ibid., 811.

79. Benjamin M. Palmer, "Thanksgiving Sermon," in *Life and Letters of Palmer,* 212, 213.

80. Ibid., 212. Jean-Paul Marat was a propagandist of the French Revolution and a close friend of Robespierre. He was also a strident antimonarchist who encouraged the September 1792 massacres of political prisoners, and he

formed the Committee of Surveillance, which was designed to root out antirevolutionaries.

81. Ibid., 212.

82. Lacon [R. S. Gladney], *The Devil in America: A Dramatic Satire* (Mobile: J. K. Randall, 1867), 111.

83. Ibid., 118–19.

84. Ibid., 123.

85. Robert L. Dabney, *A Defense of Virginia* (New York: E. J. Hale & Son, 1867), 262; Dabney, "Civic Ethics," 313–13; and Dabney, "The True Purpose of the Civil War," in *Discussions, Vol. 4: Secular* (Edinburgh: Banner of Truth Trust, 1897), 104–5.

86. Dabney, "True Purpose," 105.

87. Ibid.; and Dabney, "Civic Ethics," 312.

88. Dabney, "Civic Ethics," 313.

89. Ibid., 314.

90. Robert L. Dabney, *Life and Campaigns of Lieut.-Gen. Thomas J. Jackson* (New York: Blelock & Co., 1866), 160.

91. Ibid., 159.

92. Eugene D. Genovese, "The Southern Slaveholders' View of the Middle Ages," in *Medievalism in American Culture: Papers of the Eighteenth Annual Conference of the Center for Medieval and Early Renaissance Studies,* ed. Bernard Rosenthal and Paul E. Szarmach, 31–51 (Binghamton, NY: Center for Medieval and Early Renaissance Studies, 1989), 32.

93. Snay, *Gospel of Disunion,* 60–63.

FIVE. **The Hierarchy Responds to Political Protestantism**

1. James J. Hennesey, *American Catholics: A History of the Roman Catholic Community in the United States* (New York: Oxford University Press, 1981), chaps. 8–9; and John Tracy Ellis, *American Catholicism* (Chicago: University of Chicago Press, 1956), 44–51. See also Andrew Greeley, *The Catholic Experience: An Interpretation of the History of American Catholicism* (Garden City, NY: Doubleday, 1967); and Jay P. Dolan, *The Immigrant Church: New York's Irish and German Catholics, 1815–1865* (Baltimore: Johns Hopkins University Press, 1975).

2. Michael V. Gannon, *Rebel Bishop: Augustin Verot, Florida's Civil War Prelate* (Gainesville: University of Florida Press, 1964), 30–31.

3. Augustin Verot, *A Tract for the Times: Slavery and Abolitionism* (Baltimore: John Murphy & Co., 1861).

4. Gannon, *Rebel Bishop*, 6–7, 17, 20–21, 63.

5. Augustin Verot, *A Just Judgment on the Catholic Doctrines* (Baltimore: Murphy & Co., 1843), 11.

6. Quoted in Gannon, *Rebel Bishop*, 43.

7. *Freeman's Journal*, December 8, 1855.

8. Ibid., June 18, 1856.

9. *Catholic Mirror*, September 16, 1860.

10. The *Catholic Miscellany*, founded by Bishop John England, was the first Catholic journal published in the United States.

11. *Catholic Miscellany*, September 12, 1835, June 30, 1838.

12. John C. Murphy, *An Analysis of the Attitudes of American Catholics toward the Immigrant and the Negro, 1825–1925* (Washington, DC: Catholic University of America Press, 1940), 49–50. The only exception to the Catholic press's consistent stand against the abolitionists was the *Cincinnati Catholic Telegraph*. See Murphy, *Analysis of the Attitudes*, 51–52.

13. *Freeman's Journal*, January 7, 1860, August 27, 1859.

14. Ibid., August 27, 1859.

15. Ibid., May 7, 1864.

16. Ibid.

17. Cuthbert Edward Allen, O. S. B., "The Slavery Question in Catholic Newspapers, 1850–1865," *Historical Records and Studies* 26 (1936): 126; and Frank Luther Mott, *A History of American Catholic Magazines, 1741–1850* (Cambridge, MA: Harvard University Press, 1966), 716.

18. *Catholic Mirror*, May 10, 1852.

19. Ibid., December 1860.

20. Ibid., October 29, 1859.

21. Ibid., April 20, 1861.

22. Ibid., May 10, 1862. Emphasis original.

23. For more on Brownson's biography, see Arthur M. Schlesinger Jr., *A Pilgrim's Progress: Orestes A. Brownson* (Boston: Little, Brown & Co., 1943); Theodore Maynard, *Orestes Brownson: Yankee, Radical, Catholic* (New York: Macmillan, 1943); and Patrick W. Carey, *Orestes A. Brownson: American Religious Weathervane* (Grand Rapids, MI: W. B. Eerdmans, 2004).

24. Orestes A. Brownson, "The Church and Its Mission," in Patrick W. Carey, ed., *American Catholic Religious Thought: The Shaping of a Theological and Social Tradition* (New York: Paulist Press, 1987), 120.

25. Orestes A. Brownson, *The Works of Orestes A. Brownson*, collected and arranged by Henry F. Brownson, 20 vols. (Detroit: T. Nourse, 1882), 17:23.

26. For an excellent detailed survey of the Catholic arguments surrounding slavery, see Joseph Edward Capizzi, "A Development of Doctrine: The

Challenge of Slavery to Moral Theology" (PhD diss., University of Notre Dame, 1998).

27. *Freeman's Journal,* June 16, 1860.

28. Ibid., February 11, 1865. For a detailed analysis of Aquinas on slavery, see Capizzi, "Development of Doctrine," 157–64.

29. Gregory XVI, *In supremo apostolatus fastigio,* in Donald Shearer, *Pontificia Americana: A Documentary History of the Catholic Church in the United States (1784–1884)* (Washington, DC: Catholic University of America Press, 1933), 203–5.

30. John F. Quinn, "[TS]'Three Cheers for the Abolitionist Pope!': American Reaction to Gregory XVI's Condemnation of Slave Trade, 1840–1860," *Catholic Historical Review* 90, no. 1 (January 2004): 67–94.

31. Ibid. See also John Forsyth, *Address to the People of Georgia* (1840; Louisville, KY: Lost Cause Press, 1971).

32. John England, *Letters of the Late Bishop England to the Hon. John Forsyth, on the Subject of Domestic Slavery* (1844; New York: New Negro Universities Press, 1969), 24.

33. Joseph L. O'Brien, *John England, Bishop of Charleston: The Apostle to Democracy* (New York: Edward O'Toole Co., 1934), 119.

34. Patrick W. Carey, *An Immigrant Bishop: John England's Adaptation of Irish Catholicism to American Republicanism* (Yonkers, NY: U.S. Catholic Historical Society, 1982), 11–26.

35. Ibid. See also Peter Guilday, *The Life and Times of John England,* 2 vols. (New York: American Press, 1927).

36. O'Brien, *John England,* 149.

37. Augustine, *De Civitate Dei Contra Paganos,* bk. 19, chap. 16, "Prima ergo servitutis causa peccatum est, ut homo homini condicionis vinculo subderetur; quod non fit nisi Deo iudicante."

38. England, *Letters,* 24.

39. Ibid. England is paraphrasing Augustine.

40. Ibid.

41. Ibid., 45.

42. Ibid.

43. Ibid., "Si quis docet servum, pietatis praetextu, dominum contemnere, et a ministerio recedere, et non cum benevolentia et omni honore domino suo inservire. Anathema sit."

44. Ibid.

45. Ibid., 23.

46. Ibid., 44.

47. Ibid., 23.

48. Ibid.

49. See Dino Bigongiari, ed., *The Political Ideas of St. Thomas Aquinas* (New York: Hafner Press, 1981), 3–55; and Paul E Sigmund, *St. Thomas Aquinas on Politics and Ethics* (New York: W. W. Norton, 1988), 46–58, 82.

50. England, *Letters,* 47, 48, 73–95, 100–102.

51. Hugh J. Nolan, *The Most Reverend Francis Patrick Kenrick, Third Bishop of Philadelphia, 1830–1851* (Philadelphia: American Catholic Historical Society, 1948), 3–9.

52. Ibid., 241.

53. Francis Patrick Kenrick, *Theologia Moralis,* 2nd ed., 2 vols. (Baltimore: Mechlin, 1859), preface.

54. Capizzi, "Development of Doctrine," 252; and Joseph D. Brokhage, "Francis Patrick Kenrick's Opinion on Slavery" (PhD diss., Catholic University of America, 1955), 108–9.

55. Brokhage, "Francis Patrick Kenrick's Opinion on Slavery," 45.

56. Kenrick, *Theologia Moralis,* tr. V, cap. VI, no. 35; tr. III, cap. I, no. 6; and tr. V, cap. I, no. 2.

57. Ibid., tr. III, cap. I, no. 16.

58. Quoted in ibid., tr. V, cap. VI, no. 35.

59. Ibid., tr. V, cap. V, no. 36.

60. See Michael Felberg, *The Philadelphia Riots of 1844: A Study in Ethnic Conflict* (Westport, CT: Greenwood Press, 1975).

61. Francis Patrick Kenrick, *Pastoral Letter of the Archbishop and Bishops of the Province of Baltimore, Assembled in the Ninth Provincial Council, May 1858* (Baltimore: John Murphy & Co., 1858), 11–13.

62. O'Brien, *John England,* 60.

63. John England, "The Pope's Dispensing Power," in *The Works of the Right Reverend John England, First Bishop of Charleston,* ed. Sebastian G. Messmer, 7 vols. (Cleveland: Arthur Clark Company, 1908), 3:395.

64. Ibid., 3:396.

65. Ibid., 3:395.

66. Ibid., 3:393.

67. Ibid., 3:400.

68. Ibid., 3:402.

69. England, "Catholic Doctrine Misrepresented," in *Works,* 3:164, 172.

70. Ibid., 3:172, 174.

71. Ibid., 3:173.

72. Joseph Blanco White, *Letters from Spain and Practical and Internal Evidence against Catholicism* (London: H. Colburn, 1822).

73. England, "Calumnies of J. Blanco White," in *Works*, 2:328.

74. Ibid., 2:330.

75. Ibid., 2:382.

76. Ibid. Examples of "divine positive law" include the time and place of worship, the observance of the Lord's Day as a holy day, fast days, etc.

77. Ibid., 2:333, 382.

78. Carey, *American Catholic Religious Thought*, 7.

79. Francis Patrick Kenrick, *A Letter on Christian Unity to the Right Rev. B. B. Smith, Protestant Bishop of the Diocese of Kentucky* (Philadelphia: M. Fithian, 1836).

80. Francis Patrick Kenrick, *A Review of the Second Letter and Postscript of the Right Rev. John Henry Hopkins, D.D.* (Philadelphia: M. Fithian, 1843), 32.

81. Ibid.

82. Ibid., 34.

83. Ibid., 34–35.

84. John Lancaster Spalding, *The Life of the Most Rev. M. J. Spalding, D.D.* (New York: Christian Press Association, 1873), 23, 51.

85. Gerald P. Fogarty, ed., *Patterns of Episcopal Leadership* (New York: Macmillan, 1989), 107.

86. Ibid.; and Thomas W. Spalding, "Martin John Spalding: Building of Louisville and Archbishop of Baltimore 1810–1872" (PhD diss., Catholic University of America, 1971), 98–102.

87. J. L. Spalding, *Life*, 185.

88. Martin John Spalding, *Miscellanea: Comprising Reviews, Lectures, and Essays, on Historical, Theological, and Miscellaneous Subjects* (Louisville: Webb, Gill & Levering, 1855), 44–45.

89. Ibid., 154.

90. Ibid., 144.

91. Martin John Spalding, *D'Aubigné's "History of the Great Reformation in Germany and Switzerland" Reviewed* (Baltimore: John Murphy, 1844), 464.

92. Ibid., 437.

93. Martin John Spalding, *The Church, Culture and Liberty* (New York: J. F. Wagner, 1923), 149–50.

94. Ibid., 88, 116. Emphasis original.

95. Ibid., 88.

96. Ibid., 80, 81.

97. Ibid., 82.

98. Spalding, *D'Aubigné's "History of the Great Reformation,"* 75, 77.

99. Spalding, *Miscellanea*, 390–91.

100. Ibid.

101. Ibid.

102. Ibid., 549.

103. Ibid., 524.

104. Ibid., 576.

105. Ibid., 456, 457.

106. Hennesey, *American Catholics,* 156.

107. Martin John Spalding, quoted in David Spalding, "Martin John Spalding's 'Dissertation on the American Civil War,'" *Catholic Historical Review* 52 (1966): 81, 75.

108. Ibid., 78–79.

109. Hennesey, *American Catholics,* 157.

110. See John Webb Pratt, *Religion, Politics, and Diversity: The Church-State Theme in New York State History* (Ithaca, NY: Cornell University Press, 1967), 161–90; Vincent P. Lannie, *Public Money and Parochial Education: Bishop Hughes, Governor Seward and the New York School Controversy* (Cleveland: Press of Case Western Reserve University, 1968); Diane Ravitch, *The Great School Wars: New York City, 1805–1973* (New York: Basic Books, 1974), 3–84; John R. G. Hassard, *Life of the Most Reverend John Hughes, First Archbishop of New York* (New York: D. Appleton and Co., 1866); and Joseph P. Cinnici, "A Study in the Intellectual Acculturation of Catholicism: Archbishops John Hughes and Martin John Spalding, 1835–1865" (PhD diss., Graduate Theological Union, 1971).

111. Quoted in Hennesey, *American Catholics,* 146. For more on Hughes' biography, see Richard Shaw, *Dagger John: The Unquiet Life and Times of Archbishop John Hughes of New York* (New York: Paulist Press, 1977).

112. John Hughes, *The Decline of Protestantism* (New York: E. Dunigan & Brother, 1850).

113. John Hughes, *A Lecture on the Mixture of Civil and Ecclesiastical Power in the Governments of the Middle Ages* (New York: New World Press, 1843), 5.

114. Ibid., 6, 11.

115. Ibid., 12, 13.

116. Ibid., 14, 15.

117. Ibid., 17, 18.

118. Ibid., 19.

119. American Protestant Society of New York, *Romanism Incompatible with Republican Institutions* (New York: American Protestant Society, 1844).

120. John Hughes, *Catholicism Compatible with Republican Government* (New York: Edward Duncan, 1844), 13.

121. Ibid., 33.

122. Ibid., 35.

123. Ibid., 37.

124. John Hughes, *Complete Works of the Most Rev. John Hughes, D.D., Archbishop of New York*, ed. Lawrence Kehoe, 2 vols. (New York: American News, 1864), vol. 1, sec. 2, p. 72.

125. Ibid., vol. 1, sec. 2, p. 96.

126. Ibid., vol. 1, sec. 2, p. 129.

127. Ibid., vol. 1, sec. 5, p. 13.

128. John Hughes, *The Church and the World* (New York: Edward & Brother, 1850), 8.

129. Hughes, *Complete Works*, vol. 1, sec. 5, p. 14.

130. In particular, see Madeleine Hooke Rice, *American Catholic Opinion on the Slavery Controversy* (New York: Columbia University Press, 1944), 156–61.

131. On Lincoln and the Civil War, see James Hennesey, S.J., *American Catholics: A History of the Roman Catholic Community in the United States* (New York: Oxford University Press, 1981), chap. 12.

Epilogue

1. On evangelicals and common sense philosophy, see Mark A. Noll, "Common Sense Traditions and Evangelical Thought," *American Quarterly* 37, no. 2 (Summer 1985): 216–38; Nathan O. Hatch, "Sola Scriptura and Novus Ordo Seclorum," in *The Bible in America: Essays in Cultural History*, ed. Nathan O. Hatch and Mark A. Noll (New York: Oxford University Press, 1982), 59–87; E. Brooks Holifield, *The Gentlemen Theologians: American Theology and Southern Culture 1795–1860* (Durham, NC: Duke University Press, 1978), 72–126; George M. Marsden, *The Evangelical Mind and the New School Presbyterian Experience* (New Haven, CT: Yale University Press, 1970), 47–52; and Sydney E. Ahlstrom, "The Scottish Philosophy and American Theology," *Church History* 24 (1955): 257–72.

2. Mitchell Snay, *Gospel of Disunion: Religion and Separatism in the Antebellum South* (Chapel Hill: University of North Carolina Press, 1993), 58–61; and William Sumner Jenkins, *Pro-Slavery Thought in the Old South* (Chapel Hill: University of North Carolina Press, 1935), 234–36.

3. Laura L. Mitchell, "Matters of Justice between Man and Man: Northern Divines, the Bible, and the Fugitive Slave Act of 1850," in *Religion and the Antebellum Debate over Slavery*, ed. John R. McKivigan and Mitchell Snay (Athens: University of Georgia Press, 1998), 157–59.

4. Alexis de Tocqueville, *Democracy in America*, ed. Harvey C. Mansfield and Delba Winthrop (Chicago: University of Chicago Press, 2000), 424.

Index

W. JASON WALLACE

is assistant professor of history at Samford University.